Praise for *The Wealth Habit*

'*The Wealth Habit* shows how small, well-designed behaviours, repeated consistently, create extraordinary financial outcomes over time. This is a practical, thoughtful guide to building wealth the way it actually happens: gradually, deliberately and sustainably.'

Steven Bartlett, entrepreneur, investor, *Sunday Times* bestselling author and host of *The Diary of a CEO* podcast

'This book will open your eyes to what's truly possible when you build wealth with intention and joy. Ken and Mary prove that financial freedom isn't reserved for the few – it's a habit you can cultivate, one small step at a time.'

Nischa Shah, chartered accountant and financial educator

'The antidote to get-rich-quick culture. Ken and Mary understand what a lot of financial advice misses: wealth isn't built in dopamine spikes – it's built in the quiet compound of daily habits.'

TJ Power, neuroscientist and *Sunday Times* bestselling author of *The DOSE Effect*

'Wealth isn't built in one big moment – it's built in the habits you repeat when no one is watching. This book does a brilliant job of breaking that down in a way that feels achievable, not overwhelming.'

Patricia Bright, entrepreneur, content creator and author of *Heart and Hustle*

'In a world obsessed with shortcuts and quick wins, *The Wealth Habit* stands out as a refreshingly grounded, deeply practical guide to building real, lasting wealth. Ken and Mary blend behavioural science, lived experience and heartfelt wisdom into a system anyone can follow. This is the book to read if you want financial freedom that actually lasts and, more importantly, a life that feels meaningful along the way.'

Chris Ducker, author of *The Long-Haul Leader* and founder of Youpreneur®

'We all know the basic mechanics of money – earn more, spend less, invest the rest – but knowing isn't doing. In *The Wealth Habit*, Ken and Mary Okoroafor focus on the only thing that actually moves the needle: behaviour. It's a practical and empowering guide for anyone who wants to stop obsessing over the pennies and start focusing on the habits that truly lead to results.'
Rob Dix, *Sunday Times* bestselling author of *The Price of Money* and *Seven Myths About Money*

'This is the kind of money book I love! It's about the small, intentional habits that can change your relationship with money and, ultimately, your life. Ken and Mary are just so brilliant at making wealth feel accessible.'
Carrie Green, bestselling author of *She Means Business*

'This book shows you how seemingly simple things can drive crazy long-term returns. The best thing is Ken and Mary actually practice what they preach. This is like if your friendly, financially savvy uncle and auntie sat you down and showed you how to win the game of money. Really shows that wealth isn't a complex thing and can be attained through very simple practices anyone can do.'
Timothy Armoo, entrepreneur and *Sunday Times* bestselling author of *What's Stopping You?*

'If working out builds muscles in the gym, reading this book builds wealth habits in your mind. This book helps you build wealth, one small habit at a time, and gives you the framework to make it actionable, achievable and sustainable.'
Kristy Shen, author of *Quit Like a Millionaire*

'This book is a powerful reminder that a richer life is available to you if you are willing to make small, intentional choices when it comes to your relationship with money. If you apply the wisdom and insights that are shared in these pages, then you will be able to enjoy the rewards that come with living *The Wealth Habit* sooner than you think!'
Simon Alexander Ong, life coach, keynote speaker and author of *Energize*

'For those who are tired of chasing wealth and want to design their life with intention. This book offers a calmer, more humane approach to wealth that will equip you with the mental and emotional systems to reimagine your relationship to wealth.'
Anne-Laure Le Cunff, neuroscientist and bestselling author of *Tiny Experiments*

'A book for readers ready to take action with their personal finances. Rich in ideas, tools and tips, The Wealth Habit offers clear frameworks and concrete steps that help turn avoidance into action and chaos into structure.'

Vicky Reynal, financial psychotherapist and author of *Money on Your Mind*

'By now, there is a great deal of evidence from many decades of research that, when it comes to building wealth, two of the very most important factors in whether you will succeed or not are your mindset and your habits. In this important book, Ken and Mary Okoroafor provide you with the tools you need to make an enormous difference to your life, step by step. If you want to make this the year you get to grips with your finances, you will be well served by adding The Wealth Habit to your reading list!'

Andrew Craig, author of *How to Own the World* and founder of Plain English Finance

'The Wealth Habit discusses wealth building in the context of being human – a perspective that's so desperately needed, now more than ever. Another absolute banger from Ken and Mary, always fabulously written and research backed. This is a must read!'

Emma Edwards, author of *Good With Money* and founder of The Broke Generation

'A book full of aha money moments that will change your mindset and build your wealth.'

Helen Tupper, *Sunday Times* bestselling author of *The Squiggly Career*

'Ken and Mary have a rare gift: they make wealth building feel practical, human and achievable. The Wealth Habit isn't about shortcuts or hype – it's a practical guide to the tools, mindset and habits anyone can use to build lasting wealth.'

Rotimi Merriman-Johnson a.k.a. Mr MoneyJar

'A calm, intelligent and deeply practical guide to building wealth without burnout, shame or stress. The Wealth Habit proves that small habits, done consistently, can change everything.'

Sharmadean Reid, author of *New Methods for Women*

'As a maths teacher, I've spent years teaching students that small, consistent gains beat last-minute cramming every time – and *The Wealth Habit* proves the same is true for money. Ken and Mary have an extraordinary gift in being able to combine evidence, real life and compassion to create a system that makes wealth feel less intimidating and far more attainable. Where *Financial Joy* helped grateful readers reset their relationship with money, this book takes the next step for those still feeling left behind with money by offering a hopeful, practical path to building wealth that's achievable, human and sustainable.

Bobby Seagull, teacher, presenter and author of
The Life-Changing Magic of Numbers

'*The Wealth Habit* reframes wealth as something you build daily, not something you'll achieve "one day".'

Adrienne Adhami, author of *Decisions That Matter*
and wellness coach

'*The Wealth Habit* clearly shows the reader how real wealth can be built through small, consistent habits, over time. Grounded and practical, it reflects how Ken and Mary handle money together and what actually works in real life. I highly recommend *The Wealth Habit* to anyone who understands the basics of budgeting and is ready to choose their next best money steps with confidence.'

Hope Ware, founder of Under the Median

'*The Wealth Habit* is a refreshingly clear and practical guide to building lasting wealth. It focuses on small, consistent habits that feel genuinely achievable. One of the most practical and usable books on money habits I've read.'

Dominique Woolf, Sunday Times bestselling author and
founder of Woolf's Kitchen

'Here the simple truth is thrust not just in our faces but through our souls – consistency in simple habits of financial discipline (we used to say counting the pennies and building the pounds!) is the greatest act of logical conscientiousness – a decision which goes unnoticed because it's always there. This is matched only, ironically, by growing generosity – to give away is to grow wealth because the real discipline is holding a mindset that liberates our mood and manages our money. It's about time this book was seen by every hungry seeker.'

Lord Dr Michael Hastings CBE, Chairman, SOAS,
University of London

THE
WEALTH HABIT

SMALL CHANGES THAT WILL MAKE YOU RICH

Also by Ken and Mary Okoroafor:

Financial Joy

THE
WEALTH HABIT

SMALL CHANGES THAT WILL MAKE YOU RICH

KEN & MARY OKOROAFOR

QUERCUS

First published in Great Britain in 2026 by Quercus
Part of John Murray Group

Copyright © 2026 Ken Okoroafor and Mary Okoroafor

The moral right of Ken Okoroafor and Mary Okoroafor
to be identified as the author of this work has been
asserted in accordance with the Copyright,
Designs and Patents Act, 1988.

All rights reserved. No part of this publication
may be reproduced or transmitted in any form
or by any means, electronic or mechanical,
including photocopy, recording, or any
information storage and retrieval system,
without permission in writing from the publisher.

A CIP catalogue record for this book is available
from the British Library

TPB ISBN 978-1-52944-920-4
EBOOK ISBN 978-1-52944-922-8

10 9 8 7 6 5 4 3

Typeset in Gill Sans by CC Book Production

Cover design by Steve Leard

Printed and bound in Great Britain by Clays Ltd, Elcograf S.p.A.

Papers used by Quercus are from well-managed forests and other responsible sources.

Quercus
Carmelite House
50 Victoria Embankment
London EC4Y 0DZ

John Murray Group
Part of Hodder & Stoughton Limited
An Hachette UK company

The authorised representative in the EEA is Hachette Ireland,
8 Castlecourt Centre, Dublin 15, D15 XTP3, Ireland (email: info@hbgi.ie)

For our children, who bring love and purpose to our lives. And for every reader who has ever felt behind with money; may this mark the beginning of a new chapter of confidence, freedom and possibility.

Wealth

*A non-linear journey of peace, progress and purpose,
guided by daily choices, not society's checklist.*

Derived from the mid 12th century word *welth*, which means 'state or condition of happiness, wellbeing, joy'. Also from the old English word *weal*, which means 'welfare, wellbeing and prosperity'. *Weal* is related to the older word *wel*, meaning 'in a state of good health, soundly'.

Habit

A small action you repeat often until it happens automatically.

Derived from the Latin words *habere*, which means 'have, consist of', and *habitus*, which means 'condition, or state of being'.

CONTENTS

Introduction: The Wealth Mindset   1

Pillar 1:
Build the Mindset

1.	What is the Wealth Habit?	19
2.	The 1% Rule: Tiny Adjustments, Massive Wealth	35
3.	The Wealth-Identity Shift	49
4.	The Money-Guilt Cure	65
5.	Escaping the Scarcity Loop	81
6.	Money Triggers and How to Reprogramme Them	97

Pillar 2:
Build the Habit

7.	The Set-and-Soar System	117
8.	The Wealth-Multiplier Effect	133
9.	The Guilt-Free Spending Habit	155
10.	Your Future-Self Fund	167
11.	The 24-Hour Pause Button	181
12.	The Pay-Yourself-First Habit	193

Pillar 3:
Build the System

13.	The Effortless-Investing Habit	211
14.	The Side-Hustle Habit	231
15.	The Global-Wealth Habit	255
16.	The Financial-Freedom Calendar	275

Pillar 4:
Build the Life

17.	The Generosity Habit	293
18.	The Network Effect	305
19.	The Anti-Fragile Money Mindset	323
20.	Conclusion: Live the Wealth Habit	340

Glossary	342
Resources	345
Notes	347
Acknowledgements	355
Index	359
About the Authors	369

Introduction

THE WEALTH MINDSET

What if your journey to true wealth begins the moment you pin your dream on a wall?

It was a cold October evening in 2009 when I squeezed onto a packed London Underground train after another long day at work. I'd just come out of a breakup and despite hard graft, I felt as broke as everyone else in the wake of the global financial crisis.

Flipping through a discarded newspaper, I spotted an ad for a three-day property-investing seminar. Something about it lit a spark and I counted down the days until I could attend.

On day one, I entered a seminar hall of 400 and took the front-row seat. I scribbled notes for hours. Then, at the break, I scanned the room, and there she was: absolutely beautiful and graceful. Something within me said, 'Leave the front row and head to her table after the break', which I did. What I didn't know was that my life was about to change forever.

I felt led to buy her and her brother some sandwiches and snacks, which went down well. She'd tell me years later that this simple gesture dropped her guard. During another break, she laughed at one of my dry jokes and said, 'I'm Mary, by the way.' I grinned and replied, 'Ken, nice to finally meet you.'

On day three of the seminar, something life-changing happened. The facilitator invited everyone, table by table, to approach the 'commitment wall' and pin up their biggest dreams – no filters, just pure vision. My heart pounded as I stepped up to that wall, the thrill of declaring my deepest hope in public mingling with the risk of failure for all to see.

There we were, two strangers in the presence of many others, and we smiled as we wrote down our dreams. Mary pinned up, 'financial freedom to travel and give back', while I wrote, 'pay off a home debt-free' and 'one day quit the rat race'. Standing side by side, we realized we shared the same values: a hunger for freedom, the desire to provide for family, a passion for generosity, faith that God empowers us to create wealth and a belief in the power of small, consistent steps. In that moment, we weren't just attendees, we were co-pilots on a shared journey to live and discover the Wealth Habit.

I'd later find out that she was single (best news ever). As we walked down the escalator to the Underground, she casually pointed to a West End show she liked, *Stomp*. As soon as we swapped numbers, I went off and booked that show as a surprise, and this would become our first official date.

A year later, we were engaged and eight months after that we married, in 2011. I'd come to learn about property, but that seminar introduced to me my first and most important investment: the lifelong partnership that would fuel every habit and mindset in this book.

OUR MONEY JOURNEY

We both come from humble beginnings, having begun life with our families as first-generation immigrants to the UK with no money or connections. By applying the ideas in this book, we gradually hit milestones that matched our definition of wealth: built a loving home, paid off our £380k ($512k) mortgage in seven years and raised two wonderful children. We also invested in stocks, property, digital assets and purpose-led ventures; travelled to over 35 dream destinations; and gave back to our communities.

Over time, as we continued to level up our skillsets, toolsets and mindsets, we achieved financial independence at age 34 and, beyond that, reached financial freedom. We did this without winning the lottery or receiving an inheritance.

In all those years, we have navigated various economic challenges, such as the ramifications of the 2008 global financial crisis, the 2020 pandemic and the cost-of-living crisis, various redundancies, plus major life events, like losing friends and family, as well as health crises.

Our relationship with money has also shifted from being fear-based to purpose-driven stewardship rooted in abundance, generosity and faith.

Join us on this journey, build systems and small, habit-driven income streams now, so you're ready for whatever tomorrow brings. In an era where AI and automation are reshaping careers, *The Wealth Habit* ensures you never rely on a single paycheque.

UNDERSTANDING WEALTH: MORE THAN MONEY

Wealth isn't just the numbers on a bank statement, it's the quality of your days, the depth of your relationships and the legacy you leave behind. Across cultures, people have long understood that true wealth comes from the harmony of five pillars:

Time freedom

In Japan, the concept of *ikigai* reminds us that a life of purpose and balance is richer than one crammed with obligations. Real wealth means owning your schedule, so you can savor morning tea, attend family gatherings or simply pause and breathe. Wealth is being able to say 'no' without guilt.

Wellbeing

From the Mediterranean *la dolce vita* to Indian *sattvic* living, health is often regarded as our greatest asset. Investing in routine self-care, movement and rest compounds into energy and clarity, far more valuable than any portfolio.

Connection and community

In the African *ubuntu* philosophy, or Spain's extended family traditions, success is measured by the strength of our bonds. Building wealth without generosity or shared joy looks impressive from the outside, but can often leave you hollow on the inside.

Also within connection are lifelong partnerships. Marrying well or choosing a partner who shares your money values is like selecting a co-pilot for your financial journey. A marriage built on aligned goals, mutual accountability, shared habits and mindset is one of the highest-leverage 'investments' you can make.

Purpose and impact

Indigenous communities worldwide teach that prosperity includes giving back to the land and each other. When your financial habits fuel causes you believe in, be it micro-donations to local charities or time volunteered, you transform wealth into a force for lasting good.

Cultural wealth

Cultural wealth is the traditions, stories and collective resources we pass on, so that our children and communities inherit more than just bank balances. It's the sense of belonging, the celebration of heritage and the creation of shared experiences that outlast any paycheque.

In *The Wealth Habit*, we embrace this holistic vision. You'll learn to automate savings, become debt-free, grow your income, compound investments and master guilt-free spending, but always through the lens of a richer life. When your habits deliver financial freedom, the ability to choose your hours, health, relationships and impact, while embracing your culture, you don't just build wealth – you cultivate financial joy that uplifts your world and, by extension, enriches the human experience.

Pause and reflect

What does wealth mean to you personally?

We asked our communities @thehumblepenny to complete this sentence, 'I feel wealthy when …', and here are some of their responses:

- 'I have control over my time.'
- 'I'm strong and healthy.'
- 'I don't owe anyone anything!'
- 'My mortgage is paid off :)'
- 'My mind is at peace when I have clarity and my confidence in God is anchored.'
- 'I'm spending more quality time with my family.'
- 'I travel and see the world.'
- 'I don't have to count pennies for my food shopping and basics.'
- 'I'm sat in my garden looking at the flowers.'
- 'I have my cleaner come around.'
- 'I have financially free abundance.'

THE DECEPTION OF MONETARY WEALTH

The toxic pursuit of financial wealth at all costs has a way of destroying the soul. Perhaps you can relate to some of these examples.

- **False fulfillment:** Buying status feels thrilling, until the next upgrade beckons. That 'high' fades quickly, leaving you richer on paper but emotionally emptier than before.
- **Workaholic burnout:** Logging 80-hour weeks and sacrificing sleep, exercise and downtime to chase the next deal or meet deadlines, only to end up burned out, anxious, depressed and unable to enjoy any of the wealth you've amassed.
- **Ethical compromises:** Cutting corners to hit performance bonuses, then living in constant fear of being exposed.
- **Social isolation:** Ghosting friends and skipping family birthdays,

anniversaries and weekend football games to go on business trips or 'strategic' networking, only to end up emotionally absent from the lives of those you love, with no one to celebrate your successes.

- **Lifestyle inflation debt trap:** Expanding your lifestyle with high-interest credit – e.g. fancy cars, exotic holidays, upgrading to that mansion – only to discover your income can't keep up and you're paying interest for years.
- **Identity erosion:** When you define yourself by net worth or possessions, any market dip or broken asset becomes a personal crisis, your sense of self wavers with every financial headline.
- **Loss of integrity:** Lying on your CV, inflating your success stories or betraying colleagues to climb the corporate ladder, only to constantly look over your shoulder, mistrust others and question your own self-worth.
- **Spiritual emptiness:** That feeling that money is all you pursue but you never seem to have enough of it, and deep down you feel spiritually empty because money has become the god in your life.

Worst of all, in the toxic pursuit of wealth, it is easy to forget that when you die, no riches can accompany you beyond life's final door. Each of these scenarios shows how 'wealth at any cost' can erode the very foundations – i.e. health, relationships, values, joy – that make life worth living.

The Wealth Habit offers a different path. Rather than measuring success by what you own, we focus on who you become. By anchoring each tiny habit – for example, saving, investing, giving – on the foundations of identity, abundance, action and patience, you safeguard your values even as your wealth grows, so you never have to sacrifice your soul in the process.

INTRODUCING *THE WEALTH HABIT*™

The Wealth Habit™ is a mindset and habit system: a daily cycle of tiny, intentional money moves, which are triggered by your environment, reinforced by micro-wins and woven into your identity, and which compound into lasting freedom.

This book protects you from the deception of wealth by building habits that reinforce your core self; transforming fear of scarcity into confident, purposeful action and cultivating patience and trust that small, consistent moves compound into lasting security.

When you practise *The Wealth Habit*, wealth becomes a source of freedom, whether financial, emotional or spiritual, instead of a deceptive trap. You trade in the exhaustion of endless comparison for the steady joy of knowing you're building something that truly matters.

Why we wrote this book

Most people think that wealth is reserved for the lucky few, those born into privilege, gifted with an entrepreneurial streak or naturally skilled with money. But the truth is, financial success isn't about luck, it's about habits.

The Wealth Habit is a groundbreaking, behaviour-driven approach to wealth building that rewires the way you think about money, turning financial success into a series of effortless, repeatable actions.

Instead of rigid budgets or complex investment strategies, this book reveals how small daily financial moves compound into life-changing wealth — no matter where you start.

Whether you're struggling with money, looking to break free from the paycheque-to-paycheque cycle, or searching for a stress-free, automated way to build wealth, this book gives you a clear, habit-based roadmap to make financial success inevitable.

By focusing on small, repeatable money behaviours, *The Wealth Habit* ensures that true wealth isn't just something you achieve, it's something you sustain for life.

WHO IS THIS BOOK FOR?

No matter your background, income or stage of life, if you're ready to replace fear with clarity and build wealth that lasts, this book is for you. For example:

- **You're stuck in a paycheque-to-paycheque grind:** Small, consistent habits can transform your cash flow, no matter how little you start with.
- **You crave purpose, not just profit:** If you want wealth aligned with your values – e.g. spending guilt-free, giving generously, living with intention – this is your roadmap.
- **You need a system, not another hack:** If quick fixes haven't worked, these science-backed frameworks will build lasting momentum, step by step.
- **You face uncertainty from AI and automation:** In a world where jobs evolve or vanish, multiple income-stacking habits ensure you never depend on one paycheque.
- **You're building from scratch or feeling overwhelmed:** First-generation, immigrant or simply starting late, these habits meet you where you are and guide you forwards.
- **You value faith and generosity alongside financial gain:** If money

advice without heart feels hollow, learn how stewardship and abundance can fuel both impact and freedom.

WHAT MAKES THIS BOOK DIFFERENT?

There are excellent books about habits. There are excellent books about money. But *The Wealth Habit* is different.

- **It's global:** We've included stories and lessons from the UK, US, Kenya, India, China, Nigeria, Australia and beyond.
- **It's inclusive:** Whether you're single, married, a parent, a student or approaching retirement, this book is for you.
- **It's research-backed:** We include the latest behavioural science, neuroscience, financial psychology and global economic research.
- **It's real and timeless:** We've lived these habits, taught them and tested them. The ideas in this book will be relevant decades from now.
- **It's doable:** There's no jargon. No shame. No overwhelm.

Ken: As someone who worked in finance for 14 years and still struggles with uncertainty, I can tell you: expertise isn't the answer. Behaviour is. Once you learn to automate, track and enjoy the process, wealth becomes inevitable.

Mary: As someone who has to juggle motherhood, work and life, I want you to know: this book meets you where you are. You don't need to be perfect. You just need to start.

WHAT YOU'LL GET OUT OF THIS BOOK

Picture wealth like a house: you don't get it all at once; you build it step by step. This book is your guide to laying the foundation, raising the pillars and putting the roof in place. The roof is *The Wealth Habit* itself – the life where money works for you, where freedom and joy are no longer distant dreams but daily experiences. That's the life you're building as you turn these pages. To hold it up, you'll build four pillars, each one represented by a part of this book:

Pillar 1: Build the Mindset (Chapters 1–6)

In this section you'll rewire how you think about money, shifting your identity from 'employee' to 'wealth builder', dismantling guilt and scarcity, and learning how to master your emotional triggers. By the end of this part, you'll have the mental foundation to support every other habit in the book.

Pillar 2: Build the Habit (Chapters 7–12)

Next, you'll move from knowledge to action, using automation, stress-free cash-flow systems and simple compounding practices to make wealth building frictionless. These daily and weekly habits put your money on rails, creating momentum you can trust.

Pillar 3: Build the System (Chapters 13–16)

Here you'll scale up. You'll learn how to invest effortlessly, create new income streams, leverage geography for financial advantage and set up rhythms that keep your entire financial life humming in the background. This part turns habits into a self-reinforcing operating system.

Pillar 4: Build the Life (Chapters 17–20)

Finally, you'll ensure your wealth lasts and matters. You'll embed generosity, harness the power of relationships and develop an anti-fragile mindset that allows you not just to survive downturns but to thrive in them. This is where wealth becomes about freedom, impact and joy.

The four principles

What holds the house together? Four principles that make every habit doable and sustainable:

- Keep it simple.
- Keep it automatic.
- Keep it compounding.
- Keep it fun.

The strong pillars form the structure; the principles are the way you design and live in that house. They make it easy, liveable and worth staying in. Running through every chapter, like wiring in a home – invisible but essential – they make every framework in this book accessible, repeatable and sustainable.

Together, they form a house that doesn't just stand tall, it stands the test of time.

By the end of this book, you'll have built that house for yourself, not with bricks or mortar, but with habits – small, repeatable actions that compound into something extraordinary.

Also included

In addition to the wealth-building habits you can start immediately, you'll also find:

- Real stories from people across the globe who are applying them.
- Our signature frameworks, like The Habit Loop of Wealth™, The 1% Compound Ladder, The Joy-Spend Radar, The Set-and-Soar System and more.
- Faith-informed reflections and actions (where relevant).
- Tiny steps that become automatic and, eventually, life-changing.

Each chapter ends with a pause for reflection, small action step and chapter summary, so you're never just reading, you're moving.

THE FOUR MINDSET BLOCKERS

Before you start building a house, you have to clear the ground. You can't pour foundations on soil that's rocky, uneven or full of obstacles. The same is true for wealth habits. We've found that most people who struggle with money aren't held back by a lack of knowledge, they're blocked by invisible mindsets. These are the weeds in the ground, the cracks in the soil, the hidden barriers that stop you from building strong pillars. We have observed four of them:

- **Employee mindset**: Believing wealth only comes from trading hours for money.
- **Scarcity mindset**: Living in survival mode, hoarding every penny 'just in case'.

- **Overnight-success mindset**: Expecting big wins fast and quitting when progress feels slow.
- **Analysis-paralysis mindset**: Endlessly researching but rarely acting.

We'll help you clear these four blockers in the first part of the book and get the ground ready so you have the space and stability to lay the principles, raise the pillars and build a Wealth Habit that will stand for life.

IMPORTANT DISCLAIMER

Nothing we share in this book constitutes financial advice.

Beyond our professional expertise (Ken is a qualified Chartered Accountant, holds an MBA from Cambridge University Judge Business School and worked in the investment business for 14 years, working his way up to become a Chief Financial Officer), everything we share comes from our lived experience of working towards and achieving financial freedom, including everything we've learned from our parents, mentors and research by other experts.

In our corporate jobs, we've met others who are extremely wealthy. For example, Ken's work as a CFO in the venture capital business, helping to raise tens of millions of pounds, meant that he often interacted with high-net-worth individuals.

In addition, having coached thousands and taught millions of people through our content on how to achieve financial freedom and received tens of thousands of positive comments, emails and progress reports in the different areas we cover in this book, we know that our methods work.

All these experiences give us a unique perspective in order to bring something fresh with this book. We're confident that everything we share in this book will help you move forwards on your money journey and, beyond that, make building wealth inevitable.

OUR WORK

We are the multi-award-winning creators of The Humble Penny and Financial Joy Academy (FJA), where, so far, we've helped more than five million people to improve their relationship with money.

The Humble Penny is a personal finance and financial wellness brand, a community-driven platform that includes a blog, newsletter, YouTube channel, Instagram, LinkedIn and TikTok, reaching over 250,000 subscribers and followers every week. We help you build lasting wealth through simple, consistent financial habits, actionable insights and mindset shifts, empowering you to create financial joy. Learn more at thehumblepenny.com and follow @thehumblepenny.

FJA is a global, step-by-step membership platform and community designed to help 'Dream Makers' take action towards financial freedom while prioritizing wellbeing. FJA combines expert-led classes, tailored 'wealth paths', fortnightly coaching calls, a daily lunch-time club, monthly masterminds, accountability partnerships and a supportive community of like-minded individuals to guide you on your journey to lasting financial freedom. In addition, we deliver corporate workshops and provide a learning platform to help companies improve the financial wellbeing of their employees. Learn more at financialjoyacademy.com and follow @financialjoyacademy.

We are also *Sunday Times* bestselling authors of our debut book, *Financial Joy*, a ten-week plan to help you banish debt, grow your money and unlock financial freedom. Think of *Financial Joy* as the emotional and step-by-step practical 'reset' that helps you get unstuck and finally feel in control of your money, while *The Wealth Habit* is the 'system' that makes wealth effortless, inevitable and sustainable for life. Start with joy. Stay with habit. Finish with freedom.

STAY IN TOUCH

Send us your book shelfie or selfie on Instagram Stories @thehumblepenny and @financialjoyacademy to reshare.

Follow us on YouTube, Facebook, X and TikTok. Follow us on LinkedIn by searching 'Ken Okoroafor' and 'Mary Okoroafor'.

In addition, join over 40,000 readers of our weekly newsletter at our blog at www.thehumblepenny.com where you can also email us directly at book@thehumblepenny.com

Finally, remember that your Wealth Habit starts here. This book is a blueprint. A bridge. A challenge. But above all, it's an invitation to stop surviving and start building.

We believe wealth isn't just for the lucky few. It's for those who build it, brick by brick, habit by habit.

Let's do this together.

Love, Ken and Mary 🖤

PILLAR 1
BUILD THE MINDSET

Chapter 1

WHAT IS THE WEALTH HABIT?

The single shift that separates the wealthy from everyone else

Theme: *Foundation*
Lay your identity groundwork and shift from an 'employee' mindset to that of a 'wealth builder'.

THE WEALTH HABIT

Most people think getting rich is about knowing more, earning more or inheriting more. But what if the real secret is doing less, just more often?

Sixteenth July 1969: Kennedy Space Center, Florida. The pre-dawn sky was still inky black when the Saturn V rocket came to life. At its base, technicians finished loading five million pounds of liquid fuel, carefully measured to the gram, while engineers in the Launch Control Center felt tensions rise with each system check. In those final moments, every bolt and sensor had to be perfect; even a tiny misalignment could keep the rocket grounded.

At 9:32am, the engines ignited with a thunderous roar that rattled the control room. A wall of flame blossomed beneath Saturn V, vapour clouds billowing out like a cosmic waterfall. Slowly at first, then faster and faster, the rocket climbed, clearing the pad, piercing the atmosphere and vanishing into a trail of fire. In minutes, it had shed its first-stage boosters and accelerated past the speed of sound, and the Apollo 11 spacecraft was bound for the Moon.

But what does a moonshot have to do with building wealth? Everything.

The Wealth Habit is a mindset and habit system: a daily cycle of tiny, intentional money moves – triggered by your environment, reinforced by micro-wins and woven into your identity – that compound into lasting financial freedom.

Just as NASA stripped away all unnecessary weight so Saturn V could break free of Earth's pull, your path to financial success requires eliminating small obstacles such as decision fatigue, needless complexity and emotional roadblocks. When we overcomplicate money management, we stall before even leaving the pad.

What is the Wealth Habit?

- **Rigid budgets:** Like a rocket drenched in drag, intricate spreadsheets and endless apps slow you down.
- **Emotional turbulence:** Guilt over a purchase, fear of a market downturn or shame about past mistakes act like unpredictable wind shear, enough to knock you off course.
- **Lack of triggers:** Without a clear signal (e.g. 'After I have coffee, I'll do X') your habits never ignite, just as a misaligned valve would keep fuel from igniting.
- **Environment design:** Even the strongest resolve can't overcome a hidden cue. If your savings jar sits hidden in a drawer, you'll forget and never drop in a coin. Instead, put a bright 'rainy-day fund' widget on your phone's lock screen. Every time you unlock your phone, it reminds you to tap and save, just like seeing a glass jar on the counter. NASA didn't just remove friction, it also packed Saturn V with more propellant than strictly necessary, creating a safety buffer to handle unexpected turbulence. In wealth terms, your 'fuel' is purpose, identity and micro-wins.
- **Purposeful habits:** Every small action gets tethered to a meaningful 'why'. Just as NASA knew exactly where Apollo 11 needed to go, you must anchor each dollar, pound or euro moved and each stock purchased to a vision that pulls you forwards.
- **Identity shifts:** Declare, 'I am a wealth builder' the way an astronaut affirms, 'Failure is not an option'. That identity alone turns casual tasks (checking balances or automating transfers) into mission-critical steps.
- **Micro-celebrations:** Each habit completed, like marking off a transfer or cheering a small dividend deposit, produces a tiny dopamine surge, the equivalent of a rocket jolt at staging. Those micro-wins keep your confidence on the high.

Just as mission control stripped away every unnecessary bolt and loaded Saturn V with extra fuel to ensure Apollo 11 could escape Earth's pull, building wealth starts by shaping your environment – reducing friction from good habits, adding friction around bad habits you're trying to break, and fuelling your system with purpose and quick wins. Minimal drag, maximum fuel and tiny daily ignitions – that's how you lift off towards lasting wealth and freedom.

> **Wealth Habit Mantra 1:**
> *Habits > income*
> Your habits are the rocket fuel, not just your pay packet.

THE EMPLOYEE MINDSET

I (Ken) once had lunch with someone who worked for one of the largest investment banks in the world. He'd started as a working-class, first-generation immigrant but became an executive director by his forties. He was so successful, in terms of income, that his tax alone was a six-figure amount. During lunch, we discussed life and what I didn't expect him to say was: 'Man, things are hard, I feel broke.' I was stunned! If someone who earns a significant basic salary plus bonuses each year feels broke, what hope is there for anyone else?

You see, with the rise in income came significant lifestyle creep: a mansion over £1m (with more mortgage debt, more interest, higher property tax, insurance and maintenance costs), a sports car, private education for his children, luxury holidays, etc. The various things some of us want or feel we need, which, if we're being honest, mostly come down to society's – or potentially a partner's – expectations.

So, although he earned more than 99% of the global population, he felt trapped and still experienced financial stress every month, not only from needing to meet some high fixed costs, but also from the fear of redundancy without much to fall back on.

I've been there too. Early in my finance career, I earned well but always felt it wasn't enough. I tried keeping up, but I realized some lifestyle choices were holding me back – something had to change.

Research by Bank of America[1] found that around 35% of households with incomes below $50,000 (£38,000) a year are living paycheque to paycheque. This falls as incomes rise, but, surprisingly, 20% of households with incomes above $150,000 (£115,000) are also living paycheque to paycheque. Of course, the rising cost of living and lower incomes are key reasons why the percentage of households just making ends meet keeps rising year on year, but there is more at play.

Intelligence and hard work don't always translate to lasting wealth. Even experts fall into debt when lifestyle habits override what they know. This isn't a knowledge gap – it's a mindset gap. We call this the 'employee mindset' – the belief that your financial future depends solely on your job. It centres on dependency: a cycle of trading time for money, waiting for the next salary, raise or bonus to get ahead, rather than creating or growing wealth daily.

We believe there is another way, that of the 'wealth builder', which focuses on small, cumulative habits and building systems and assets. By focusing on habit design rather than income boosts, you will build a foundation that sustains wealth through life's ups and downs.

The Employee Mindset	The Wealth-Builder Mindset
'I trade time for money.'	'I use money to buy back time.'
Waits for pay rises, promotions or bonuses	Creates income through habits, assets and systems
Spends in proportion to income	Builds in proportion to income
Focuses on job security	Focuses on financial security and freedom
Money is a reward for hard work	Money is a tool for creating options
Financial life is reactive	Financial life is intentional and designed
Fears losing income	Builds resilience through multiple income streams

WHY HABITS, NOT INCOME, DETERMINE LONG-TERM WEALTH

Research in behavioural science shows that consistent routines have more impact on outcomes than one-off efforts (e.g. getting a pay rise).

Self-control drives saving and investment behaviour

Self-control is a better predictor of long-term wealth than income because it shapes how money is managed, saved and invested, not just how much is earned. In our experience, self-control can be achieved by optimizing your environment to reduce the cue that triggers a bad habit.

For example, let's say you have a habit of impulsively buying things late at night after scrolling on Instagram. The cue is boredom or stress, the routine is browsing and buying, the reward is a dopamine hit or short-term comfort. To apply self-control through environment optimization, you could:

- Remove saved cards from shopping sites. This adds friction, making purchases less instant.
- Use app blockers or time limits for Instagram or TikTok during peak temptation hours.
- Keep your phone out of your bedroom at night, reducing the cue (mindless scrolling in bed).

However, reducing temptation isn't easy. In our Nigerian culture expensive cars signal success, and seeing family and friends in expensive financed cars once made us question our modest second-hand vehicle. We couldn't avoid them – and willpower wasn't enough – so we reframed the car's place in our identity: not a status symbol, but an enabler of freedom. Eight years on, that shift has saved us thousands, which we've invested or enjoyed instead.

Research shows that people with strong self-control tend to save consistently from each paycheque, invest for the future and avoid impulsive spending, no matter how much they earn. Over time, this builds financial security and long-term wealth. On the flip side, even high earners with poor self-control often spend more as their income grows, making it harder to accumulate real wealth.

In addition, studies show that people with strong self-control feel less anxious about money and are more confident and secure about both their current finances and future plans.[2]

Behaviour and mindset shapes financial decisions

Financial habits start forming from childhood. The way you manage money is rarely just about numbers, it's shaped by your mindset, beliefs and the money stories you've absorbed over time, often without realizing it.

If you grew up seeing money disappear quickly, you might cling to it tightly or avoid taking risks, like investing, out of fear of losing it. On the other hand, a person raised to see saving as normal, even rewarding, is far more likely to carry that habit into adulthood without much effort.

Our financial behaviours often have deep, emotional roots. Understanding those roots is the first step to changing them.

Wealth grows in the space between wanting something now and choosing to wait

Decades of research shows that people who can delay gratification tend to experience better financial outcomes later in life. In Stanford's famous marshmallow experiment, children faced a choice: eat one marshmallow now or wait for two later.[3] Around 75% didn't wait. It tested delayed gratification and revealed that patience wasn't a natural or pre-determined trait, but was shaped by their experiences and the reliability of their environment.[4] The same applies to our finances. It's not about how much you earn, but about how consistently you choose long-term rewards over short-term indulgence in any economic circumstance.

Wealth is grown with multiple income streams

Most millionaires don't rely on one income stream. They build a mix — dividends, businesses, investments, property — that creates stability and momentum. But this isn't just for the rich. Even on a modest income, you can build the habit of thinking beyond one source, layering new ways to earn over time. It's consistency and creativity, not cash alone, that drive diversification. We'll explore this in Chapters 9 and 14.

Lifestyle choices dictate where you arrive

Research shows our daily spending and lifestyle choices predict wealth more than income.[5] Two households can earn the same yet end up worlds apart – one intentional, the other inflated. It's the quiet consistency of saving, investing, budgeting and planning that builds lasting wealth. Higher income helps, but without good habits, more money just means more spending.

THE SCIENCE BEHIND COMPOUNDING SMALL FINANCIAL BEHAVIOURS

What if we told you that moving just $1 into savings each morning could be more powerful than a one-off $1,000 bonus? That's the quiet power of habit-driven compounding.

Neuroscience shows that when we repeat a tiny action in response to the same daily cue – say, transferring $1 right after your morning coffee – those neural pathways strengthen. Over time, the brain stops questioning the move entirely. By the end of a year, you've saved $365 without having to debate or budget for it, and each deposit, like a reinvested dividend, grows quietly in the background.

Behavioural economists have found that frequency beats size when it comes to saving.

In a real-world experiment conducted by a bank in the Philippines, clients were encouraged to make smaller, more frequent deposits using behavioural nudges like SMS reminders and a weekly savings calendar.[6] Those who saved little and often grew their account balances by 37% more than those who didn't receive the nudges.

The real advantage comes when consistency meets scale – as your regular savings naturally grow in size and begin earning returns of their own. That's when momentum compounds and wealth accelerates.

THE HABIT LOOP OF WEALTH™

To make the science real, we created the Habit Loop of Wealth™ to help you turn small money actions into automatic habits. It's built on four parts: **trigger**, **action**, **reinforcement** and **identity**. Each repeated action strengthens your identity as a wealth builder – until wealth becomes your default, not your goal.

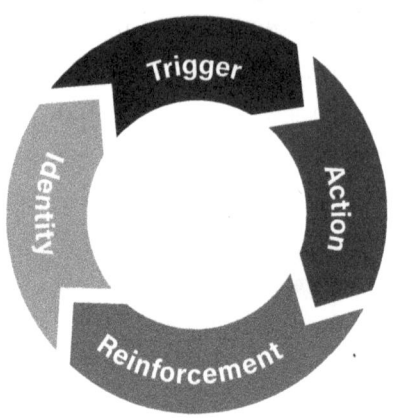

Identify your trigger

Choose a cue you already do daily (for example, making coffee or checking emails) in order to tie this to a simple action. 'When my mug is full, I do X.' Create triggers by designing your environment to place visual cues such as a sticky note on the coffee machine, a savings widget or a calendar reminder.

Choose the tiny action

Make it so small you can't say no (e.g. transfer $1, read one money article, round up a purchase). Example: '$1 feels trivial, but it proves I can show up.' Remove friction: keep your banking app one tap away and skip extra logins.

Create immediate reinforcement

Celebrate with a one-second fist pump, tap the habit tracker or jot a note. This small reward cements the loop. Like NASA monitored each stage separation to confirm success. The positive reinforcement tells your brain, 'That felt good', making it more likely you'll repeat the habit tomorrow.

Let identity fly (repeat until automatic)

Repeat this loop for at least 21 days. Your thoughts shift from, 'I'm an employee scraping by' to 'I'm someone who automatically saves.' Handle slip-ups gracefully. If you miss a day, identify what broke the loop (no trigger, no reward), adjust and restart. Once $1 is effortless, automate it or bump it to $2. This mirrors a rocket's stage separation system: initial small thrust escapes low orbit, later stages add more fuel for the journey.

Behind our Habit Loop of Wealth sits decades of behavioural science, from Charles Duhigg's emphasis on the cue, routine, reward loop (*The Power of Habit*) to James Clear's insight that 1% improvements add up (*Atomic Habits*) to B J Fogg's tiny-behaviour approach (*Tiny Habits*). We've adapted the best of each into a single, unified loop designed specifically for wealth.

By repeating this loop – trigger, action, reinforcement, identity – you'll build an invisible wealth machine. Over days, weeks and months, these micro-actions compound into real financial progress without you having to remember or muster willpower every single time.

The framework in action

We use this framework in our own lives. Two years into our mortgage, after adjusting our lifestyle (the trigger), we called the bank to overpay by £500 a month (the action). That one call wiped nine years off our term – nine years of life, debt-free. When our initial mortgage deal ended, we switched to one without overpayment penalties, giving us full freedom to accelerate progress. We gamified the process, tracking it on a mortgage-free chart and celebrating milestones with dinners out (the reinforcement). When our balance dropped from six figures to five, we marked it with a weekend in the Algarve. Gradually, we shifted from mortgage slaves to wealth builders (the identity shift) and paid off our home in seven years instead of 25 – free at last, we increased our investment in stocks each month.

HOW TO START BECOMING A WEALTH BUILDER TODAY

True wealth begins in your mind long before it ever shows up in your bank balance. Neuroscience confirms that identity drives behaviour: when you see yourself as a wealth builder, your brain automatically scans for opportunities to save, invest and grow. To shift your identity, you will need to flip your internal script.

Declare your new identity

Change 'I wish I could save' to 'I am a wealth builder.' Wealth builders don't wait for someday, they act now. Stand in front of a mirror and say it out loud. Your tone, posture and conviction rewire your brain, so every dollar moved strengthens that identity. Repeat it daily – morning, evening and before any money decision.

Reframe every choice as a win

Swap, 'I'm giving up $5' for, 'I'm investing $5.' Next time you pause before a daily purchase think, 'I'm choosing growth.' That mental flip turns FOMO (fear of missing out) into JOMO (joy of missing out); you don't feel deprived, you feel powerful. Within weeks, you'll start craving the pride of seeing your freedom fund rise.

Embed a three-second anchor ritual

    Trigger: every time you unlock your phone.
    Action (i.e. an affirmation): whisper, 'My habits make me rich.'
    Reinforcement (i.e. a micro-win): tap your thumb and forefinger once.

This tiny ritual links a daily trigger (unlocking your phone) to your wealth identity. The tap gives a small dopamine hit, wiring the affirmation faster. Within days, it primes your brain to spot micro-saving or investing moments as automatically as checking the weather.

PAUSE FOR REFLECTION

Think back to your last three pay days:

- **Trigger:** What do you naturally do on pay day? Grab a coffee or open your banking app?
- **Action:** What tiny habit could follow this? For example, you could transfer £10 or $20 to your freedom fund.
- **Reinforcement:** How will you celebrate? Tick your tracker and savour that moment of pride.
- **Identity:** How does it feel to act as a wealth builder rather than an employee spending a paycheque? Write one word capturing this sense of agency.

You already have the ability to build wealth. Not just by earning more, but by repeating small actions that align with who you want to become. One tiny shift, done consistently, will change everything. Wealth doesn't start with money, it starts with habits. Start small. Repeat often. Let the habit lead the way.

> *Small action step*
> Choose one habit you want to build (e.g. checking your balance daily or moving $1 to savings). Identify your trigger (e.g. brushing your teeth). Perform the action. Reinforce it (e.g. tracking it on a visible calendar).

Chapter summary

- The Wealth Habit is a mindset and habit system: tiny, intentional money moves – triggered by your environment, reinforced by micro-wins and woven into your identity – that compound into lasting freedom.
- Reducing friction (streamlining your environment, reducing emotional turbulence and inertia) and adding fuel (purpose, identity and celebrations) creates steady momentum towards wealth and freedom.
- True wealth isn't about how much you earn but what you consistently do with your money.
- Habits beat income: tiny, repeated or automated actions outpace pay rises through the power of compounding.
- The Habit Loop of Wealth is a cycle of trigger, action, reinforcement and identity that rewires your mindset from employee to wealth builder.

Chapter 2

THE 1% RULE: TINY ADJUSTMENTS, MASSIVE WEALTH

How to make wealth building effortless with micro-changes

> **Theme: Patience**
> Once you see yourself as a builder you learn to trust tiny daily gains rather than chasing big wins.

THE WEALTH HABIT

Wealth isn't built in leaps, it's built in layers. If you've ever wondered how the rich get richer, the answer may surprise you: small, invisible steps, repeated with consistency.

Imagine standing by a serene lake at dawn, the water smooth like glass. You pick up a small pebble, barely noticeable, and toss it gently into the lake. At first, the impact is tiny, just a quiet plop, but soon the ripples spread outwards, softly expanding, until they touch every corner of the water's surface. Each ripple amplifies the pebble's initial small action into something visible, powerful and far-reaching. This encapsulates the lasting impact of small changes.

To see this principle in action in the real world, consider the remarkable journey of Eliud Kipchoge, the Kenyan marathon runner who shattered records and famously became the first person to run a marathon in under two hours. On 12 October 2019, in Vienna, he completed 26.2 miles in 1 hour, 59 minutes and 40 seconds, a feat once considered beyond human limits. To put that in perspective, Kipchoge ran 100 metres in just over 17 seconds, 422 times in a row, maintaining a pace of around 4 minutes and 34 seconds per mile for the entire marathon.

But what's most remarkable isn't just the outcome, it's how he got there. Kipchoge achieved this not by seeking some radical breakthrough, but by stacking dozens of microscopic gains on top of each other: refining his posture, calibrating his nutrition, rotating elite pacemakers in precise formations to reduce wind resistance, selecting the perfect weather window and even training in custom-engineered shoes designed for maximum efficiency. Each adjustment on its own was almost imperceptible. But together they shattered what the world thought was possible.

While not every change was strictly a '1% improvement', the compounding effect of these tweaks was crucial to his success. He later said,

'No human is limited.' His achievement wasn't magic; it was the triumph of compounding micro-improvements.

Imagine applying this principle to your financial actions, i.e. those tiny, nearly imperceptible adjustments you can effortlessly make each day. What if, instead of expecting a sudden financial windfall, you focused on becoming just 1% better each day at managing, saving or investing your money?

Most people chase overnight successes, believing that wealth is created through big leaps or lucky breaks. Yet the truth, the quiet secret of genuine wealth, is far simpler: it's built through tiny, consistent changes compounded over time. This is the essence of the 1% Rule, and exactly why it's profoundly powerful. One small adjustment today, another tomorrow, and soon enough these micro-changes cascade into massive financial outcomes.

Let's discover how small becomes mighty when harnessed correctly, and why patience is your greatest wealth-building ally.

> **Wealth Habit Mantra 2:**
> Small steps, big freedom.

MICRO-HABITS IN MONEY MANAGEMENT

Before we explore the mechanics of compounding, we need to zoom in even closer on the micro-habits that quietly power it all. These aren't grand gestures but small, repeatable behaviours that quietly rewire your financial future.

We often underestimate the astonishing impact of small, repeated actions. Science and real-world experience both prove that sustained financial wellbeing hinges not on grand gestures but on tiny, habitual improvements.

A recent Government of Canada study of 1,119 young women (aged 16–25) found that even brief five-minute online activities – such as sharing a short story about a money win, explaining a financial concept in their own words or reading another woman's story – significantly boosted financial confidence within a week and led to more saving, budgeting and debt repayment over the month.[7] The takeaway: low-friction actions, repeated, build capability and control.

Take Sophie, a young professional in Manchester who struggled to save. Traditional budgeting advice felt overwhelming. So, she started small: each morning she'd spend two minutes checking her banking app and moving a few pounds – like the odd £1.37 – into a savings pot. Weeks later, she discovered her app's auto round-up feature, which saved spare change from her everyday spending. Within three months, she'd quietly built up over £250 entirely through small, effortless daily actions.

This concept aligns perfectly with modern neuroscience research. Neuroscientists describe habits as neural shortcuts, which form through repetition. Each time Sophie performed her simple saving habit, she reinforced a neural pathway. Eventually, it became as automatic as brushing her teeth. Researchers at University College London found that habit formation takes, on average, around 66 days,[8] significantly reinforcing the effectiveness of small, consistent actions in embedding lasting financial habits.

This approach is accessible globally, whether you're a young family in Sydney cutting takeaway expenses, a retiree in London automating small pension contributions or a student in Nairobi setting aside just a few shillings each day. Micro-habits scale effortlessly because they demand minimal effort and adapt naturally to individual lifestyles.

Crucially, the psychological impact of micro-habits surpasses mere financial gains. They transform identity. With each small win you reinforce your powerful self-image as a wealth builder. Soon, managing money shifts from something daunting to an empowering daily practice. This identity shift, as insignificant as it may feel initially, is your secret weapon in maintaining long-term wealth-building momentum.

Ultimately, embracing micro-habits in money management isn't just about financial growth; it's about transforming your relationship with money, one small daily action at a time. Like Kipchoge's meticulous marathon preparations, your consistent financial adjustments will yield extraordinary results.

WHY IMPROVING BY JUST 1% DAILY CAN LEAD TO EXPONENTIAL FINANCIAL GROWTH

Now that we've seen how micro-habits shift our mindset and behaviour, the next question is: why does this seemingly insignificant 1% matter so much over time? The answer lies in the surprising science of compounding and how tiny gains today unlock exponential growth tomorrow.

The principle behind the 1% daily improvement is remarkably straightforward, yet astonishingly powerful: small, consistent changes, compounded over time, yield exponential results. Mathematically, improving by just 1% each day for a year doesn't simply yield modest progress, it creates an outcome almost 38 times greater than the starting point. Conversely, declining by 1% daily diminishes your capabilities almost down to zero. This concept, well-articulated by author James Clear in his book *Atomic Habits*, highlights the stark reality of how tiny, incremental actions compound significantly over time.

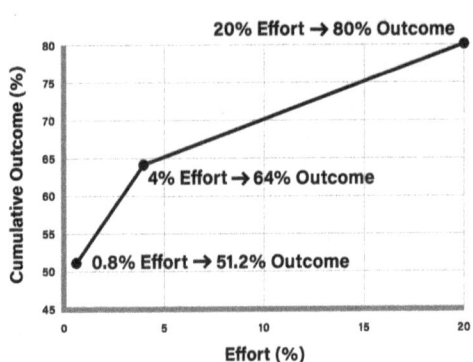

The Compounding Power of the Right 1%

As you apply the 80:20 rule recursively, you find that just 0.8% of the right actions can produce over 50% of your results. This is the hidden math behind high-leverage habits and why finding your 'right 1%' matters more than doing more.

Here's another, lesser-known compounding insight worth noting. The famous 80:20 rule, also known as the Pareto principle, says that around 20% of your actions drive around 80% of your results. The 80:20 rule isn't just theory — it shows up everywhere. Around 80% of traffic flows on about 20% of roads. Roughly 20% of destinations receive around 80% of all international tourists. About 20% of the world's countries produce around 80% of global GDP.[9] But what happens when you apply that rule in layers more than once — say, three times? You begin to see the compounding power of leverage in action.

If 20% of your actions drive 80% of your results, then 20% of that top 20% (just 4% of your total actions) could be creating about 64% of your outcomes:

20% (0.2) × 20% (0.2) = 4% (0.04)
80% (0.8) × 80% (0.8) = 64% (0.64)

Go one layer deeper and it gets even more powerful: the top 20% of that again – around 1% of what you do – could be responsible for roughly 50% your results.

20% (0.2) × 20% (0.2) × 20% (0.2) = 0.8% (0.008)
80% (0.8) × 80% (0.8) × 80% (0.8) = 51.2% (0.512)

In other words, not all effort is equal. A tiny fraction of your actions carries almost all your leverage. Focus on those few, and you'll multiply progress with less strain and more intention.

This is why your 1% habits matter. The right micro-action isn't just 'better than nothing', it's often the difference between noise and real progress. It's about doing things that are smarter, because one well-chosen habit can quietly produce half your long-term results.

Take Mark, for example, a software engineer living in San Francisco. Initially, Mark could only afford to save a small fraction of his income – around 2%. Rather than attempting ambitious jumps, he chose a modest strategy: increasing his savings by a mere 1% every few months. At first, these small increments barely felt noticeable. But within just five years, Mark's savings rate reached nearly 20% of his income, effortlessly achieved without significant lifestyle disruption. The result? Mark accumulated substantial savings that provided financial security and flexibility he had never anticipated.

Mark's experience reflects something researchers have confirmed across millions of people. The real-world impact of small, sustained improvements is best exemplified by the Save More Tomorrow™ (SMarT) programme by Shlomo Benartzi and Richard Thaler.[10] Employees who commit to gradually increasing their pension contributions, usually by just a few percentage points, automatically over successive pay raises saw their retirement savings jump from around 3.5% to nearly 13.6% within 40 months. This programme proves that financial transformation often doesn't come from heroic effort, but from designing small systems that steadily push you forwards.

In the UK, auto enrolment has built on similar behavioural principles. Since 2012, more than ten million people have been automatically enrolled into workplace pensions.[11] While participants didn't actively choose to increase contributions, the government introduced a phased approach, gradually raising minimum contributions from 2% to 8% between 2018 and 2019. These increases were timed to coincide with tax and minimum wage changes to soften the impact, mirroring the behavioural insight of the SMarT framework: make progress feel painless. Research from Nest and Vanguard confirms how effective this behavioural design is.[12] Even after a five-fold increase in required contributions, opt-out rates stayed low, especially among long-term members. Those saving for over nine months were significantly more likely to stick with the higher rates. In many cases, people simply adapted. The higher contribution became the new normal.

Globally, from New York's financial centres to communities in Lagos, people everywhere are discovering the power of small, steady improvements. Whether it's adjusting your savings, growing your investments or trimming spending, daily tweaks quietly compound into big results. And because these shifts don't require major lifestyle changes, financial growth becomes accessible to anyone.

At its core, the 1% Rule isn't about overnight success, it's about patience, consistency and intention. A quiet financial revolution anyone can join, one small, achievable step at a time.

HOW TO APPLY THIS RULE TO SAVING, INVESTING AND EARNING MORE

Understanding the theory is one thing, but how do you actually live it out? You don't need more spreadsheets or willpower to apply the 1% Rule to your finances. What you need is a small, consistent shift in how you save, invest and earn. Think of it like turning a dial, not flipping a switch.

Saving: start with a tiny transfer

Most people save backwards, waiting to see what's left at the end of the month. A better approach? Automate a 1% increase in your saving rate today. If you earn $5,000 a month, that's just $50. Over time, this can grow into thousands with little effort, especially if you increase it gradually each year as your income rises.

Alternatively, use a standing order or banking app to round up your spending and sweep the spare change into a savings pot.

Investing: build your knowledge and your contributions

Already investing? Try increasing your contribution by 1% a month, either in value or as a share of income. Most platforms make this easy to automate.

New to investing? Start smaller. A 1% daily improvement could be five minutes a day learning investing basics: read a blog, watch a video or explore your pension. That steady habit builds confidence, and confidence moves you from hesitation to action.

You might begin with $10 a month in a global index fund. As your comfort grows, so will your investment habit.

Earning: 1% more value, 1% more income

Earning more doesn't require a big leap. A 1% improvement might mean learning a new skill on LinkedIn Learning, spending ten minutes improving your AI prompts, pitching an idea at work or connecting with one new professional a week. Small steps like these can open doors to promotions, freelance gigs or new income streams.

One member at the Financial Joy Academy (FJA) sent one outreach message per weekday to potential property clients. It took 15 minutes a day. Within three months, she had a side income, recouped her investment and was on track to match her full-time salary.

Your version might be asking, 'What's one small way I can grow my value or visibility today?' Then doing that on repeat.

Ensure simplicity and sustainability

Applying this principle takes only small tweaks: automate your savings, spend a few minutes a day learning or schedule consistent professional growth. Its power lies in keeping it simple and sustainable.

The psychological win is just as strong – each small step affirms your identity as someone in control of their financial future.

By embedding the 1% Rule into how you save, invest and earn, you create a steady, sustainable engine for financial growth. It's not about overnight miracles, it's about consistent, exponential progress.

FRAMEWORK: THE 1% COMPOUND LADDER

To make 1% daily improvements a way of life, we created the 1% Compound Ladder, a step-by-step guide to building financial momentum through small actions. It has four rungs: **awareness, action, accumulation and autopilot**. Each rung moves you from knowing what to do to having your finances run themselves – simply, sustainably and with minimal effort. It's a behavioural roadmap built on clarity and progress.

The 1% Rule: Tiny Adjustments, Massive Wealth

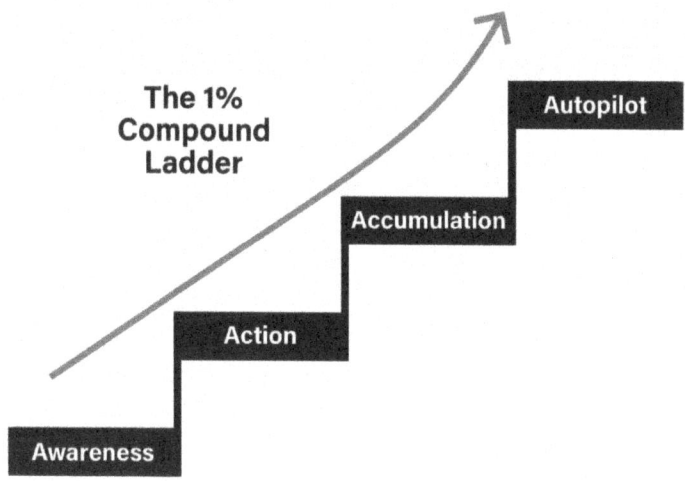

Framework illustration

Let's bring this to life with a real-world example. Alex earns a steady income but has always struggled to save or invest consistently. He decides to use the 1% Compound Ladder to build better money habits:

- **Awareness:** He starts by noticing that he spends $10 on takeaways three times a week. That's $120 a month. He becomes aware of the habit and its long-term impact.
- **Action:** Alex decides to divert just $10 of that each week into a savings pot instead. This is his 1% action – small enough to be sustainable, significant enough to start momentum.
- **Accumulation:** As the weeks pass, his $10 becomes $20, then $30 weekly. He's not only saving more but building confidence. His account grows quietly in the background, and his consistency builds a rhythm.

- **Autopilot:** After a few months, Alex sets up a direct debit to automatically transfer $120 monthly into an investment account. Now, he doesn't need to think about it; his system does the work for him.

This ladder could just as easily apply to increasing income (freelancing one hour more per week) or investing (learning one concept per day or investing $1 more monthly).

How it works

The genius of the 1% Compound Ladder lies in its design: it meets you where you are and grows with you. Most systems fail because they demand too much, too soon. This one thrives on modesty and momentum.

- **Awareness is the gateway:** You can't change what you don't notice. Tracking your habits, even just observing, is enough to shift your mindset.
- **Action is where progress begins:** Pick one small behaviour to tweak. Make it specific and easy. This is not about discipline, it's about direction.
- **Accumulation is where confidence kicks in:** Small wins build trust in yourself. Each repeated behaviour reinforces your identity as someone who handles money well.
- **Autopilot is your freedom phase:** By now, the habit is locked in. Systems are running. You're no longer trying, you're maintaining.

We've seen this ladder transform lives across income levels, ages and cultures. It works because it honours human nature: we resist big, we embrace small. And when small is repeated with intention, it becomes unstoppable. This isn't just a framework, it's your financial staircase to sustained, automatic wealth.

PAUSE FOR REFLECTION

Think back to the last time you told yourself, 'I'll start saving or investing when things calm down' or 'when I earn more'. What's one tiny financial action you could take today – even if your life is busy or income is tight – that would move you 1% forwards? Write it down and name the specific moment in your day it will happen.

> *Small action step*
> Open your banking app and create a new savings pot, name it '1% wealth fund'. Transfer just £1 or $1 (or your local currency equivalent) into it. That's it. Let the habit begin, not with pressure but with proof that you're in motion.
>
> Let's make this more fun. Take a screenshot of your '1% wealth fund' pot and post it on Instagram Stories and tag @thehumblepenny so that we can celebrate your 1% leap.

Every wealthy person you admire didn't start with millions. They started with a system. The 1% Rule is your system, it's quiet, powerful and compounding beneath the surface. Trust the small steps. Trust yourself. Over time, this tiny habit creates a life-changing ripple.

Chapter summary

- Small daily habits have a massive cumulative impact on your finances.
- Micro-habits, like checking your account or saving spare change, rewire your brain and build momentum.
- Improving by just 1% each day creates exponential results through the power of compounding. Just 1% of your efforts can drive roughly 50% of your outcomes.
- The 1% Compound Ladder (awareness, action, accumulation, auto-pilot) gives you a simple roadmap to automate wealth building.
- Start small, stay consistent and let the system carry you forwards, even on days when motivation doesn't show up.

Chapter 3

THE WEALTH IDENTITY SHIFT

You don't need a raise,
you need a new identity first

> **Theme: Deepening identity**
> Solidify your new self-image as a wealth builder and break limiting beliefs so you can own your goals.

> 'Don't ask your child what they want to be when they grow up. Ask them what they can be.' Idris Elba

What do you want to be when you grow up? Chances are you were asked that question more than once as a child. I (Ken) didn't know exactly what I wanted to be, but I did know what the 'respectable' options in my Nigerian household were: doctor, lawyer, accountant or engineer.

I chose to train as an accountant and that single decision shaped a massive part of who I thought I was. Whenever I met someone new at a networking event, a dinner party or even the school gate, the question always came: 'So, what do you do for a living?' And without missing a beat, I'd reply, 'I'm a chartered accountant.'

But here's the truth: I didn't feel like an accountant. Deep down, I felt like I had so much more to offer the world. Yet I had boxed myself into an identity that defined how others saw me and, more dangerously, how I saw myself. That one title dictated what I focused on professionally, how I earned money and what I believed was possible.

Because I saw myself as 'just' an accountant:

- I relied on my job as my only source of income for years.
- I neglected other talents and passions that deserved attention.
- I eventually began to stagnate, losing confidence and growing afraid of stepping outside the nine-to-five box.

Everything changed the day I met a life coach who challenged me to ask: what if you saw yourself not just as an accountant but as a creator of value? That one identity shift transformed my life. Today, I'm an author, investor, international speaker, entrepreneur, YouTuber, blogger, financial coach, chartered accountant, teacher, mentor, parent, husband and still expanding.

You might be wondering, what does all this have to do with wealth? Here's the truth: you'll never out-earn the identity you hold in your mind.

Your financial identity – how you see yourself – controls more of your future than your salary ever will. If you see yourself as someone who's bad with money, every smart financial move will feel unnatural. Shift that identity? Gradually, building wealth becomes the most natural thing in the world.

Over time, with this shift in my identity has also come a significant upwards shift in our household financial wealth, as well as other dimensions of wealth, including giving me a sense of purpose and confidence about the future.

Melissa's story

Melissa Westgate, a life coach and entrepreneur based in Adelaide, Australia, spent over a decade working traditional nine-to-five jobs. Despite succeeding professionally, she always sensed a pull towards something more expansive. As she later reflected: 'I've always had the mindset of an entrepreneur.'

That mindset began to show itself more tangibly 15 years ago, when she and her then-husband made the intentional and difficult decision to invest early in their first property. She said, 'It wasn't just about owning property; it was about learning how to make money work for me.'

Back then, Melissa never imagined she'd one day be the person handling tenants, managing property upgrades and making financial decisions with long-term impact. At the time, she didn't see herself as someone capable of managing investments or owning a business. But gradually, that changed. Through consistent action of researching, saving, making tough calls and taking small risks, Melissa's identity shifted from employee to investor.

One week, as a tenant moved out, she found herself confidently reviewing what repairs and upgrades would add value. Painting, new carpets, market positioning – all decisions she once thought were for 'other people'. Now, they're part of who she is.

Over time, Melissa realized she had quietly transitioned from being just an employee to thinking like a business owner and investor. She wasn't just working for money anymore; she was learning how to make money work for her. 'I wouldn't have seen myself as someone who could handle this,' she reflected. 'But now, it's just part of who I am.'

Melissa's transformation wasn't overnight and she's quick to admit that she's still growing. But what's clear is this: her financial shift began with an identity shift. She chose to see herself differently. And in doing so, she unlocked a new financial future.

Melissa's financial identity shift mirrors her broader journey of personal transformation. She's lived and worked across Canada, Japan and Australia, summited Mount Fuji and Kilimanjaro, and built a life around pushing past her comfort zone. She often says the real summit isn't external, it's becoming the kind of person who owns her value and multiplies it. Her love of personal development, paired with global resilience, has fuelled not just her income but her sense of purpose and self-trust.

Even if property isn't your path, Melissa's story shows that identity, not income or asset class, is the foundation of all financial growth.

> **Wealth Habit Mantra 3:**
> You don't become wealthy and then act like it. You act wealthy first through habits and the wealth follows.

IDENTITY-FIRST WEALTH BUILDING

In a world obsessed with numbers – such as net worth, income and investment-portfolio value – we often miss the root cause of sustainable wealth: self-perception.

Wealth isn't merely built through action. It's built through actions aligned with identity. That's why people who win the lottery often go broke and people with modest salaries can become millionaires. It's not about what they have. It's about who they believe they are.

This chapter fits into the larger Wealth Habit journey as a turning point. In Chapter 1 we introduced the Habit Loop of Wealth (see page 28) and in Chapter 2 the 1% Compound Ladder (see page 45). These gave you the systems and taught you to trust tiny daily gains. But without the right identity? Even the best system stalls.

Globally, this idea is transformative. Across cultures and income levels, people carry limiting money identities and have been programmed to believe:

- 'Hard work alone leads to wealth.'
- 'It's rude to talk about money.'
- 'I'm not smart enough to start investing.'
- 'People like me don't get rich.'
- 'Rich people are greedy.'
- 'We can't afford that.'

But what happens when we challenge those stories? We unlock a future not defined by our past.

THE SCIENCE BEHIND SELF-IMAGE, MINDSET AND FINANCIAL OUTCOMES

Self-image, the internal narrative and perception you hold about yourself, directly influences financial behaviours and outcomes. Research consistently shows that individuals who perceive themselves as capable, worthy and financially competent are more likely to engage in positive financial behaviours, set ambitious goals and persist through setbacks. Conversely, a negative self-image can lead to avoidance, self-sabotage and chronic underachievement.

Studies indicate that self-esteem and self-image are critical mediators between financial satisfaction and financial behaviour,[13] shaping how individuals relate to money and their ability to build wealth. For example, someone with positive self-esteem is likely to engage in desirable financial behaviour and have a good sense of financial satisfaction. However, someone with low self-esteem is more likely to pay for status-symbol products that attract attention, which can ultimately lead to a cycle of debt and financial struggle.

In addition, a foundational body of research by psychologist Carol Dweck demonstrates that the way we view our abilities – i.e. our mindset – profoundly shapes our motivation, resilience and achievement across life domains, including finances.[14] Dweck distinguishes between a fixed mindset (believing abilities are static) and a growth mindset (believing abilities can be developed through effort and learning).

Individuals with a growth mindset are more likely to embrace challenges, persist after setbacks and see failures as opportunities to learn, all traits linked to financial success. Whereas those with a fixed mindset may avoid risks and give up easily. This difference is critical in financial contexts, where setbacks and learning curves are inevitable. The ability to reframe failures as learning opportunities can make the difference between giving up and ultimately achieving financial goals.

A good example of this need for a reframe is seen with the impact of AI on jobs. A growing number of people fear AI is taking their jobs and, as such, remain in a state of inaction. However, a simple mindset reframe, such as, 'AI is a tool for creating opportunity and more financial abundance', is necessary to help us adjust to the change in our situations.

PRACTICAL STRATEGIES TO REFRAME YOUR SELF-IMAGE

If your self-image hasn't caught up with your goals, you'll keep sabotaging your progress. Here's how to reframe your self-image one practical step at a time.

Identify and challenge limiting narratives

Reflect on your earliest money memories and the beliefs you've internalized. Are they empowering or restrictive? For example, one of our restrictive internalized beliefs was that we needed to work twice as hard to succeed as Black people, relative to other ethnicities. Over time, we've reframed this to a need for us to work smarter to get ahead.

Journalling and cognitive-behavioural techniques can help surface and challenge these beliefs. For example, if you believe, 'I'm just not good with money,' look for evidence to the contrary and reframe it as, 'I can learn to manage my finances effectively.'

Use visualization and affirmation

Visualization is a proven psychological tool. Imagine yourself making confident financial decisions, negotiating pay rises or investing wisely. Pair this with daily affirmations such as, 'I am worthy of financial abundance.'

Surround yourself with positive influences

Your environment shapes your self-image. Seek out mentors, communities and content that reflect the wealth mindset you wish to adopt. This was one of our biggest motivations for creating a community at the Financial Joy Academy (FJA), where we learn and grow wealth together. Exposure to positive role models normalizes financial success and offers new templates for what's possible.

Take small consistent actions

Identity is built through repeated behaviour. Start with manageable financial habits, for example, automating savings, tracking expenses or reading one finance article per day from a reliable source. Each action reinforces your new self-image as someone proactive and capable with money, in line with growth-mindset principles.

Practise self-compassion

Changing self-image is a gradual process. Celebrate progress, forgive setbacks and remind yourself that growth is non-linear. Self-compassion reduces shame and builds resilience, allowing you to stay the course when challenges arise.

THE PSYCHOLOGY OF LIMITING BELIEFS

Limiting beliefs are subconscious convictions that restrict your potential. They originate from family, culture and personal experiences and often operate outside conscious awareness. Financially, these beliefs can manifest as self-doubt, fear of success or chronic financial struggle, regardless of income or education.

Cognitive-behavioural research shows that beliefs drive behaviour. If you believe, 'I'm not the type of person who gets rich,' you're less likely to pursue opportunities, negotiate or invest. Over time, these beliefs become self-fulfilling prophecies.

Several core beliefs frequently block wealth creation:

- **Scarcity mindset:** The conviction that resources are limited, leading to thoughts like, 'There's never enough money' or 'If I get more, someone else gets less.' This mindset fosters fear, risk aversion and reluctance to pursue opportunities. We'll explore this mindset further in Chapter 5.
- **Unworthiness:** Internalized messages such as, 'I don't deserve to be wealthy' or 'Rich people are greedy' undermine self-worth and can cause self-sabotage when financial opportunities arise. We'll explore this further in Chapters 4 and 6.
- **Learned helplessness:** Growing up in environments where financial struggle is the norm can instill a belief that wealth is unattainable, resulting in resignation and a lack of initiative.
- **Fixed identity:** Statements like, 'I'm just not good with money' or 'People like me don't get rich' reflect a static view of personal capability, discouraging learning and growth.

STEPS TO BREAK LIMITING BELIEFS

Beliefs are powerful. But it is possible to change them. For example, I (Mary) grew up believing that Christians shouldn't try to build wealth. This limiting belief came from hearing 'money is the root of all evil' and resulted in me feeling guilty for wanting to progress in life. But, over time, I learned that wealth was not the issue, but the love of money above everything else. This reframe helped me to see money as a matter of the heart and an opportunity to steward what we've been blessed with.

Breaking limiting beliefs clears the mental and emotional blocks to wealth. Here are some of the tried-and-tested approaches we've used to dismantle those inner barriers.

Awareness and identification

Reflect on your financial behaviours. For example, do you avoid checking your bank account for fear you might see a negative balance? Shy away from investing or feel uncomfortable discussing money? These actions often point to underlying beliefs. List your recurring financial thoughts and behaviours. For each, ask, 'What belief is driving this?'

Challenge and reframe

Actively dispute the validity of each belief. Seek out counter-examples, such as stories of people from similar backgrounds who have achieved financial success. Replace limiting beliefs with empowering alternatives. For example, if you believe, 'I'll never be good with money,' reframe it as, 'I can learn to manage my finances, just like I learned to cook or read.'

Small behavioural experiments

Test new beliefs through small, low-risk actions. For instance, if you fear investing, start with a small amount in a diversified fund. Positive experiences will gradually weaken old beliefs and reinforce new ones. Begin to visualize the future you as a confident investor. Visualization activates the brain's reward system and increases motivation.

Leverage social proof and mentorship

Surround yourself with people who embody the beliefs you want to adopt. Iron sharpens iron. Your environment and the people in it influence your mindset. Read biographies, join communities or mastermind groups of like-minded individuals, or seek mentorship and friendships from those who have overcome similar barriers, encourage ambition and celebrate progress.

Address emotional roots

Limiting beliefs are often tied to fear, shame or guilt. Practices like prayer, mindfulness, journalling or therapy can help process these emotions, making it easier to adopt new beliefs. Gratitude shifts focus from scarcity to abundance, while generosity reinforces the belief that there is always more to give and receive.

FRAMEWORK: THE WEALTH IDENTITY SHIFT

We created The Wealth Identity Shift as a simple three-step model designed to help you reset your financial self-image.

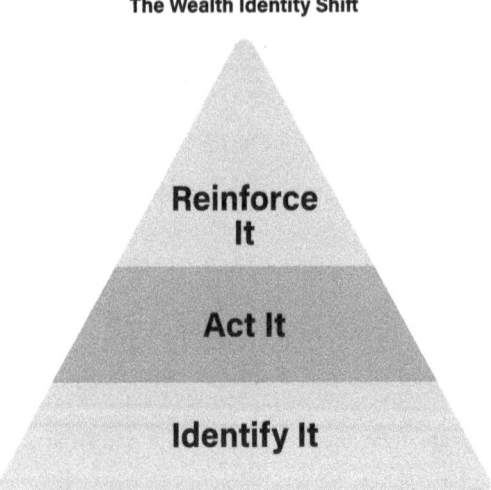

The Wealth Identity Shift

From the base:

- **Identify it:** Without naming the old belief, you can't change it.
- **Act it:** Daily habits aligned with the new identity.
- **Reinforce it:** Wins, language and community strengthen the shift.

Each level supports the one above. When the triangle holds, the identity becomes unshakable.

Identify it

Begin by noticing the financial identities you carry or live out. These often come from childhood, failure or culture. Ask yourself:

- What are my money beliefs?
- Where did they come from?
- Are they serving or sabotaging me?

These identities act like mental walls, blocking any habit that contradicts them.

Act it

Your behaviour reshapes your belief. Start acting like the person you want to become, even before you believe it fully. Want to be an investor? Start by transferring £1 or $1 to a new account. Want to be financially disciplined? Review your spending weekly.

Begin acting out the new identity in small but consistent ways. Each action sends a message to your brain and reinforces the belief, 'I am someone who builds wealth.'

Reinforce it

Identity solidifies through repetition. To solidify the shift, surround yourself with reinforcements:

- **Visual:** A savings tracker, a future-self vision board, track small wins and share them.
- **Social:** Join communities that reflect your new identity or follow creators aligned with your goals.
- **Verbal:** Daily affirmations like, 'Every dollar I manage multiplies with purpose.'

PAUSE FOR REFLECTION

Think back to the last financial decision you made. What identity were you acting from? Were you a spender, a survivor, an avoider or something else?

Now imagine your highest Wealth Identity, one who is intentional, confident and purpose driven. What would they have done differently?

Write down one sentence that reflects that version of you. Repeat it each morning this week.

> *Small action step*
>
> Choose one symbolic action that your Wealthy Identity would do and do it today.
>
> - If that person invests, open an account and move £1 or $1.
> - If that person manages money weekly, schedule a 15-minute money meeting.
> - If that person gives, donate £1 or $1 to a cause that you believe in.
>
> Small actions create big identities. Start now.

Let's be clear: this model isn't about pretending. It's about psychology and programming. When you take action consistent with your desired identity, the brain rewires your self-image. And when your identity shifts, your actions become natural. You don't fake it till you make it. You practise it till you believe it.

You don't need a higher salary to become wealthy. You need a higher identity. Everything in this book makes sense when you accept one truth:

wealth is something you practise becoming, one habit at a time. Start calling yourself what you truly are: a builder. A multiplier. A steward. Speak it. Act it. Reinforce it. And watch as your results rise to meet your new self. You don't wait to feel wealthy. You choose to become it.

Chapter summary

- Your identity shapes your financial destiny. Without an upgrade in self-perception, even the best habits won't stick.
- Reframing your self-image, breaking limiting beliefs and adopting a rich mindset are interconnected steps that form the foundation of lasting financial success.
- By understanding the psychological roots of your money story, challenging inherited narratives and embodying the habits of wealth builders, you can transform your financial destiny, regardless of your starting point. The journey begins in the mind, is reinforced by action and is sustained by community and purpose.
- The Wealth Identity Shift helps you move from limitation to liberation in three steps: identify it, act it, reinforce it.
- This identity shift is the invisible engine behind all visible success.

Chapter 4

THE MONEY-GUILT CURE

Why we fear wealth (and how to embrace it)

> **Theme: Emotional clearance**
> With your identity reset and belief in small wins planted, you clear away any shame or unworthiness that could hold you back.

Money guilt is the echo of an old story, not the truth of your worth. To silence it, you must rewrite the narrative not with numbers, but with courage and compassion.

In the quiet dawn before the city stirred, Amina sat on the edge of her bed in Lagos, her first paycheque trembling in her hands, a symbol of both achievement and the invisible weight she had carried for years. As the eldest daughter in her Nigerian family, Amina was more than a child; she was a caretaker, a mediator and often the silent pillar holding everyone together. From a young age, she absorbed the unspoken rule that her needs were secondary to those of her siblings and parents. Praise came when she sacrificed, when she put others first and when she made herself useful, teaching her that love and worth were earned through selflessness.

Now, with her own income, Amina found herself caught between pride and guilt. Every time she considered spending on herself — a new dress, a celebratory meal or even a small treat — she heard the echoes of her upbringing: was this selfish? Shouldn't she save for her siblings' school fees or contribute more to the household? The pressure to provide, coupled with the fear of appearing indulgent or ungrateful, kept her locked in a cycle of self-denial.

Amina's turning point came when she began to recognize that her feelings were not unique but part of a larger pattern known as 'eldest-daughter syndrome'. This is where the first-born girl in many African (and other) families is expected to shoulder an 'invisible load' of extra responsibility and self-sacrifice; they are conditioned to believe that financial independence is a privilege to be used for others, not for themselves. By reading the stories of other eldest daughters across the world and speaking openly with friends, Amina realized she was living out a cultural narrative, not a personal failing. Through honest reflection and gentle boundary setting, Amina learned that honouring her own needs was not a betrayal of her family but an act of self-respect and, ultimately, a healthier way to support those she loved. With each small act of self-care, she chipped away at the feelings of shame and undeservedness that had held her back, discovering that true abundance meant permission to thrive, not just survive.

Money is not just a currency; it is a mirror reflecting our deepest beliefs, fears and aspirations. For many, financial success brings not only abundance but also an invisible burden: guilt. This guilt can manifest as a quiet voice whispering, 'You don't deserve this' or a pang of anxiety when spending on yourself, even when logic says you've earned it. In a world where wealth is often conflated with morality, learning to navigate and heal money guilt is a critical step towards true financial freedom.

As we embark on this chapter, let's remember: guilt is not a badge of honour, nor is it a sign of weakness. It is simply a signal, a call to examine our relationship with money and ourselves.

> **Wealth Habit Mantra 4:**
> Guilt is not a punishment.
> It's a compass, guiding you to grow.

THE HIDDEN REASONS PEOPLE FEEL GUILTY ABOUT FINANCIAL SUCCESS

Money guilt is far more common than most realize, and its roots are often buried deep within our past experiences, family values and societal messages. When we peel back the layers, we find that guilt about financial success is rarely about the money itself. Instead, it is a complex interplay of emotions, memories and expectations that shape our financial identity.

In many communities – especially immigrant families, faith-based upbringings or working-class backgrounds – money is associated with morality. Being 'too rich' can be framed as selfish, detached or even sinful.

In psychological terms, this is linked to cognitive dissonance: the mental stress of holding two conflicting beliefs. For example, 'I want financial freedom' and 'I don't want to be seen as greedy.'

Research demonstrates that cultural background profoundly shapes financial guilt and decision making. In collectivist cultures, such as those in Nigeria, China and India, family and community wellbeing are prioritized over individual desires and financial choices are often made with the group in mind.[15] For example, it's common in India for multiple generations to live together and pool resources for shared goals like education or property, while in Nigeria and Ghana, money is deeply intertwined with kinship, social responsibility and long-term reciprocity.[16]

Studies show that people from these backgrounds are more likely to experience guilt when their financial success outpaces that of their peers or relatives and this guilt can lead to under-investing, overspending to maintain social acceptance or delaying important financial moves.[17] Ultimately, these behaviours reflect the powerful influence of cultural norms and social networks on economic decisions.

In the last chapter, we explored how to reprogramme the limiting beliefs that quietly shape your financial identity. But even when your mind has caught up, your heart may still carry guilt, shame or a lingering sense that you don't deserve abundance. This chapter helps you release that weight, to make peace with money so that you can move forward freely.

We'll now explore some of the reasons why people feel guilty about financial success.

The scarcity mindset

Money guilt often stems from a scarcity mindset, the belief that resources are limited and any spending is a permanent loss. If you grew up in a household where money was tight or unpredictable, this fear of not having enough can linger long after your finances improve. Even when you can afford something – a new outfit or a meal out – you might still feel uneasy. That's your subconscious clinging to lack, not reality. We'll explore this further in Chapter 5.

Financial trauma and past experiences

Financial trauma, such as growing up in poverty, losing a home or experiencing sudden job loss, can leave lasting emotional scars. These experiences can create a sense of unworthiness or fear around money, leading to self-sabotage or chronic guilt. This trauma is not always obvious; it can manifest as anxiety, avoidance or even arguments with loved ones about money.

Social comparison and shared finances

In a world of constant comparison, seeing others spend luxuriously or feeling like you're financially 'behind' can fuel guilt and self-doubt. The pressure can intensify in shared finances. Spending on personal treats might feel selfish, especially if you're not the primary earner. You might feel like you're not contributing enough or that your partner's hard-earned money is being 'wasted' on you.

Perfectionism and self-worth

For many, financial guilt is tied to perfectionism and self-worth. You might believe that you should have achieved more by now or that your financial stability isn't 'good enough' compared to your peers or your own expectations. This can lead to a cycle of guilt and self-criticism, where every financial decision is scrutinized and judged.

Inheritance guilt: the weight of unearned wealth

Inheriting wealth can bring unexpected guilt and internal conflict – especially when that fortune was built in ways that clash with your values, such as exploitative industries or even the slave trade.[18] The discomfort often comes from knowing the money wasn't earned by you and may carry a moral cost.

This guilt is compounded by pressure to honour the legacy and reconcile the source of your wealth with one's own moral compass. Many inheritors fear appearing tone-deaf or ungrateful, leading to feelings of unworthiness, anxiety or isolation, as discussing such guilt is often taboo. Some feel compelled to give it away through philanthropy just to ease the discomfort.[19]

Martine's story

Martine Warmann, a former British and European powerlifting champion, lives in Northamptonshire, UK, with her husband Okiem (a classical pianist and composer) and their two daughters. After 15 years in health and wellness, supporting over 10,000 mums and co-owning an award-winning gym, she now manages her husband's orchestra while building two side hustles: a natural oral-care Etsy shop and a Kindle Direct Publishing business. Here is how she unlearned negative associations with money, undeservedness and unworthiness:

> My parents were successful in business, and we lived in a beautiful seven-bedroom house with a sauna, jacuzzi, gym, bar, snooker table, jukeboxes – the lot. On the outside, it looked like we had everything. But from a young age, I learned to read people. And what I noticed was this: people didn't want to play with me, they wanted to play at my house. That hit me hard. It shaped how I saw friendships, trust and my own value. I started to hide. I wouldn't let people come over. I'd lie about where I lived and what my parents did. I arranged playdates elsewhere, anything to avoid being judged or treated differently.
>
> I didn't fully understand it, but I was forming a belief: having money – or even appearing to – made people treat you differently, and not in a good way. That programming stayed with me and wired me to repel abundance. I came to think that being seen as 'having' meant being judged, used or excluded. It made me shrink and doubt my worth.
>
> Cultural programming shaped me, too. My dad's from the Caribbean, he's Black, and though he was successful, he often said, 'As a Black person, you have to work twice as hard. You have to be better. Do more.' I know he meant to prepare me for the world, but there's a fine line between educating a child about inequality and unintentionally teaching them they'll always be at a disadvantage. When you hear, 'You have to work ten times harder' over and over, success starts to feel out of reach. Like perfection is the bare minimum. Instead of empowering you, it creates pressure. You begin to believe that every reward is conditional – that being 'good enough' isn't enough.

Things began to shift after I attended a Tony Robbins seminar. One of the biggest takeaways was learning to approach situations with intention. Instead of thinking, 'I have to work twice as hard to be taken seriously' or 'They won't give this to me because of my skin colour' (and I'm really fair for being mixed race, too!), I started asking: what do I want to create here? How do I want to be seen?

That mindset freed me. I stepped out of fear and into purpose. I began showing up with confidence and clarity – and people responded. I stopped assuming rejection and started expecting alignment. Because when you stop hiding and own your story, you give others permission to see the real you – not what they think you represent but who you truly are.

HOW TO REFRAME MONEY AS A TOOL FOR IMPACT AND SECURITY

Once we understand where money guilt comes from, we can begin to shift our relationship with money. Rather than seeing it as a source of anxiety or self-worth, we can start to view it as a tool – for impact, security and a life aligned with our values.

Money as a means, not an end

Money's value lies in how we use it. Like a hammer, it can build or destroy. It can create opportunities, support loved ones and shape our future; or it can fuel waste and destructive habits. When we see money as a tool, we reclaim agency and start building the life we desire.

Creating impact through conscious spending

One powerful way to reframe money is to focus on its impact. Supporting local businesses, giving to your church or place of worship, or investing in causes and communities you care about turns money into a force for good. Even small acts, like tipping generously or buying fair-trade coffee, can align spending with your values and ease guilt.

Building security and peace of mind

Money is also a tool for security. Savings, insurance and a solid financial plan offer peace of mind and reduce future anxiety. When you reframe money as protection – for yourself and your loved ones – spending on essentials or even indulgences feels less guilt-inducing. Emergency funds or investing in your health become acts of self-care, not selfishness.

The power of gratitude

Practicing gratitude for what you have shifts your mindset from scarcity to abundance. Focusing on what you've achieved and the opportunities money affords you helps you see it as a tool for empowerment, not guilt.

RELEASE THE GUILT AND MAKE PEACE WITH MONEY

The final step in curing money guilt is to confront and release the negative beliefs that keep you trapped in cycles of guilt and self-doubt. This process requires self-compassion, awareness and practical strategies to rewrite your money story.

Confronting past mistakes without judgment

Everyone makes money mistakes. Harsh self-judgment only deepens guilt. Instead, treat mistakes as lessons. For example, if you overspent on a holiday, ask what you learned and how you'll do it differently next time. Self-forgiveness is key to a healthy money mindset.

Challenging scarcity thoughts

Scarcity thoughts like, 'I'll never have enough' or 'I don't deserve this' often stem from childhood or societal messages. To break free, challenge those beliefs and replace them with affirmations like, 'I manage my money wisely' or 'I deserve to enjoy my financial success.' Visualizing your goals can also help to reprogramme your subconscious mind.

Embracing financial knowledge and empowerment

Ignorance breeds fear, and fear feeds guilt. But financial education builds confidence. Reading books like *The Wealth Habit* and *Financial Joy* or attending courses or in-person seminars gives you the tools to manage money well. Learning about managing cashflow, investing or debt can reduce anxiety and help you feel more in control and less guilty.

The role of therapy and financial coaching

For some, money guilt is deeply rooted in trauma or self-doubt. In these cases, working with a therapist or financial coach can help uncover the source, provide the support needed to heal and develop healthier coping mechanisms.

FRAMEWORK: THE MONEY-GUILT CURE

The signature framework for this chapter is the Money-Guilt Cure: a three-step process designed to help you release shame, rewire your beliefs around wealth and break free. The steps are: notice it, name it, grow from it. This isn't just about ideas, it's about transformation through action.

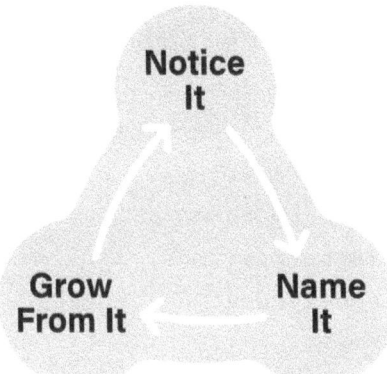

Step 1: Notice it

Start by tracking your emotional patterns. Use a money journal or voice note app to capture how you feel during these moments:

- Receiving unexpected income (a gift, bonus, raise).
- Making large purchases (for yourself or others).
- Saying no to a financial request.
- Talking about your success in front of friends or family.

Write down the emotions and their intensity. Guilt, shame, anxiety, pride, awkwardness – everything counts.

Next, look for patterns. Does guilt spike when you enjoy something your parents never had? When you spend on convenience or luxury? When you don't give?

Awareness alone creates space between stimulus and response.

Step 2: Name it

This is where you unearth the story behind the emotion. Often it's inherited, absorbed or attached to an identity.

Some common money-guilt scripts include:

- 'We're not the kind of people who spend money on things like that.'
- 'My worth is tied to my sacrifice.'
- 'If I shine, someone else dims.'

Give each belief a name, for example, 'The Martyr Script', 'The Loyalty Guilt' or 'The Class-Climber Shame'. Naming disempowers the narrative; it helps you treat it as something external, not intrinsic.

Step 3: Grow from it

Now we rewrite. Ask yourself:

- What belief do I want instead?
- What's a small, safe step I can take to live this new belief?
- Who can support or mirror this shift?

Examples:

- If your old belief was, 'Success isolates me', your new one could be, 'Success connects me to more opportunities to lift others.'
- Your action might be to join a wealth-focused book club or mentorship group.
- Your support might be a therapist, coach or accountability partner.

Make it visible. Write the new belief somewhere you'll see it daily. Affirm it. Speak it into your identity.

Integrating the cure into your daily life

Transformation is sustained through repetition. Here are some ways to make the Money-Guilt Cure part of your everyday habits:

- **Wealth-wins journal:** Every week, list three financial actions you took that aligned with your values. Reflect on how they felt.
- **Celebration rituals:** Celebrate income or milestones with intention, not apology. Share them with people who affirm your growth.
- **Generosity flow:** Set a monthly or quarterly 'impact budget' to give or support a cause that matters to you. This channels your abundance meaningfully.
- **Language shift:** Watch your words. Replace, 'I'm lucky' with, 'I've made choices I'm proud of.' Replace, 'I don't deserve this' with, 'I've prepared for this.'

Over time, your nervous system begins to accept wealth without panic; guilt fades and is replaced by grounded responsibility and peace.

PAUSE FOR REFLECTION

Think about a recent financial win such as a pay rise, a debt paid off, an investment return or even a luxurious treat you allowed yourself.

Now pause. What were your first three thoughts?

- Did you feel joy?
- Did you feel the need to hide it?
- Did you worry about how others would perceive you?

Write those thoughts down. Then ask: what belief do they point to?

Once you've named that belief, write a sentence that starts with: 'A more empowering belief would be...'

Let your answer guide your next money decision.

> *Small action step*
>
> Open your phone or grab a sticky note. Write this statement and put it somewhere visible:
>
> 'I am allowed to build wealth and enjoy it without guilt.'
>
> Now choose one small action to reinforce that belief today:
>
> - Transfer $50 into a dream vacation fund.
> - Share a financial win with someone who celebrates you.
> - Say no to a money request that doesn't align.
>
> Small actions break big patterns. Today is your cue to start.

You were never meant to shrink in the presence of wealth. You were meant to expand, to stretch into generosity, into possibility, into the fullness of what your life can be.

Money guilt will whisper that you should feel bad for rising. It will mask itself as humility, responsibility or care. But guilt is not the same as integrity. Guilt says, 'Stay small to stay loved.' Integrity says, 'Rise well so others can too.'

You don't need to apologize for building wealth. You need to get better at receiving it, using it and sharing it.

That is what the Money-Guilt Cure is about. It's not about letting go of who you are. It's about embracing who you're becoming without shame.

Let this chapter be your turning point. Not into greed. Into growth.

Chapter summary

- The emotional undercurrent that silently blocks wealth is guilt.
- From inherited beliefs to survivor's shame, money guilt can prevent even the most disciplined earners from truly enjoying or using their wealth.
- The Money-Guilt Cure helps you: notice it, name it, and grow from it.
- Reframe money as a tool, a neutral force for impact and security, not a symbol of ego.
- By rewriting your internal money scripts, you don't just feel better, you make clearer choices, invest with confidence and give with purpose.

Chapter 5

ESCAPING THE SCARCITY LOOP

How to break free from paycheque-to-paycheque thinking

> **Theme: Abundance**
> Having permission to succeed, you dismantle the fear of never having enough, freeing up both funds and psychology for growth.

THE WEALTH HABIT

The real test of wealth isn't how much you earn but how free you feel. True abundance begins the moment you stop measuring your life by what's missing and start building it around what's possible.

John's story is a powerful lens into the silent struggle faced by many people at every income level, a struggle that numbers alone can't explain. In his early forties, John and his wife Isobel live in Oxford, UK, and have built what, from the outside, looks like a life of financial security. Together, they bring home £120,000 ($160,000) after tax each year, live in a comfortable home and are raising two young children. They've worked hard, overcome obstacles and steadily climbed the ladder of professional success.

Yet, beneath this picture of prosperity, John's family is caught in a relentless financial balancing act. Once debt-free, they now carry £80,000 ($105,000) in debt, a figure that crept up with the arrival of children and the cost of education. Their monthly outgoings of £9,000 ($12,000), nearly swallow their whole income, leaving little room for error or unexpected expenses.

Looking ahead, John and Isobel are facing projected private-education costs of over £380,000 ($500,000) for their two children over the next decade, a figure that highlights how even high incomes can be rapidly absorbed by long-term choices and commitments.

Some may wonder why John and Isobel are committed to private education given the extraordinary costs, especially when finances are so tight. For them, as for many families, this is not a decision taken lightly. It reflects their personal values, hopes for their children and a willingness to make sacrifices elsewhere. But it also highlights a wider truth: financial stress and the Scarcity Loop are not always about reckless choices or mismanagement, they often stem from deeply held aspirations and the rising costs of modern life.

With one child about to start independent school and another in full-time nursery, their commitments are only set to rise. Despite their best efforts, paying down debt, chipping away at a £300,000 ($400,500) mortgage and trying to invest for the future, progress feels elusive.

Every new expense chips away at their savings or adds to their debt. Their pension pot is modest and the idea of being unable to work for even a few months is a real source of anxiety. Yet, amid this, John and Isobel still want to enjoy the fruits of their labor: 'We feel it is only right that we treat ourselves to some of the niceties of life before we become too old, so we sometimes do.'

This is not a story of financial mismanagement or lack of ambition. It is a story of modern life, of families doing everything 'right' and still feeling as if they are running on a treadmill. John's questions are the questions of a generation: should we focus on clearing debt, paying off the mortgage or investing? How do we balance enjoying life now with preparing for an uncertain future? Is it possible to break free from this cycle or is the Scarcity Loop an inevitable part of striving for a better life?

John's experience reveals a crucial truth: escaping the Scarcity Loop is not simply a matter of earning more or spending less. It's about the deeper patterns – psychological, emotional and behavioural – that shape our financial lives. His story is a call to look beyond the numbers, to understand the hidden drivers of financial stress and to forge a new path towards genuine abundance.

While John's challenges highlight that even high earners are not immune to the Scarcity Loop, Lisa's story shows how these patterns play out for those on a more modest income. Lisa is a single mother living in Detroit, USA, working full-time as a cashier and earning around $26,000 (£19,500) a year. Her monthly income barely stretches to cover rent, groceries, childcare and utilities. There's rarely anything left. A car breakdown or school expense can throw everything into chaos.

But for Lisa, the hardest part isn't just the numbers, it's the constant vigilance. The guilt of saying 'no' to her son. The anxiety of checking her balance before buying toothpaste. The constant fear that one wrong move could unravel everything. She isn't irresponsible – she's running on empty with no room for error. Even small decisions feel heavy when you're stretched thin.

Lisa's story is a powerful reminder that the Scarcity Loop cuts across income levels and that the emotional and psychological toll is just as real for those living on the edge as for those with higher incomes.

> **Wealth Habit Mantra 5:**
> Your old story said, 'Not enough.' Your new one begins with, 'I already have something to build from.'

WHY FINANCIAL STRESS IS MORE ABOUT MINDSET THAN MONEY

Financial stress is often mistaken for a numbers problem. On the surface, it's easy to believe that if you just had a bit more income or a little less debt, peace of mind would follow. But research and real-life stories, like John's and Lisa's, show that the roots of financial anxiety run much deeper into the soil of our beliefs, habits and emotional wiring.

The mindset trap

When you're caught in the Scarcity Loop, your brain is hijacked by a constant sense of 'not enough' – not enough money, time, opportunity or security. This mindset doesn't just affect your wallet, it alters your physiology and decision making.

Studies show that financial scarcity can lead to a more inflexible, short-term mindset,[20] narrowing your focus to immediate problems (e.g. needing to pay rent) and making it harder to plan for the future. Chronic financial stress is linked to anxiety, reduced wellbeing and even impaired cognitive performance.[21] In a study published in *Science* by researchers from the universities of Warwick, Princeton, Harvard and British Columbia, they found that low-income individuals working through a difficult problem in their finances, led to a cognitive strain that's equivalent to a full night's sleep lost or a 13-point deficit in IQ.[22]

The stories we inherit

Our money mindset is shaped long before we earn our first paycheque. Family attitudes, cultural narratives and early experiences with money all leave their mark. In the UK, for example, cultural attitudes towards debt and home ownership are deeply ingrained, with many feeling pressure to get on the property ladder. By contrast, in Germany[23] long-term renting is the norm – more than half the population rents – and home ownership isn't seen as a milestone of success in the same way.

If you grew up hearing phrases like 'money doesn't grow on trees' or witnessed adults arguing over bills, you may unconsciously carry these scripts into adulthood. These inherited beliefs can create self-fulfilling prophecies: if you believe you'll never get ahead you're less likely to take risks, negotiate for more or invest in your future.

The loop of stress and behaviour

Financial stress doesn't just cause worry, it drives behaviour. When you're anxious about money you're more likely to procrastinate on financial decisions, avoid looking at your accounts or make impulsive purchases for temporary relief.

This avoidance only deepens the cycle, leading to more stress and poorer financial outcomes. Research shows that financial scarcity is linked to financial avoidance, increased risk-taking and a tendency to focus on short-term relief rather than long-term solutions.[24]

This explains why John, despite his high income, finds himself trapped in this loop. The constant pressure of expenses and debt triggers anxiety, which sometimes leads to short-term spending to relieve stress, undermining his long-term goals. Lisa, on the other hand, often avoids opening bills or budgeting, feeling overwhelmed by the relentless demands on her limited resources.

The science of mindset

Neuroscience confirms that our brains are wired for survival, not abundance. The 'negativity bias', which is our tendency to 'attend to, learn from and use negative information far more than positive information',[25] means we naturally focus on threats and shortages; an evolutionary mechanism that once kept us alive but now keeps us stuck.[26] But the brain is also plastic, i.e. it can be rewired. By becoming aware of our money stories and consciously choosing new beliefs, we can start to break the loop.

> *Key takeaway*
> Financial stress is less about your current bank balance and more about the beliefs and habits you bring to every financial decision. Changing your mindset is the first and most crucial step to escaping the Scarcity Loop.

HOW TO SHIFT FROM SURVIVAL MODE TO ABUNDANCE THINKING

Moving from survival mode to an abundance mindset is not about wishful thinking or ignoring reality. It's about retraining your brain to see possibilities, opportunities and resources, even when circumstances are tough.

Scarcity versus abundance: the mental models

A scarcity mindset is like wearing blinders: it narrows your focus to immediate problems and short-term fixes. You become hyper-aware of what you lack and overlook what you have or what's possible. In contrast, an abundance mindset expands your field of vision. You start to notice opportunities, build resilience and make decisions that serve your long-term goals.

Scarcity mindset:

- Focuses on limitations and competition.
- Triggers anxiety and short-term thinking.
- Leads to hoarding, jealousy or self-sabotage.

Abundance mindset:

- Focuses on possibilities and collaboration.
- Triggers optimism and long-term planning.
- Leads to generosity, creativity and growth.

The power of perspective

The shift begins with awareness. Start by observing your automatic thoughts about money. Do you catch yourself thinking, 'I'll never get ahead' or 'There's just not enough'? These are signals of scarcity thinking. Challenge these thoughts by asking: 'Is this really true?' and 'What evidence do I have for the opposite?'

When faced with an unexpected expense, someone in scarcity mode might panic and say, 'That's just my luck! This always happens to me. I can't get a break.' Someone with an abundance mindset might pause and ask, 'What resources or solutions do I have in my hands? Who can I ask for advice? What can I learn from this?'

The power of language

One simple way to begin this shift is through language. Take this sentence: 'I can't afford that.' Now try this: 'That's not a priority for me right now.'

The first implies helplessness. The second reinforces agency. This small reframe is powerful – it reminds your brain that you have a say in your financial story. You're not just reacting; you're choosing.

I (Mary) used to say, 'I really struggle with the weather in the UK – especially in winter.' But underneath that was a deeper truth: I felt stuck in a routine that I hadn't designed.

Then came the reframe: 'What would it look like to create a life I don't need to escape from?' That question led to more intentional goals, income streams and eventually the freedom to spend part of the winter abroad – not to escape, but to align with the life we truly wanted.

We've also come to embrace the cosy beauty of British winters – hot chocolates, warm blankets and slow evenings by the fire. For us, abundance isn't about choosing one or the other. It's about having the option to enjoy both. Abundance is designing a life you love – and seeing beauty in every season.

Future anchoring

Another abundance-building habit is future anchoring. Abundance thinkers make decisions based not just on what they need today, but who they want to become tomorrow. They ask: 'What would my future self thank me for?' It's not always grand gestures. Sometimes it's choosing to transfer £20 or $50 into your tax-advantaged account instead of spending it on another takeaway. It's choosing to learn one new money skill a month instead of bingeing on another trending series. Remember: abundance isn't about how much you have. It's about how you direct what you have.

Practising gratitude and generosity

Gratitude is the cornerstone of abundance. Research shows that regularly practising gratitude rewires your brain to focus on what's going right, rather than what's missing.[27] We personally love to start the day with prayer with our children and enjoy keeping a gratitude journal, where we list up to three things we're thankful for each day.

We also discuss these with our children during dinner time as a way of teaching them to adopt this practice. Reflecting and discussing what you're grateful for boosts optimism and reduces stress. Even often unnoticed things, like laughter with a friend, the joy of eating vanilla ice cream in the sunshine or a stranger's kindness, all matter.

Generosity is the next step. When you give time, money or support, you reinforce the belief that there is enough to go around and you create a ripple effect of abundance in your community.

To return to our real-life examples, John and his wife, while managing tight finances, choose to celebrate small wins and occasionally treat themselves, which helps them to maintain motivation and a positive outlook. Lisa, despite her limited budget, volunteers to help organize food drives for families like hers. Giving her time doesn't change her finances, but it lifts her spirits and expands her sense of possibility.

Redefining success and value

Society often equates wealth with status symbols such as cars, houses, luxury goods. But true abundance is about freedom, peace of mind and the ability to pursue what matters to you.

Redefine what success means for you. Is it having time for your family? The ability to travel? The freedom to choose meaningful work or create your own income? When you focus on these deeper values, you start to see wealth in all areas of your life.

Building resilience and openness

An abundance mindset doesn't mean ignoring challenges. It means facing them with curiosity and confidence. People with this mindset are more resilient, they bounce back from setbacks, adapt to change and see failures as learning opportunities.

They also celebrate others' successes, knowing that someone else's gain (e.g. a pay rise, business success or investment growth) is not their loss. This mindset of genuinely celebrating others is so important, especially in cultures characterized by the 'tall poppy syndrome', where people criticize, attack or resent someone due to their success. I recall the chairman at an old workplace warning me about the unwritten 'crabs in a bucket' mindset, where people in a group, such as a workplace, actively sabotage each other's attempts to escape or advance, whether at work or with business and so on. To move ahead and escape the Scarcity Loop, we have to move differently.

> *Key takeaway*
> Shifting to abundance thinking is a conscious, daily practice. It starts with awareness, is fuelled by gratitude and generosity, and is sustained by redefining success on your own terms.

FRAMEWORK: ESCAPING THE SCARCITY LOOP

To move from theory to action, we created a simple three-step framework anyone can use to break free from the Scarcity Loop. It replaces financial stress with **redirection, automation** and **celebration**:

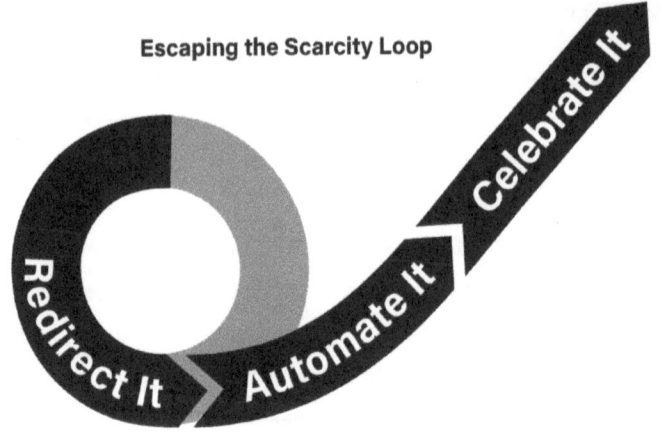

Escaping the Scarcity Loop

Step 1: Redirect it

Instead of letting money flow reactively towards short-term comfort or avoidance, consciously redirect a small amount of that energy towards long-term gain. This redirection isn't about deprivation. It's about decision.

Choose one area of your finances where money typically leaks unconsciously. Common places include emotional eating or takeaways, subscriptions you barely use and late-night Amazon browsing.

Now, pick a redirection amount. Not big. Start with $1 to $10. Set up a new savings pot or envelope. Name it something that makes you smile or signals growth, like 'abundance jar' or 'overflow account'.

Link the redirection to a trigger. For example, 'Every time I'm tempted to order in, I'll redirect $5 to my overflow account.' This creates a behavioural interruption, a financial fork in the road. You're no longer reacting. You're choosing.

Step 2: Automate it

The new direction becomes a habit only when it's automatic. Automating your actions removes the emotional resistance and decision fatigue that keeps people stuck. It makes your best choices your default choices. What gets automated, grows. You don't need a complex system. In fact, the simpler, the better.

Start with any of the following:

- Weekly automatic savings transfers.
- Round-up investing apps.
- Standing orders into a separate 'overflow account'.

Next, link automation to calendar rituals. Every Friday afternoon? Wealth review. Every first of the month? Redirect review.

Remember, consistency beats intensity. You want small automated steps that require zero willpower.

Step 3: Celebrate it

Most people skip this step. But without positive reinforcement, your brain won't attach pleasure to the new habit. Celebrate every micro-win. Feel the shift. Share the progress. That's how your mindset rewires.

When practised consistently, these three steps reprogramme your nervous system from one of survival to one of possibility. You stop asking, 'How will I make it to the end of the month?' and start asking 'How far could this grow?'

The Scarcity Loop is a psychological pattern. But, like any loop, it can be disrupted. This framework shows you exactly how.

How it all comes together

Each loop strengthens the next. Eventually, these loops grow into a financial flywheel. You stop budgeting in fear and start designing in confidence. You stop asking, 'Can I afford this?' and start asking 'Is this aligned with my values?' You escape the Scarcity Loop not in a single moment, but in hundreds of tiny upwards loops. That's the Wealth Habit.

PAUSE FOR REFLECTION

Think back to the last time you felt financially stuck or anxious. What triggered that feeling? Was it a bill, a conversation, an unexpected cost?

Now, imagine you could go back and insert one redirection, however small. What would you have done differently? What symbolic act could you have taken to reinforce agency instead of helplessness?

Journal this: 'The next time I feel scarcity creeping in, I will...' Let it be your new reflex.

> *Small action step*
>
> Create your first 'scarcity breaker'. Choose a money leak, just one.
>
> 1. Rename it. Reframe it.
> 2. Redirect £5 or $5 into a new savings pot. Name it something powerful.
> 3. Celebrate. Fist pump, smile or share it.
>
> This is your first loop. Lock it in before the end of today.

Scarcity wants to keep you small. It whispers, 'There's never enough.' But you've now seen what it really is: a loop. Not a life sentence.

You've learned how to interrupt it. Redirect the narrative. Automate your escape. Celebrate the wins. You can begin with whatever you have in your hands right now.

This isn't about perfection. It's about pattern breaking. It's about choosing belief over fear. Direction over reaction.

You're not behind. You're beginning. And every upwards loop you complete is evidence of the future you're building.

Scarcity trained your brain to expect less. Now, teach it to expect overflow.

Chapter summary

- Financial stress is often a mindset loop, not a maths problem.
- Reframe financial stress as a narrative issue, not just an income issue.
- Build abundance thinking with the power of language, perspective, future anchoring, gratitude, automation and micro-actions.
- The Escaping the Scarcity Loop framework can be used, regardless of income, to get unstuck and start building real abundance: redirect it, automate it, celebrate it.
- Scarcity ends not when income triples but when belief shifts. When action becomes automatic. When your identity changes from, 'I never have enough' to 'I build from what I have.'
- You are not bound by your bank balance but by your beliefs. Change your story and you will change your wealth.

Chapter 6

MONEY TRIGGERS AND HOW TO REPROGRAMME THEM

The secret behind emotional spending
and financial self-sabotage

> **Theme: Emotional mastery**
> Now that guilt and scarcity are addressed,
> you learn to spot and reroute impulse cues,
> so your habits stay on track.

THE WEALTH HABIT

Have you ever noticed how a stressful day at work can end with an unplanned 'treat yourself' splurge, clicking 'add to cart' or tapping your card again and again, only to regret it later? What if the real barrier isn't your income or willpower but survival signals wired deep in your brain, nudging you to spend whenever stress strikes?

In Tokyo, Japan, mid-morning crowds flood the city's underground malls, lured by the bright glow of convenience stores and vending machines. Rina, a 34-year-old copywriter, once found herself trapped in a cycle of midday snack runs she couldn't explain. A rice ball here, a matcha latte there, her spending spiked and, with it, her anxiety. It wasn't until she learned about emotional-eating cues that she made the connection: loneliness and stress from her high-pressure job were hijacking her brain, driving her to comfort purchases that delivered a fleeting hit of dopamine.

Halfway across the world in São Paulo, Brazil, Marcos, a 29-year-old startup founder, faced the same invisible tug. Pre-launch jitters sent him scrambling to purchase expensive tech gadgets he neither needed nor used, always chasing a thrill he'd already lost. When a mentor introduced him to the concept of trigger-action loops, he began mapping his impulses. By journalling every purchase and tracing the emotion behind it, he discovered that boredom, not business strategy, was steering his credit card.

From Shinjuku's neon lights to São Paulo's co-working spaces, emotional spending isn't a cultural quirk, it's a universal neurochemistry phenomenon. Recognizing the pattern is the first step to breaking it.

In Chapter 4 you uncovered the money-guilt scripts that taught your brain to soothe shame with spending. In Chapter 5 you broke free of the Scarcity Loop that made every purchase feel like a life raft. Now, in Chapter 6, we're going under the hood to see exactly how those old survival patterns hijack your Wealth Habit loop and how to reprogramme them for lasting abundance.

> **Wealth Habit Mantra 6:**
> Impulse is the enemy of progress. Spot it, own it, reroute it and build new paths to wealth.

UNDERSTANDING THE PSYCHOLOGY BEHIND IMPULSIVE SPENDING

Impulsive spending is rarely a shout, it's a whisper from your wallet: subtle enough to dismiss, persistent enough to unravel months of careful planning. But that whisper is actually a roar from ancient brain circuits, designed to protect you but now misfiring in a world engineered for instant gratification. Emotional spending isn't a moral failing; it's a survival mechanism playing out on the wrong stage.[28]

The neurochemistry of urge

Picture this: you're scrolling late at night, tired from a long week. A 'limited-time offer' flashes across your screen. Instantly, your amygdala, the brain's alarm centre, flares up, signalling scarcity and urgency.

Cortisol, the stress hormone, surges. At the same time, your nucleus accumbens, part of the brain's reward system, anticipates a dopamine hit if you act. Neuroscience shows that dopamine spikes not just when you make a purchase but even as you anticipate it, priming you for the rush.[29] This is why the 'buy now' button can feel irresistible, especially when you're tired, stressed or seeking comfort.

Daniel's Friday night escape

For Daniel, a project manager in his thirties, Friday evenings became a ritual of self-sabotage. After a week of relentless meetings and deadlines, he'd order expensive takeaway and scroll for 'treats', e.g. gadgets, clothes, anything to break the monotony. The real reward wasn't the item but the fleeting sense of control and comfort. By Sunday, regret would set in, but the cycle was already primed for next week. Daniel's story is not unique, it's a modern echo of a universal pattern.

Emotional contexts and cognitive shortcuts

Our brains are wired to conserve energy. When an emotional trigger strikes, such as loneliness, anxiety or just a mid-week slump, your rational prefrontal cortex goes quiet. Decision making shifts to the limbic system and basal ganglia, which care only about immediate relief.[30] Laboratory research shows that when cognitive resources are depleted (from stress, fatigue or emotional strain) people are far more likely to make impulsive purchases. For example, a study in the *Journal of Consumer Research* found that participants with depleted self-control spent more and felt stronger urges to buy, regardless of product type.[31] Similarly, research demonstrates that people excluded from social groups spent significantly more on 'treat yourself' items, in order to signal status, mimic group trends or simply to restore a sense of belonging.[32]

Universal yet personal

The science is universal, but the triggers are deeply personal. Across cultures and income levels, impulsive buying is a global phenomenon. Research shows that 88% of Brits make an impulse purchase at least once a month, with each Brit making 40 impulse buys a year, spending an average of £50.43 a month or £605.16 a year.[33] In the US, 89% have a history of impulse buying, with 54% spending $100 or more and 20% spending over $1,000 on a one off item.[34] In Australia and Canada, 80%[35] and 63%[36] of shoppers say they shop impulsively. Worldwide, 57% of women have impulsively bought clothes or shoes, while 49% of men have impulsively purchased electronics.[37] Single shoppers make 45% more impulse buys compared to married shoppers.[38]

In China, where the convenience of e-commerce has totally revolutionized the way people shop, a survey of middle-class consumers found that 53% of the respondents said that social media is the main trigger for their impulse buying and 70% of Gen Z consumers are more inclined to buy products through social media (compared to a global average of 44%).[39]

One micro example: Lihua, from Shanghai, China, was asked why she purchased five new pairs of shoes during JD's popular 618 Festival; she said:

> No specific reasons actually. My friends usually share their newly purchased shoes or outfits on their WeChat Moments, together with their reviews. At that time, I thought – wow, this pair of shoes is really nice, so many people have got it, I must buy one for myself. Then, I clicked on the sharing post, was directed to a WeChat store and completed the transaction in the blink of an eye.[40]

Whether it's stress at work, childhood money scripts, FOMO or social comparison on Instagram, the neurobiology is the same.

Community voices: what triggers us

When we asked our Instagram @thehumblepenny community about impulsive spending their responses echoed this universality:

- 'Ice cream/make-up/clothes. Triggered by feeling out of control or like we are all doomed anyway.'
- 'Make-up, skin care, homeware and flights. Triggered when I am overwhelmed.'
- 'Food (takeaways usually). Triggered by feeling stressed, tired or burnt out by work.'
- 'Stress, sadness. I buy anything from clothes to beauty. Lately I have been returning items.'
- 'Mainly clothes. If I'm annoyed by something or just feeling YOLO. Spent so much.'

These stories reveal that the urge to spend is rarely about the item, it's about soothing emotions, escaping discomfort or reclaiming a sense of agency.

The self-sabotage moment

Every time you spend to soothe an emotion, you're unwittingly telling your brain that short-term relief beats long-term reward.

- **Sabotage trigger:** A stressor or emotional void.
- **Sabotage action:** An unplanned purchase.
- **False reward:** A dopamine spike, quickly replaced by guilt.
- **Regret loop:** Reinforces the belief, 'I'm not in control', making the next impulse stronger.

From guilt to curiosity

Before you can change, you must first see your triggers as information and each impulse purchase as a data point, a clue to which emotions you're seeking to soothe or which needs are going unmet. A luxury coffee isn't inherently bad, but buying one out of boredom at 3pm every day signals a pattern worth exploring. The key is shifting from, 'Why am I so weak?' to 'What is this moment teaching me?'

Bridging to reprogramming

Understanding the psychology behind impulsive spending is the foundation for lasting change. It transforms guilt into curiosity and self-judgment into self-inquiry. When you recognize the neural fireworks behind each urge, you reclaim your power of choice.

IDENTIFYING YOUR SELF-SABOTAGE TRIGGERS AND ELIMINATING BAD HABITS

Emotional spending isn't just a random lapse, it's financial self-sabotage. Every impulse purchase chips away at your long-term goals, trading real progress for a fleeting sense of relief and, often, lasting regret.

To break this cycle you need to shine a light on what's really happening beneath the surface and use a system that transforms vague guilt into actionable insight.

Step 1: Map your personal trigger-action loop

Start with a simple but powerful tool: a spending trigger log. For one week, every time you make a purchase beyond your routine essentials, pause and jot down the following:

- **Trigger:** What happened and what emotion did it spark? For example, received a stressful email and felt anxious; scrolled past a friend's holiday pics and felt envy; felt lonely after lunch.
- **Action:** What did you do in response? For example, bought a high-caffeine drink, a new gadget, an online dress.
- **Reinforcement:** What immediate feeling or outcome did this action create? For example, brief excitement, guilt, relief.
- **Identity:** What belief or self-perception did this reinforce? For example, 'I'm someone who shops to cope,' 'I'm not in control' or 'I'm learning to break this pattern'.

Within days, you'll start to see patterns emerge.

Step 2: Categorize your triggers

Once you've gathered enough entries, group your triggers into three main buckets:

- **Emotional triggers:** Stress at work, arguments with loved ones, loneliness or anxiety.
- **Situational triggers:** Seeing a sale ad, walking past a favourite shop, hearing a pitch from an influencer or simply being bored at home.
- **Social triggers:** Peers' purchases, social-media envy or FOMO.

This step is crucial. When you know which category your triggers fall into, you can design targeted countermeasures. For example, if you're triggered by stress after a tense call with your manager, you might schedule a five-minute breathing exercise before opening any shopping app. If you're tempted by situational cues, like passing your favourite store, you could take a different route home or set your phone to a mode that shuts down all apps during peak temptation hours.

Step 3: Interrupt the habit loop

Research shows that breaking just one link in your habit loop can significantly weaken the entire cycle.[41] Here are three proven interruption techniques:

- **Physical barriers:** Remove saved payment details from your browser, delete shopping apps or keep your wallet in another room.
- **Mental barriers:** Impose a three-question rule before buying, e.g. 'Am I purchasing this for survival, joy or status?' If the answer isn't a clear 'survival' or 'true joy', delay the purchase. More on this in Chapter 12.
- **Social accountability:** Share your spending goals with a trusted friend and ask for a check-in when temptation strikes.

By inserting even one barrier after a trigger, you disrupt the automatic flow. Over time, your brain forms a new association – trigger, interruption, no purchase – weakening the original pattern.

Step 4: Audit and eliminate junk-finance habits

Once a quarter, perform a subscription spring clean. Pull up your bank and card statements and list every recurring payment. For each, ask:

- **Value check:** 'Does this subscription help me build wealth, save time or support my goals?'
- **Engagement check:** 'Am I actively using it?'
- **Cost-benefit check:** 'Is the cost justified by the return I get?'

Keep only subscriptions that build wealth, improve wellbeing or support your goals – for example, an investing app, an education membership you engage with or a productivity tool you rely on.

Check your card for auto-renews – snack boxes, beauty or novelty services – and switch them to one-off purchases you only buy deliberately. You could reclaim hundreds, even thousands, a year.

Jessica's journey from emotional spending to intentional living

Jessica Williams is a Brit who lives in Paris, France, and a self-described recovering emotional spender.[42] She used to find herself wandering lifestyle stores or endlessly scrolling her favourite brands online whenever she felt overwhelmed or caught in a spiral of negative emotions. She shares, 'You can bet I'm right back filling up my imaginary dream cart on Cult Beauty, then feeling oh so tempted to think "**** it" and buy the lot without even checking my bank account.'

Over time, Jessica realized that managing her emotional spending wasn't just about controlling her finances, it was about understanding and managing her feelings. By raising her awareness and focusing on her emotions, she gradually became a more intentional shopper. Now, she says, 'Learning to manage my emotional spending tendencies has benefitted my wallet, mental health and life in general.'

Her journey highlights how intentional habits can replace impulsive ones, leading to better financial and emotional wellbeing.

REPLACING HARMFUL FINANCIAL BEHAVIOURS WITH WEALTH-BUILDING ACTIONS

You've learned to spot self-sabotage and disrupt the cycle. Now it's time to move from insight to action, using your triggers as launchpads for practical, forwards-looking Wealth Habits. Lasting wealth isn't just about resisting old habits, it's about rehearsing new ones until growth becomes your default.

Wealth trigger actions: turning cues into growth

Rather than simply resisting old spending cues, use them as prompts for small, positive Wealth Habits, rewiring your brain's default pathway from 'trigger, spend' to 'trigger, grow'.

One of the most effective ways to do this is with personalized 'if–then' wealth plans, a behavioural technique known as implementation intentions. For example:

- If I feel stressed after a work call, then I will open my budgeting app and review my spending in the last 24 hours.

- If I open a shopping app after 9pm, then I'll put $5 or $10 into my weekend getaway savings.

Research consistently shows that such clear, pre-committed statements significantly increase follow-through on new habits by making the desired action automatic when a trigger occurs.[43]

Next-level micro-investing: automate and escalate

You may have started with rounding up spare change or applying the 1% Rule (Chapter 2). Now escalate your micro-investing by automating increases and diversifying your platforms. Behavioural science demonstrates that automating small incremental changes reduces friction and increases long-term savings.[44] For more on automating savings and investments, see Chapter 7.

- Set your investment app to increase contributions by a small percentage every quarter.
- Try windfall investing. Send, say, 30% of any unexpected refund or bonus straight into long-term investments.
- Use platforms that allow for fractional investing in diverse assets, not just cash savings.

Elevate your Joy Spend

Upgrade your discretionary spending bucket by linking it to personal growth or shared experiences, making every pound or dollar a conscious investment in happiness. Research confirms that spending on experiences and relationships brings more lasting satisfaction than material goods.[45] For more on joyful spending, see Chapter 9.

- Replace 'retail therapy' with 'experience therapy'. Allocate your joy budget to activities that build memories or skills (e.g. workshops, travel or group experiences).
- Do a value audit. After each Joy Spend ask, 'How did this boost my wellbeing or relationships?' Then tweak next month's plan.

Aisha, a project manager, replaced her £50 monthly shopping splurge with a rotating dinner series with friends. Over three months, she spent 40% less and reported a 60% boost in post-treat wellbeing on her reflection scale.

FRAMEWORK: THE WEALTH TRIGGER RESET

At the heart of this chapter is the Wealth Trigger Reset framework: a four-step loop – **notice, name, neutralize, nurture** – that turns emotional spending cues into deliberate choices. Used consistently, it rewires your reward circuitry so urges become prompts for action, not derailments, and each trigger becomes a moment to compound your wealth.

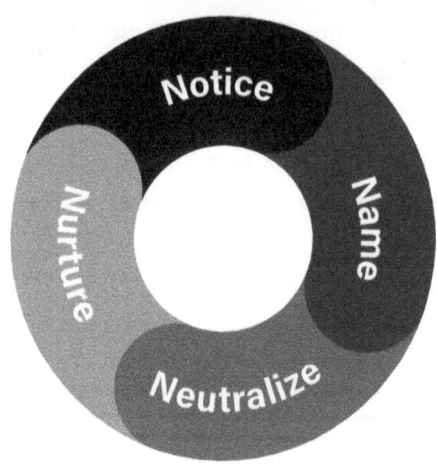

Notice

Cultivate moment-to-moment awareness of impulses. Train yourself to notice the exact cue – envy on social, post-work stress or a flash-sale ping – and set hourly phone reminders labelled 'notice'. When it pings, take one breath and ask, 'Am I feeling an urge to buy?' Do this consistently and your brain will learn to spot cues before you act.

Name

Label the underlying emotion. Are you anxious? Bored? Lonely? Envious? Proud? Seeking approval? By accurately naming your feeling, you shift decision making from your limbic system to the prefrontal cortex, engaging rational insight over reflexive action.

Neutralize

Interrupt the automatic spend. Employ a barrier, this could be physical (remove saved cards), mental (impose a cooling-off rule) or social (text a financial friend), to weaken the established habit loop.

Nurture

Replace the void with a small Wealth Habit. Whether it's a micro-investment, a scheduled Joy Spend or a trigger-linked momentum builder, you reinforce a new neural pathway that rewards long-term growth rather than instant gratification.

PAUSE FOR REFLECTION

Find a quiet ten minutes. Take out your spending trigger log and review the past week's entries. Circle the three most frequent emotions you named. For each:

- What underlying need was it signalling?
- How often did you successfully neutralize the urge?
- What Wealth Habit did you nurture instead?

Write a brief paragraph on one trigger you still struggle with. Then answer: 'If this trigger appeared tomorrow, what exact neutralize barrier and nurture action would I deploy?' This reflection, which could be done once a week, anchors your learning in a real-world context, turning insight into resolve.

> *Small action step*
>
> Today, before your next non-essential purchase, enact a five-minute pause. Set a timer, close your eyes and breathe deeply. Ask yourself:
>
> - What am I feeling right now?
> - What exactly am I about to buy?
> - What mini Wealth Habit can I perform instead?
>
> After five minutes, decide whether to delay, proceed mindfully or press 'add to savings'. Celebrate whichever choice you make. Each conscious decision rewires your habit pathways, bringing you one step closer to emotional mastery and lasting wealth.

Mastering emotional spending is not about deprivation, it's about empowerment. Each impulse you tame, each trigger you reprogramme, is a victory over the invisible forces that keep so many chained to stress-buy cycles.

Remember, your brain craves reward and by deliberately nurturing Wealth Habits you gift it a higher-order thrill – the satisfaction of growth, security and control.

Be patient, habits deepen with practise. Celebrate every pause, every named emotion, every micro-investment. You're not just resisting temptations, you're forging a new identity: one of a calm, deliberate wealth builder who masters money's emotional undercurrents.

Chapter summary

- Your ancient survival wiring, cortisol-fuelled scarcity alarms and dopamine-driven reward loops mistake retail therapy for relief. Reframe impulses as valuable information.
- Name unplanned 'treat yourself' splurges for what they are – financial self-sabotage – and shift from guilt to strategy.
- Keep a spending trigger log to pinpoint your unique cues (e.g. stress, envy, boredom), the purchases they spur and the fleeting relief they deliver.
- Interrupt automatic spends by deploying barriers, deleting saved cards, applying the three-question rule and leaning on accountability.
- Swap impulse buys for growth rituals: micro-investing, purposeful Joy Spends and 'if–then' wealth actions that satisfy your brain's craving for reward with progress.
- Practise reflective and real-time pauses: a weekly ten-minute review to map triggers and script responses, plus a daily five-minute pause before non-essential buys.
- The Wealth Trigger Reset teaches you to notice, name, neutralize and nurture, turning every impulse into an opportunity for growth.

> ### Building The Wealth Habit
>
> ## Pillar 1: Build the Mindset
> **Principle lens: Keep it simple**
>
> You've rebuilt how you think about money, shifting identity before behaviour.
>
> Through this pillar, complexity was never the goal. Clarity was.
>
> Ask yourself: *What belief about money feels lighter, clearer or simpler than when I started?*

PILLAR 2
BUILD THE HABIT

Chapter 7

THE SET-AND-SOAR SYSTEM

The Wealth Habit's number one tool:
Set it and forget it

> **Theme: Action**
> You move from knowing your triggers to automating micro-habits, embedding them so deeply that choice fatigue disappears.

Every decision you automate frees up time and energy you can pour into true wealth. Imagine if every cup of your morning coffee fuelled not just your savings, but also your wellbeing, relationships and personal growth.

On 2 April 2025, a.k.a. Liberation Day, the US president announced a series of tariffs that sent global stock markets into a meltdown. By 8 April, more than $8.56tn (£6.72tn) had been wiped off the value of global stock markets and the S&P 500 had fallen by 12.1%. London's Financial Times Stock Exchange (FTSE) tumbled 10.8% in a single week.[46]

Across continents, households faced the same gut-wrenching uncertainty: some panic sold at steep losses, while others hesitated, waiting for the 'perfect' moment, only to watch markets rebound a few weeks later without them.

One member at the Financial Joy Academy (FJA) captured the dilemma:

> I got caught up in this whole drama. The stock market went down and there was still a lot of noise about it and I thought, 'I'm sure it's going to go further down'. I had a lump sum amount of money to invest and I didn't invest because I kept saying, 'Surely this is going to go down further'. But I've just sat watching it over the last three weeks and it has been flying and flying higher than it ever was and I missed the opportunity to buy. Now, I'm thinking, 'Should I buy it now or not?' The thought that kept crossing my mind with a lump sum was, 'Surely I should try and gauge the market?'

This exposes a universal truth: every choice we defer in the hope of perfect timing risks eroding both our returns and our peace of mind. In moments of chaos, our instincts betray us: panic, regret and indecision take over, leading to an analysis-paralysis mindset.

But what if we could sidestep these pitfalls entirely? What if our savings and investments simply flowed according to rules we set once, quietly building wealth while we lived our lives?

Imagine waking up to find your bills paid, savings growing and investments compounding, all without lifting a finger. This is the automation advantage: the silent engine that banishes decision fatigue, locks in disciplined growth and lets your money work while you sleep.

Automation isn't about surrendering control; it's about reclaiming your life and letting your systems work for you. From London, to Dubai, to Singapore and beyond, ordinary people are using automation to turn crisis into opportunity and to reclaim their financial freedom, come rain or shine.

> **The Wealth Habit Mantra 7:**
> Wealth isn't about willpower; it's about building systems that work while you live.

HOW AUTOMATION REMOVES DECISION FATIGUE FROM MONEY MANAGEMENT

In the modern world, not only are hundreds of things vying for our attention every second, we're also bombarded with decisions every day, from what to eat for dinner to which work emails to answer first. This is compounded for parents who not only have to deal with their own mental loads but also have children with lots of questions to look after and feed.

This relentless barrage drains our mental reserves, a phenomenon known as decision fatigue.

When it comes to money, decision fatigue is especially costly. Research shows that the more choices we face, the more likely we are to procrastinate, make poor decisions or avoid action altogether.[47]

Money management is a minefield of micro-decisions. Should I save or spend? Is now the right time to invest or should I overpay my mortgage? Did I pay that bill? Each question chips away at our willpower, leaving us vulnerable to impulse purchases, missed payments and abandoned goals.

Over time, even the most disciplined among us can falter, not because we lack intelligence or motivation, but because our brains are wired to conserve energy and avoid complexity.

Automation is the antidote. By converting repetitive financial decisions into automatic processes, we reclaim our mental bandwidth for what truly matters. Instead of wrestling with the same choices, month after month, automation locks in positive behaviours, such as saving, investing or paying bills, so that they happen without conscious effort.

As behavioural scientists have shown, defaults are incredibly sticky. People are far more likely to continue with automated contributions than manual ones, simply because the path of least resistance is now the path to wealth.

But automation isn't just about convenience. It's about protecting yourself from your own worst instincts. We've seen first-hand how, when one is tired, stressed or distracted, it's easy to forget to make that mortgage payment, for example, which could lead to a late payment fee and a negative impact on your credit report, which then spirals.

Beyond the convenience, your automated system keeps you on track. High performers, successful investors and entrepreneurs have long understood this secret. They ruthlessly eliminate trivial decisions, reserving their energy for high-impact choices.

By automating routine financial tasks – for example bill payments, savings transfers, investment contributions – you free up mental space for creativity, relationships and growth.

The result? Less stress, fewer mistakes and a steady march towards your goals.

SETTING UP A FINANCIAL SYSTEM THAT GROWS WEALTH WHILE YOU SLEEP

Warren Buffett famously said, 'If you don't find a way to make money while you sleep, you will work until you die.'[48] The essence of this wisdom is simple: wealth isn't built by relentless effort alone, but by creating systems that quietly work for you, even when you're not paying attention. Here's how to transform your finances into a self-driving engine that works around the clock.

Step 1: Consolidate, categorize and clarify your money

Start by bringing all your accounts into one place. Use financial aggregators (like Plaid) or your bank's dashboard to see every balance and transaction at a glance.

Next, automate your categorization. Tools like YNAB or Emma tag your bills, essentials and discretionary spending, turning raw transactions into insights without manual sorting.

Finally, set a clear money hierarchy. Pay yourself first (emergency fund, retirement, key goals), followed by essentials like mortgage, rent and utilities, then discretionary and 'fun money'. This order shapes how your automated transfers run each month.

You will need a minimum of six different bank accounts:

1. Current or checking account for salary and household bills.
2. High-yield savings for emergency.
3. Retirement savings.
4. Tax-free accounts, e.g. Individual Savings Account (ISA), Roth Individual Retirement Account (Roth IRA), Tax Free Savings Account (TFSA) or equivalent.
5. Savings account for targeted goals (e.g. travel or side hustle).
6. Savings account for fun money.

Tweak this example to suit your personal circumstances, for example you may need more bank accounts or pots for other savings such as children's education, giving or a car purchase, etc.

Step 2: Automate your cash flows

Day 1: It's payday. After your employer withdraws pension contributions (e.g. 5–10%), taxes and potentially student loans, your net pay hits your bank account.

Day 2: The morning after payday, trigger multiple automated transfers. For example:

- 5% to emergency fund or high-yield savings account.
- 10% to debt payoff: minimum payments plus extra towards highest-interest balance.
- 10% to retirement (e.g. private pension/Self Invested Personal Pension (SIPP) or equivalent).
- 15% to tax-free accounts (e.g. ISA, Roth IRA, TFSA or equivalent).
- 5% to targeted goals (e.g. travel or a side-hustle fund).
- 2–5% to fun money.

The remaining balance flows into your everyday account for bills, living expenses and giving.

Stagger your bill payments across the month to smooth cash flow and avoid overdrafts. For example:

Day 3: Rent or mortgage via standing order.
Day 5: Utilities, household and insurance debits.
Day 10: Credit card repayment in full (if possible).

If your income varies, use the balance-trigger rules your bank or app provides to avoid overcommitting on lean months; nearly every major provider worldwide now supports them or conditional transfers ('if balance >$1,500, then transfer $200').

Step 3: Harness compound growth automatically

Make your investments work overtime:

- **Dividend reinvestment:** Any dividends or interest earned in your brokerage account are automatically reinvested. Most platforms (e.g. Fidelity, Vanguard, etc.) offer Dividend Reinvestment Plans (DRIPs) so dividends automatically buy more shares (ideally in a tax efficient account), compounding your returns without lifting a finger.
- **Auto-rebalance:** Use robo-advisors like Wealthify, Nutmeg or Betterment to auto-rebalance your portfolio when allocations drift beyond your chosen risk bands.
- **Channel windfalls:** Automatically direct any bonuses, tax refunds, freelance income or large one-off payments into your chosen bucket,

whether that's high-interest debt payoff, an emergency fund or a growth reserve, so you never miss the chance to put surplus cash to work.

Step 4: Build guardrails and checkpoints

Set low-balance alerts via SMS or app notifications. These pause discretionary transfers if your main account falls below a safety threshold (e.g. £500 or $500). This prevents bounced payments and keeps your buffer intact.

Schedule regular five-minute tune-ups. At the beginning, we recommend a five-minute weekly check for the first six to eight weeks, then you can reduce to monthly tune-ups. Glance at your aggregated dashboard, confirm transfers executed, check for unusual spikes or dips, and adjust percentages if your life circumstances change.

Every quarter, perform a deeper review. Has your emergency fund reached three to six months of expenses? Are you on track for your home deposit or retirement goals? Adjust your automated transfers accordingly.

Real-world example: Aisha's sleep-mode system

Meet Aisha in Cambridge, UK, who gets paid on the last working day of each month. She's set up:

- **Payday + 1:** 12% to emergency fund, 8% to private pension (retirement pot), 5% to 'Ikea Fund' (targeted goals).
- **Day 3:** Rent via standing order.
- **Day 5:** Utilities debit.
- **Day 10:** Credit-card paid in full.

- **Weekly:** Review that everything is working as it should.
- **Quarterly:** Dividend reinvestments and robo-advisor rebalance.

The result? Within a year, Aisha's emergency fund reached three months' expenses, her pension contribution rose from 8% to 10% and she never missed a bill or felt squeezed mid-month.

By consolidating your accounts, automating cash flows, compounding returns and adding simple guardrails, your money moves towards your goals even while you sleep. That's the automation advantage: a system that turns daily money management into something effortless.

A well-designed system isn't 'set and forget'. It's 'set it, review it weekly in five minutes and let compounding do the rest'.

THE BEST TOOLS AND STRATEGIES FOR AUTOMATING SAVINGS AND INVESTING, INCLUDING AI-DRIVEN FINANCIAL ASSISTANTS

The rise of digital technology has ushered in a new era of automation, one where AI-driven tools and smart platforms make it easier than ever to build wealth on autopilot. But with so many options, where should you start?

We wanted to share a practical guide to the best tools and strategies for automating your financial life. The mention of these tools is for illustration purposes only and is not a personal recommendation to you. Please do some more research about their pros and cons, paying close attention to fees, service, choice, usability and performance.

Whether you're in Lagos, London or Lima, these tools are at your fingertips.

Category 1: Banking and bill-pay automation

Many banks offer built-in banking features such as scheduled transfers, standing orders (externally and internally between accounts) and auto-payment for external bills.

Open banking plugins like TrueLayer (Europe/UK) let your favourite money apps talk directly to your bank – only with your permission, of course. That means your app can check your balance before moving money and trigger smarter rules (e.g. 'if balance >£1,500, move £200 to ISA'), reducing failed transfers and overdraft scares.

Category 2: Budgeting and cash-flow automation

Here are a few tools to consider for budgeting and managing your cash flow:

- **Emma:** Combines budgeting with financial wellness coaching.
- **Personal Capital:** Offers a comprehensive dashboard for tracking income, expenses and investments.
- **YNAB:** Auto-categorizes, sends alerts, visualizes trends.

Category 3: Round-up and savings automation

These apps are ideal for people who struggle to save consistently, shoppers who want to see spare change add up over time and anyone looking for an easy 'set-and-forget' buffer without changing their spending habits. For specific examples, the table on page 345 highlights popular apps and banking features around the world that turn your everyday spending into effortless savings.

Category 4: Investment automation

For recurring investments, most brokerages now allow you to set up automatic monthly investments in index funds, Exchange Traded Funds (ETFs) or stocks. This 'dollar-cost averaging' or 'pound-cost averaging' approach smooths out the ups and downs of the market and builds wealth steadily.

Consider the example at the start of the chapter where the Standard and Poor's 500 (S&P 500) plunged 12.1% on Liberation Day. An investor who bought exactly at the low with a lump sum would see a 13.8% gain simply to get back to where the plunge started.

Since no one can pick that perfect low in real time, dollar-cost averaging by committing a fixed amount on a regular schedule, regardless of whether stocks are up or down, captures much of that recovery without the guesswork. You automatically buy more shares when prices dip and fewer when they rise.

Over time, this lowers your average purchase price and helps you own more units for the same investment. Think of it like stocking up when the market 'goes on sale' – no stress, no second-guessing.

Alongside automated dollar-cost averaging, the table on page 346 highlights robo-advisors and AI-driven platforms that handle portfolio building, rebalancing and dividend reinvestment for you. From tax-loss harvesting in the US to Sharia-compliant options in the Middle East, these tools use smart rules to match your risk level and long-term goals.

Who it's for: Investors who want hands-off, professional-grade management, have medium- to long-term goals and prefer to take emotion out of their decisions.

Category 5: AI-driven financial assistants

As AI continues to evolve, expect even more personalized and proactive financial automation. Imagine a digital assistant that not only pays your bills and invests your money, but also anticipates upcoming expenses, flags opportunities and coaches you towards your goals. Some examples you could explore:

- **OneMain Trim:** An AI-powered assistant that finds and cancels unwanted subscriptions, negotiates bills and helps you save money effortlessly.
- **Origin Financial:** Provides tailored financial recommendations based on your habits and goals, making planning accessible and actionable.

Some of the benefits of using AI-powered assistants are:

- **Dynamic savings rules:** AI models can forecast income and expenses, adjusting savings percentages automatically – saving more in surplus months, pausing in lean months.
- **Behavioural nudges:** Rather than bland alerts, AI chatbots can frame suggestions in your voice: 'Hey, I noticed you have $200 extra this week, want me to stash it into your travel fund?'
- **Tax-loss harvesting automation:** Robo-advisors automatically sell losing positions to offset gains, all without you lifting a finger.

The future of wealth building using AI tools is frictionless, personalized and global.

FRAMEWORK: THE SET-AND-SOAR SYSTEM

Now you're familiarized with the tools at your disposal we want to share a powerful framework at the heart of the automation advantage: the Set-and-Soar System. This is a simple, actionable framework for embedding automation into your financial life, consisting of three steps: **set it, anchor it, soar.**

Set it

Choose key dates, define your goals (e.g. savings percentages, bill auto-payments, investment allocations) and set up automated flows for savings, investments and bill payments. Plug in rules on your bank, budgeting app or investment platform to schedule transfers and allocate funds according to your priorities.

You can do it in phases, for example:

1. Essentials (e.g. savings and bills).
2. Investments (e.g. auto-invest and dividend reinvest).
3. Sophisticated tactics (e.g. dynamic AI-driven adjustments).

Anchor it

Integrate automation into your daily routine. Tie rules to reliable triggers: payday deposits, incoming invoices, account balance breaches. Use apps that sync with your bank and anchor your system to life events (e.g. annual raises or tax refunds). Use calendar reminders for monthly reviews (no more than ten minutes).

Soar

Let your system run and observe compounding in action. Monitoring, feedback and accountability are critical to avoid surprises: review and optimize periodically; communicate with your partner if you have one, adjust annually or upon major life changes.

As your wealth grows, increase your automated contributions and expand into new investment opportunities. Celebrate small wins (e.g. your savings account balance just crossed $5,000).

This framework transforms automation from a one-time task into a lifelong habit. It's not about doing more, it's about building a system that does the work for you, so you can get closer to your dreams with confidence.

PAUSE FOR REFLECTION

Where in your financial life do you feel the most friction or fatigue? Which decisions drain your energy or cause you stress?

Write down three areas where automation could lighten your load and free you to focus on what matters most.

> *Small action step*
> Choose one financial task you perform manually each month such as saving, investing or paying a bill.
> Today, set up an automated process for that task. Even a small step, like automating a £10 or $10 transfer to savings, is a victory. Notice how it feels to remove that decision from your mental to-do list.

Automation isn't about surrendering control, it's about reclaiming your life. By building systems that work while you live, you unlock the freedom to pursue your passions, support your loved ones and create the future you deserve.

The journey to wealth doesn't require superhuman discipline or endless hustle. It requires the courage to trust in small, consistent actions and the wisdom to let your systems soar.

Chapter summary

- Automation banishes decision fatigue by turning repetitive financial choices into set-and-forget rules.
- Build a self-driving financial engine by consolidating accounts, categorizing spending and establishing a savings-first hierarchy.
- Automate cash flows with next-day transfers, staggered bill payments and balance-trigger rules to smooth your month and avoid overdrafts.
- Harness compound growth through dividend reinvestment, auto-rebalancing robo-advisors and channel windfalls into debt-paydown or investment.
- Modern tools from round-up savings apps to AI-driven assistants, remove manual effort in saving and investing, globally.
- Dollar-cost averaging outperforms market timing by buying more on dips without guessing the bottom.
- The Set-and-Soar System ties it all together – set your rules, anchor them to reliable triggers and let your money grow while you enjoy your life.

Chapter 8

THE WEALTH-MULTIPLIER EFFECT

The power of making money
while doing nothing

> **Theme: Scale**
> With your money on autopilot, you now harness compound interest and passive strategies to let wealth grow even when you're not thinking about it.

THE WEALTH HABIT

> '*Compound interest is the eighth wonder of the world.*'
> Attributed to Albert Einstein

But what if you don't have time for compound interest to do its thing?

Most people don't. Not really. Most people reading this book didn't start investing at 23. You probably didn't build a rental portfolio in your twenties. Maybe you didn't even know what an ETF was until your forties. And now you're being told to wait 30-plus years for wealth to compound? No. That's not the answer for most people. We started in our late twenties, felt behind and had to approach things differently.

This chapter is your pivot. It's about multiplying your money now, in realistic, practical, habit-driven ways. Yes, compound interest plays a role. But in a high cost-of-living world, with little spare cash and a shorter timeline, you need more than just time. You need automation, stacking and smart income flows. You need a system that grows wealth while you focus on living. Let's build that system.

Meet Nike, who started investing at the age 54 in 2022. She's a mum, wife and long-time member of the Financial Joy Academy (FJA). For years, Nike believed property would be her pension. She'd built a few investments and assumed that was enough. But then something shifted. 'It suddenly dawned on me that retirement is around the corner,' she said. 'And with the tax changes in UK property, I knew I needed a better plan.'

A conversation with a friend at church planted the seed and sparked a complete mindset shift. 'I used to think pensions were pointless. I had no idea how powerful they could be, especially with the tax benefits.'

That's when Nike joined FJA. Through our coaching calls and by reading our first book, *Financial Joy*, she began learning how to invest with clarity and confidence. 'I started researching funds and dividend stocks. The education changed everything.'

Nike opened two Self-Invested Personal Pension (SIPP) accounts, merged old pensions to reduce fees and began investing monthly, automatically. She chose a mix of funds and individual stocks, including one standout: Rolls Royce, which she first bought at just 89p a share. It's since grown over 300% overall, with her earlier shares exceeding 1,000% as of the time of writing. She now receives dividends from four to five different stocks and reinvests every penny. 'It's a good feeling,' she says. 'Like getting free money. And I don't even have to think about it.'

To create more freedom, she took on a second job with a focused mission: to pay off her mortgage before she turns 60. She's also saved over two years' worth of living expenses, giving her peace of mind and financial flexibility.

But her journey isn't just about herself. Inspired by an FJA coaching call where we shared that we were opening Junior SIPPs for our sons, Nike opened both a Junior SIPP and an Individual Savings Account (ISA) for her daughter, then aged 16, so she could start early and avoid the same mistakes. 'This all happened because of FJA,' she says. 'That one insight changed everything.'

All of this happened while Nike juggled two jobs, raised her daughter, led multiple teams at church, managed her properties and stayed committed as a wife and community leader. Her life was and is full. But she chose to learn, automate and act anyway. 'Automating my investments changed everything. The money is ring-fenced. It's growing, even while I focus on everything else.'

Today, she's also rethinking her property strategy by selling some, flipping others and paying down mortgages to boost retirement income. But perhaps most inspiring of all? Her new vision: Nike now sees a clear path to financial independence and she's intentionally enjoying the journey. 'I invest, but I also take two to three holidays a year. I make time for family and fun now.'

Her advice to others is simple: 'It's never too late. Start where you are.

If you don't start now, when will you?' Nike didn't start early. She started with purpose. And that made all the difference.

> **Wealth Habit Mantra 8:**
> You don't need decades, you need direction. Wealth multiplies when your money earns, compounds and grows even when you're not watching.

HOW COMPOUND INTEREST ACCELERATES WEALTH

What is compound interest, really? It's when the money you make from your investments starts making its own money and that new money starts earning too. Over time, your growth snowballs, even if your contributions stay the same.

Compound interest is powerful, but it's often misunderstood and oversold. Yes, it can multiply your money. But only if you give it time, consistency and discipline.

For many readers of this book, time is not your luxury. So, what do you do? You compress what others stretch. You do in 20 years what others try in 45. How? By doing this:

- Automate contributions so you never skip.
- Invest in growth-oriented stocks, Exchange Traded Funds (ETFs) or funds.
- Reinvest every dividend.
- Avoid high-fee platforms and tax drag.
- Stay open to alternative investments like gold, Real Estate Investment Trusts (REITs) or Bitcoin, etc., understanding that each plays a different role in your portfolio.

Let's be clear: starting at 40, if you invest £500/month in a tax-free account earning an average 7% return, it could still grow to around £400,000 by retirement at 65.

If you stopped adding new money at 65 and left the pot invested while you began withdrawing 5% a year to live on – about £20,000 annually and rising – your portfolio could still be worth roughly £520,000 by age 85, after 20 years of withdrawals. And that's before factoring in any state pension. If you withdrew the more typical 3.5% to 4% a year used in retirement calculations, the portfolio would likely be even larger.

If £500/month feels unrealistic, that's okay. Even £25/month builds the habit and gets the compounding engine started. If you truly can't spare any cash yet, your first multiplier is your time: offer a service, create a small product or start a side hustle to seed your first flow.

Compounding only works if you stay invested, especially during market dips. It's less about timing and more about consistency and behaviour. Compound interest is still part of your toolkit. But now you need tools that accelerate it.

Before we move on, let's be honest about why real-life wealth rarely grows in a perfect curve.

WHY REAL-LIFE WEALTH DOESN'T ALWAYS COMPOUND LIKE THE THEORY

In theory, compound interest is smooth and exponential, a perfect upwards curve.

In reality, life happens, creating a gap between expectations and reality. Here's how wealth typically plays out between ages 20 and 85.

Age 20-25: Low income, high expenses

You're just starting out: first job, student loan repayments, expensive rent. There's little to no surplus for investing. Many aren't even aware of investing, let alone compounding.

Result: No investing = no compounding.

Age 26-35: Life set-up phase

House deposits, weddings, babies and career changes. Income may rise, but so do responsibilities. Savings are often liquid (for emergencies), not invested long-term.

Result: Compounding is inconsistent or delayed.

Age 36-45: Rising income meets rising pressure

Higher income begins, but so do bigger homes, possible private-school fees or family obligations. You might start investing seriously, but often feel 'late'. Many are paying off debt and saving simultaneously.

Result: Catch-up mode begins, but time is already compressed.

Age 46-55: Peak earnings, 'last chance' investing

Kids are older, career peaks and the urgency of retirement grows. This is the golden window for serious investing and some finally max out pensions/401(k) or ISAs/Roth Individual Retirement Arrangements (Roth IRAs) or local equivalent. But even then, the lost compounding years can't be reclaimed.

Result: Growth finally accelerates, but under pressure.

Age 56-65: Preservation, not acceleration

Many reduce risk to 'protect' their capital, fearing market crashes. Retirement planning becomes top priority. Big investments may stop, especially if one partner retires or downsizes income.

Result: Wealth stabilizes but growth slows, compounding tapers off.

Age 66-75: Drawdowns begin

Retirement is here. You start withdrawing from pensions and savings. Income relies on a mix of pensions, investments and possibly rental income. Costs can be unpredictable, for example, travel, grandchildren, lifestyle.

Result: Wealth stops compounding as it now funds life.

Age 76-85: Care costs and spending spike

Health and care expenses often rise sharply in these years. If long-term care is needed, even six-figure savings can vanish quickly. Many face the risk of outliving their money, especially without passive income or property support.

Result: Wealth decays, often faster than expected.

The wealth gap

If your wealth hasn't grown like a textbook curve, it's not because you've failed, it's because you lived. That gap between what's possible and what's typical? It's not meant to shame, it's meant to show what happens when you put your system on autopilot, instead of default. You may have missed the early years, but you haven't missed the chance to compound differently.

THE WEALTH HABIT

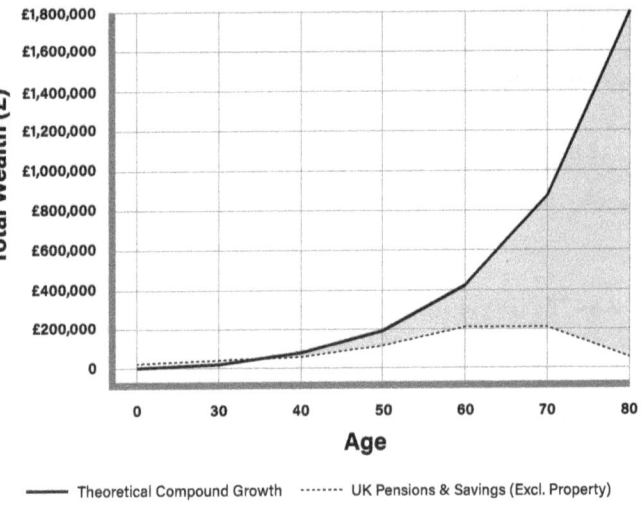

The gap between compounding potential and median UK wealth by age.

To make your money move even when you're resting. To close the gap without needing to be perfect.

This chart illustrates the 'wealth gap' between what's possible and what's typical. It compares the growth of consistent investing (£200/month at 7% from age 23) with the actual median UK pension and savings (excluding property) data by age.[49] The widening gap reflects how few people compound consistently or invest early enough. Closing that gap doesn't require perfection, it requires a system that multiplies money even when you're not watching.

Where the two lines meet around age 35 is symbolically powerful. It's the point at which someone who invested steadily now matches the typical UK saver. Beyond this point, the compound growth curve begins to soar and most people's savings flatten. This is where urgency begins.

The longer you delay, the wider the gap. But even now, with smart systems and layered income, you can still compress time and reclaim lost ground.

Although most people unknowingly follow the typical path, you're not most people. You're here because you're ready to break that pattern and make your money work differently. The Wealth-Multiplier Effect exists to close this gap with time-smart, system-led strategies that meet you where you are.

We know, because we've done it, starting as resource-poor, working-class first- and second-generation immigrants to the UK. We found ways to avoid this typical path and achieve financial independence in our thirties by investing in assets, including paying off our mortgage in just seven years, while raising two children.

We're also not alone in defying the odds. But changing your path begins by accepting that another path exists for you and that we're not all doomed to a worsening quality of life each year.

Crucially, we're not all fighting over one fixed pie where if someone else takes a slice, there's less left for you. If you sit in your room, lean into your creativity and create a new piece of art or digital product that earns you income online, that wealth didn't exist before. New pies and new opportunities are created every day. But it all begins with a shift in mindset.

PASSIVE INCOME STRATEGIES THAT MULTIPLY YOUR EFFORT

If compound interest is a long game, passive income is your mid-game accelerator. The goal isn't to quit your job and live on a beach. The goal is to create cash flow with low maintenance, so you can redirect it into wealth-building systems.

In the past, passive income came from land, labour or capital. Today, it also comes from leverage, especially digital and AI-powered media leverage. We now live in a time where a single idea, recorded once, written once or coded once, can generate income for years.

But passive income isn't one-size-fits-all. Some strategies start actively, i.e. requiring your time or skill, then evolve into income-producing assets. Others are designed to be passive from day one. Understanding both helps you choose your path based on your time, resources and risk appetite. This isn't about hype, it's about options.

If you've ever thought, 'Where do I even start?', the following two tables give you a clear roadmap. Whether you have more time than money or more knowledge than capital, there's a path that meets you where you are.

- **Table 1:** These income paths start with your time or skills – like offering a service, creating content or consulting – but can be systematized or productized over time to become passive. Ideal if you're starting with limited capital but want to earn now and scale later.
- **Table 2:** These income models are designed to earn passively from day one, often through automation, digital products or investments. There's set-up work upfront, but once built, the income flows in with minimal ongoing input.

Use these tables to spark one action. You don't need to start with ten income streams, just one that works with your energy, skills and season of life.

Table 1: Build first, then multiply

Here are some AI ideas that start active but can scale passively.

The Wealth-Multiplier Effect

	Idea	Example	Tech stack	Why it works
1	AI-powered client services	A health coach uses AI to create personalized meal and fitness plans, then explains them in videos shared through a private portal.	ChatGPT, Canva, Loom, Google Drive	Starts as one-on-one service, saves hours and delivers a premium personalized service. Over time, common client questions can be turned into guides or a course.
2	Build personal brand with AI	A YouTube channel documenting your journey to becoming debt-free, sharing lessons learned, tools used and tips for others.	YouTube, TikTok, LinkedIn, CapCut, Jasper, TubeBuddy	Your story builds trust. Trust builds community. Community builds income streams: affiliate links, digital products, sponsorships.
3	AI-driven side hustles	An AI-powered CV polishing service targeting recent grads.	ChatGPT, Copy.ai, Resume.io, Canva	Use AI to deliver fast, high-value services in niche markets.
4	Tiny service-based AI-powered tool people pay for monthly	A blog headline generator or YouTube video to blog converter that charges $10/month.	OpenAI, API, Bubble, Stripe, Zapier	Software solves one problem well. AI does the work; you earn recurring revenue.
5	Use AI in your existing business	Automate onboarding emails for a coaching programme.	Zapier, Kit.com, Make.com, ChatGPT	AI multiplies your time, reduces errors and boosts profit margins.
6	Freelance or consult using AI	Offer AI automation set-up for solopreneurs.	Upwork, Fiverr, ChatGPT, Loom	AI increases the value of your service. Clients want results and speed.
7	Social media marketing with AI	Facebook ad agency using AdCreative.ai to speed up content creation.	AdCreative.ai, Jasper, Systeme.io	AI allows you to scale client delivery without increasing team size.
8	Sell AI courses or coaching	A '30-day AI side hustle launch' course built in a weekend.	ChatGPT, Teachable, ThriveCart, Zoom	Use AI to build fast. Sell knowledge in repeatable, scalable ways.
9	License prompts and frameworks	Sell your own 'money planning prompt pack' for finance creators.	ChatGPT, PromptBase, Canva, Gumroad	Digital intellectual property. No delivery or stock. Just sell and repeat.

Table 2: Multiply from day one

These ideas are designed to be automated or earn while you sleep from day one, but require initial upfront work.

	Idea	Example	Tech stack	Why it works
1	AI digital products	A digital net-worth tracker for busy parents sold on Etsy.	ChatGPT, Canva, Etsy, Gumroad	No customer service, no shipping. Just automated digital delivery and sales.
2	Evergreen affiliate content	Blog posts reviewing top AI tools for content creators and repurposed to distribute in other formats, e.g. video, newsletter, etc.	YouTube, WordPress, TikTok, Jasper	Create content once, earn every day. Search and social bring traffic long after publishing.
3	AI-generated journals	A guided 'side hustle journal' published on Amazon KDP.	ChatGPT, Canva, Amazon KDP	Print-on-demand means you earn royalties forever with no inventory or fulfilment.
4	Custom GPTs or AI agents	A 'meal plan and grocery budget GPT' embedded on your website.	ChatGPT GPT Builder, Zapier AI Agents, Voiceflow	Works 24/7. Monetize access or use to upsell services.
5	Prompt packs	A 'grant-writing prompt pack' sold to non-profits.	ChatGPT, PromptBase, Canva	Easy to create and sell. Prompts are a growing digital asset category.
6	Evergreen AI-powered courses	An automated course: 'Build a personal brand with AI – even if you're camera shy'.	ChatGPT, Loom, ThriveCart, Teachable	Sell it while you sleep. AI helps you build fast and automation delivers it forever.
7	Invest in AI ETFs or stocks	£100 or $100 a month into a global Technology ETF for growth and dividend income.	Vanguard, iShares, Fidelity	Simple, passive exposure to tech-sector growth with minimal effort and long-term return.
8	AI content sites (blogs)	A niche blog on AI tools for teachers, monetized with ads and affiliates.	KoalaWriter, WordPress, Google AdSense	Use AI to write 100 plus blog posts. SEO traffic monetizes on autopilot.
9	AI YouTube channels	A faceless YouTube channel on 'best AI tools of the week'.	Pictory, ElevenLabs, ChatGPT	AI scripts, edits and voices. Videos get views and earn ad plus affiliate income passively.

Not based in the UK or US? No problem. The principles are universal. Use local equivalents of tax-advantaged accounts or tools like Gumroad, Kindle Direct Publishing (KDP) or Teachable – the systems still work.

WHICH PASSIVE INCOME PATH IS RIGHT FOR YOU?

The key to building passive income isn't just picking the 'best idea', it's choosing the right idea for your energy, skills and season of life.

Take this quick quiz to find your starting path and gain momentum. For each question, write a score from 1 (low) to 5 (high). Total your score and see which path suits you best. Then use the table on page 146 to find the income idea that matches your results.

Step 1: Score yourself on these five questions

Question	Score (1–5)
1. How comfortable are you creating content (writing, video, social media)?	
2. How much time can you realistically commit weekly to building a new income stream?	
3. Are you comfortable learning and testing new tech tools (e.g. AI, Canva, Zapier)?	
4. Do you prefer fast wins or building a long-term income machine? (1 = fast cash now, 5 = long-term scale)	
5. Do you already have an audience, network or email list to promote to? (1 = little or no existing platform or audience, 5 = large existing business with significant reach)	

THE WEALTH HABIT

Step 2: Add up your score

Total score: _____ / 25

Step 3: Now find your path

- **Low score?** You need simplicity and speed. Focus on cash flow first, then layer in scale.
- **Medium score?** You're ready to put the work in and build. Mix action with asset creation.
- **High score?** Build digital machines that pay you forever.

Score range	Path to start with	What to focus on
5–10	Starter path: quick cash with AI services or micro products.	Begin with easy, low-cost wins: offer freelance services (e.g. CVs, content, admin) or sell simple AI-created planners and templates. Start in Table 1: Rows 1, 3, 6 or 9.
11–15	Builder path: mix action with asset creation.	Run workshops, document your learning, then turn your service into a product (e.g. course, prompt pack). Ideal bridge between Table 1 (active) and Table 2 (passive).
16–20	Passive creator path: digital assets first.	You're ready to focus on scalable, evergreen income: build AI digital products, journals, blogs or YouTube content. Look to Table 2: Rows 1–6.
21–25	Brand and scale path: AI as a business engine.	You have an audience or platform already. Use AI to create leveraged products, GPTs, evergreen courses and automated income. Focus on Table 2: Rows 1–9 and layer in Table 1: Rows 2, 4, 5, 8.

Your next move

Now flip back to the two AI income tables on pages 143–144 and circle the ideas that match your score bracket. Start with one. Build it fully. Then move to the next.

Whether you build once and sell forever or layer AI onto an existing skillset to create income assets, the principle remains the same: create systems that make money while you're not working. That is the Wealth-Multiplier Effect. And thanks to AI, it's more accessible than ever.

Start by building with effort. End by earning with ease.

READY TO TAKE ACTION? USE THESE AI PROMPTS BASED ON YOUR PATH

Now that you know your ideal path, use one of the tailored AI prompts below to take your first step. Copy and paste the one that matches your score into ChatGPT or Perplexity (or your preferred AI tool) and let the journey begin. However, always remain in the driving seat; AI is your co-pilot but your in-built human creativity will always be the fuel of your progress.

Try adding your own interests to the prompt such as 'around parenting', 'around fitness', 'for new graduates', 'for small business owners', etc. This will help tailor these ideas to your personal experience and strengths.

This book isn't just about learning, it's about experimenting in small ways and building a life that earns while you sleep. Let these prompts be your next move, not just your next idea.

Starter path: quick cash with AI services or micro products

Prompt to experiment with: 'Act as an online business coach. What are three simple AI-powered services or digital products I could offer based on my existing knowledge or skills to earn $200 to $500 this month?'

Builder path: mix action with asset creation

Prompt to experiment with: 'I want to run a small workshop and then turn it into a digital product. Help me plan a simple three-step workshop idea using AI that solves a specific problem for my target audience.'

Passive creator path: digital assets first

Prompt to experiment with: 'Give me five profitable digital product ideas I can create using AI tools (like ChatGPT, Canva or KDP) that match my interests or expertise. Prioritize ones that can earn passively.'

Brand and scale path: AI as a business engine

Prompt to experiment with: 'Help me map out a simple 90-day plan to build a personal brand around a topic I'm passionate about or experienced in. Include three weekly content ideas and one digital product or service I could create using AI tools to generate passive income.'

A QUICK NOTE ON PROPERTY INCOME

Property is often seen as a classic passive income stream and, for some, it can be. But today, with high interest rates, tax changes and tighter regulation, property requires more capital and more hands-on management than many realize.

If you already own property, great, optimize it. But if you're starting from scratch, don't assume bricks and mortar are your only path. Digital income and investment systems can build wealth faster and with far less friction, especially when you're short on time or capital.

We explore six practical property strategies in-depth in Week 9 of our other book, *Financial Joy*. If that's a path you'd like to pursue later, it's there for you. But for now, focus on multiplying your money in ways that match your season of life.

FRAMEWORK: THE WEALTH-MULTIPLIER EFFECT

The Wealth-Multiplier Effect is not about waiting. It's about wiring. It operates on building a self-reinforcing system: invest, automate, reinvest.

You earn, whether through work, a side hustle or a small passive income stream. You automate the flow of money, so it doesn't sit stagnant or get spent by default. Then you multiply that money by channeling it into systems that grow it automatically.

This isn't theory. This is how late starters catch up. The beauty of this framework is that it doesn't require big capital or early starts. It rewards action, consistency and reinvestment. Whether your income is £1,000 or $10,000/month, you can set your money to move, stack and grow, even while you focus on other things. This loop turns linear effort into exponential effect.

Step 1: Invest

What's your mix? Compound interest, digital income, property income? Pick one low-maintenance stream to begin with.

This might be a monthly investment into a global dividend ETF, a digital product on Gumroad, a monetized newsletter, hobby blog or YouTube channel. The key is to start something that builds value over time.

You don't need to be tech-savvy to start. Some of the best multipliers are offline, like renting a spare room, tutoring or hosting workshops. It's not about being digital. It's about being intentional.

Step 2: Automate

Once your flow is set, automate it. For example:

- Auto-invest £50–500/month into a Stocks & Shares ISA, or the equivalent into a Roth IRA, Tax-Free Savings Account (TFSA) or your local equivalent.
- Route your Etsy, Teachable or YouTube payouts into your business or personal account, then set up a standing order to auto-invest a portion into your ISA or pension.
- Auto-reinvest every dividend or payout.

Automation removes hesitation and makes growth consistent.

Step 3: Reinvest

As your income streams grow, don't inflate your lifestyle, stack your gains instead. Some examples of this are:

- Airbnb income pays down mortgage.
- Spare room income buys ETFs.
- Digital sales are reinvested into better tools, marketing or an AI-assisted virtual assistant to help drive sales.
- Business profits (dividends) fund your next asset.
- Stock dividends get reinvested automatically.

This turns small wins into larger flywheels over time.

Worried about tax? In the UK, ISAs and pensions (like SIPPs) allow you to grow your money tax-free up to generous limits. And if you're outside the UK, look into your local tax-advantaged accounts (e.g. Roth IRA, TFSA, etc.) – a lot of countries have them.

Step 4: Track and recalibrate

Use a simple tracker (e.g. Google Sheet, Notion). Monitor:

- Percentage of income automated.
- Passive inflows versus expenses.
- Growth of reinvested capital.

Review monthly to track progress. Adjust quarterly, but don't over-intervene.

Our stacking approach

In our twenties and thirties, we couldn't afford to wait for stock market compounding alone.

So, while living on mostly one income, we wired the other income, pay rises, side hustles (e.g. passive digital product sales, consulting, tutoring, etc.), spare room income and redundancy pay straight into our tax-advantaged savings accounts, pension, property and some alternative investments. We reinvested every dividend. And every small stream, even the odd idle petty cash, flowed into the system.

That's how we paid off our mortgage early; not through blind hustle, but through stacked systems, which gave us a guaranteed return and slowed the compounding force of debt working against us. Once the mortgage was gone, we didn't inflate our lifestyle. Instead, we redirected the money we had been putting towards the mortgage into the stock market and other assets, further accelerating our wealth creation.

PAUSE FOR REFLECTION

Ask yourself these three questions:
1. What's one income stream I already have that I'm not using to multiply wealth?
2. Where is money leaking because it's not automated or redirected?
3. If I could design a system where $1 today becomes $5 in ten years, what habits would I need to build this month to make that real?

Then ask the deeper question:

- 'Who benefits when I stop working for every pound or dollar I earn? My family? My community? My future self?'

Write down what comes up. Your clarity begins there.

> *Small action step*
>
> Feeling overwhelmed? Don't be. Start with one stream, one investment, one system. Let it grow as you grow.
>
> Now set up your Wealth-Multiplier system:
>
> 1. Choose one compound-growth investment and automate it (e.g. a monthly global ETF contribution).
> 2. Pick one passive income idea and launch a first draft (e.g. a digital product, affiliate page or downloadable guide).
> 3. Schedule a 15-minute monthly 'wealth review' calendar alert to track progress and recalibrate.
>
> Done right, this set-up could run and grow for years without major changes.

Remember, you're not too late. You're just early to your second act. Let go of the myth that wealth is only for those who start young or earn six figures. The truth is, the most powerful wealth habit is building a system that works when you don't.

You don't need more time. You need momentum. You've already worked hard. Now, let your money and systems do the heavy lifting.

This chapter isn't about becoming rich overnight. It's about no longer being the only engine of your financial growth. You're building a loop, one that earns, automates, multiplies and flows back in. And once that loop spins, it changes everything.

The wealthy aren't lucky, they're looped in. They've built systems that multiply quietly while they live fully. Now it's your turn.

Chapter summary

This chapter wasn't about theory. It was about designing your own Wealth-Multiplier Effect, no matter when you started or how much you earn. Here's what to do now:

- Reframe your story. You haven't missed your chance. You've just outgrown old approaches. Now you get to build smarter.
- Pick one passive income idea from the chapter and launch a simple first version.
- Automate one investment. Set up a reinvestment loop so income flows back into growth.
- Review your system monthly, adjust quarterly and let it run.
- Stop being the sole driver of your wealth and start letting systems do the work.
- Accelerate compound interest by compressing time through consistency.
- Use the signature framework – invest, automate, reinvest – to give yourself the edge as a late starter.
- The first move doesn't need to be big. It just needs to be wired.

Chapter 9

THE GUILT-FREE SPENDING HABIT

How to enjoy money while still building wealth

> **Theme: Balance**
> After automating growth, you reclaim joy in spending, learning to align treats with values, so no purchase triggers guilt.

THE WEALTH HABIT

Wealth without joy is just numbers in a bank account.

Picture this: it's a Friday night. You've just tapped your card for a perfect meal at your favourite restaurant, the kind that makes you close your eyes after the first bite. The laughter is flowing, the conversation deep and, for a brief moment, you feel rich in every sense.

Then, on the way home, your phone pings. A bank notification flashes: 'Payment of $120 (£84) processed.' In that instant, the warmth fades. You feel a twinge of guilt. You wonder, 'Should I have saved that instead? Was that reckless?'

This is the silent tax on pleasure, the guilt that sneaks into moments you've earned. But here's the truth: money is meant to be enjoyed. The problem isn't the joy, it's the lack of alignment between your spending and your values.

Those who build and keep wealth learn to master this balance. They spend with purpose, so joy lingers and guilt never takes root. And you can too.

A few years ago, I met Sofia, an entrepreneur from Lisbon, Portugal, who ran a thriving digital marketing agency. By her mid-thirties, she had savings many would envy but she lived under a self-imposed austerity plan. No eating out. No travel. Clothes only from second-hand shops.

Why? She'd grown up during Portugal's financial crisis, watching her parents scramble to keep the lights on. Even when her bank balance proved she was safe, her mindset stayed stuck in survival mode and she was miserable. 'I realized,' she told me, 'that I was living as if I was still broke, even though my bank account said otherwise.'

The turning point came one autumn afternoon in Lisbon. Rain streaked her office window as she stared at an email invitation from a friend: 'Join me for a hiking trip in Patagonia.' She imagined the jagged peaks, the crunch of gravel underfoot, the thin, cold air filling her lungs and then immediately shut it down. Too expensive. She filed the email away and got back to work.

But that night, she found herself on YouTube, watching drone footage of Patagonia's glaciers. Something shifted. The next day, she dipped into her rainy-day fund and booked the ticket.

The trip was transformative. It matched her love of nature and physical challenge, deepened a friendship that later turned into a business partnership and inspired a blog series that drew in new clients who valued her adventurous side. Her takeaway? 'It wasn't indulgence. It was an investment in joy, relationships and myself.'

Today, Sofia still saves diligently, but she also maintains a 'joy fund' for experiences that match her values. And here's the paradox: her net worth has grown faster since, because she no longer burns out or makes scarcity-driven money decisions.

From Portugal to South Africa to Canada, we've seen the same truth: guilt-free spending isn't a threat to wealth, it's fuel for it.

> **The Wealth Habit Mantra 9:**
> Spend with joy on what matters most and you'll never feel guilty about money again.

WHY CUTTING OUT ALL LUXURIES IS A RECIPE FOR FAILURE

Many people imagine wealth building as an all-or-nothing pursuit. Cancel the Netflix subscription. Skip the morning coffee. Avoid restaurants. Delay joy for decades.

The problem? Humans aren't wired to delay all pleasure indefinitely.

Psychologists call it the willpower depletion effect;[50] the more you resist something enjoyable, the more likely you are to cave later, often in ways that undo your progress.

Mary and I learned this first-hand when we were paying off our mortgage in seven years. At first, we cut everything non-essential. We took packed lunches to work or bought cheaper meal deals, skipped every café and tracked every grocery penny. After three months, we rebelled with a spontaneous weekend away, wiping out most of that month's surplus. That's when we realized: perfection is brittle; sustainability is flexible.

Luxury, in this context, isn't extravagance. It's planned joy. A monthly dinner with friends, a theatre ticket, a short trip; these aren't 'failures', they're investments in your energy and motivation.

The wealthy don't avoid luxuries, they plan for them as deliberately as they do for investments. As the University of British Columbia found, purchases aligned with personal happiness – for example, paying for time-saving services like cleaning, shopping or cooking, or investing in meaningful experiences like a weekend getaway with loved ones – lead to higher life satisfaction, regardless of income.[51]

Self-denial isn't discipline if it leads to self-sabotage. Cutting all luxuries is just scarcity thinking dressed up as discipline. The goal is not a joyless existence, it's a joyful one that still compounds wealth.

HOW TO ALIGN SPENDING WITH VALUES AND LONG-TERM GOALS

The secret to guilt-free spending is alignment. Without it, luxuries become random impulses. With it, they become part of your wealth plan.

Use the 'joy–value filter' before every discretionary purchase:

- Does this align with my top three life values?
- Will this bring joy beyond the purchase moment?
- Does it conflict with my long-term goals?

If family connection is a core value, a Sunday roast with loved ones is a worthwhile spend. If health is a priority, investing in high-quality produce or a gym you actually use fits the bill.

Sandra, one of our Financial Joy Academy (FJA) members, loves to travel. In the past, she booked trips on credit and came home to debt. Now, she plans and pays for trips a year in advance. Research from Cornell University shows that the anticipation of an experience can boost happiness as much as the experience itself.[52]

To keep your spending aligned with your values, try this simple tool: keep a 'Joy Spend list' of five to ten items in your phone. Each item should include an item and its purpose, for example, 'a monthly dinner out – to deepen connection with my partner or friends'. When you feel the urge to buy, check if it's on the list. If yes, go ahead guilt-free. If no, give yourself a short cooling-off period before deciding.

When your spending matches your values, you buy more than a thing, you buy alignment. When every dollar or pound spent reflects who you are and where you're going, there's no buyer's remorse, only satisfaction.

HOW WE ALLOCATE OUR MONEY AND SPEND GUILT FREE

In 2011, just before getting married, we always had a sense of anxiety and uncertainty around our finances, especially as we were living separate lives and had different incomes and expenses, assets and liabilities.

However, we wanted to combine our finances, making sure we were able to cover our monthly outgoings, save and invest for future goals and leave room for fun. At that stage, our biggest goal was to buy a house together to start a family and that meant saving aggressively towards it and reducing expenses in some categories to achieve it. Thankfully, we still have our Budget For Life spreadsheet[53] from 2011 and so we've had a look to see how we used to split our money then versus now:

Expense category	Actual percentage allocation in 2011	Actual percentage allocation at the time of writing
Essentials	47.76% 25.72% on housing plus 22.04% on all other essential expenses (e.g. work travel, energy, council tax, insurance, food, phone bills, etc.).	26.01% No mortgage, although essentials are more expensive due to rising cost of living.
Joy Spend	6.40% Holidays.	20.80% Holidays and experiences, date nights, etc.
Overflow	45.84% Saving for a new house, investing, giving and pocket money.	53.19% Saving and investing more for our children, some for us to strengthen our freedom pot and giving more freely.

We've shared this for illustration purposes only. In the years between 2011 and now, the percentages in each of the three flows has varied, especially while raising our two sons, but also at times when we worked hard on minimizing our essential expenses (simplifying our lifestyles and avoiding lifestyle creep) and maximizing our take-home pay. Some years, the overflow rose to as high as 65%, in others it dropped to a low of around 20%. The key takeaway is that we've kept it simple, both in process and in lifestyle.

Keeping things simple and automating where possible has given us peace of mind and allowed us to work towards our unique goals while also enjoying more of our money year after year, with around 20% of after-tax income currently allocated to guilt-free spending.

STRATEGIES FOR MINDFUL SPENDING WITHOUT GUILT OR STRESS

Here's where alignment meets execution. Mindful spending means every choice is intentional and supported by systems. Use these strategies to make mindful spending automatic. Freedom isn't in the amount you spend, it's in knowing your spending is intentional.

- **Automate essentials first:** housing, bills, savings, investments. With the future secured, you can spend freely on the rest.
- **Create a Joy-Spend account:** a separate pot for discretionary spending. When it's empty, you stop. No guilt, no debt.
- **Practise purchase presence:** pause before buying and ask, 'How will I feel about this tomorrow?' If the answer is positive, proceed.
- **Choose experiences over excess stuff:** research shows experiences produce longer-lasting happiness than possessions.
- **Celebrate creatively:** milestone moments don't have to default to expensive dinners, sometimes a handwritten letter or home-cooked feast carries more meaning.

Over time, practising these habits rewires your relationship with money. Spending shifts from being a reflex driven by guilt or impulse to a conscious expression of your values.

And it's not just high earners who benefit from guilt-free spending done right. In Accra, Ghana, I met Kwame, a secondary-school science teacher earning the equivalent of $425 (£320) a month. For years, every cedi he didn't spend went straight into savings, but he constantly felt deprived.

His breakthrough came when he created a 'Saturday treat' budget, consisting of just 3% of his income. Most weeks, it was a shared meal at a small chop bar with his brother. The air was thick with the smell of grilled tilapia, the hum of conversation rising with the steam from simmering stews. They'd sit on plastic chairs, laughing over plates piled high, the week's worries melting away with each bite.

That tiny, regular joy became his anchor. And, to his surprise, he found he was more committed to saving the rest because he no longer felt trapped by his own plan. 'It's strange,' he told me. 'Spending that little bit makes it easier to save a lot.'

> ### The art of quiet wealth
> Quiet wealth is the freedom to enjoy money on your terms, rich in meaning, not in display. Quiet wealth isn't about what the world sees, it's about the freedom you feel.
>
> You spend in ways that reflect your values, not other people's expectations. You buy back time, invest in memories and build security quietly in the background. You don't need to signal wealth; you live it guilt-free, meaningfully and sustainably.
>
> This is the deeper promise of the Guilt-Free Spending Habit: to live richly on the inside, without needing to prove it on the outside.

FRAMEWORK: THE JOY-SPEND RADAR

The Joy-Spend Radar has three layers that guide you in deciding not just what to spend on, but why, so every purchase feels intentional and guilt-free: **desire, value, impact**.

While the joy–value filter is your quick, in-the-moment checklist for deciding whether a purchase fits your priorities, the Joy-Spend Radar is your bigger-picture tool. It's a visual, layered framework for planning and reviewing spending in a more deliberate way, the kind you might use when mapping your monthly Joy-Spend budget or considering a larger purchase. Think of the joy–value filter as a pocket compass and the Joy-Spend Radar as the full map.

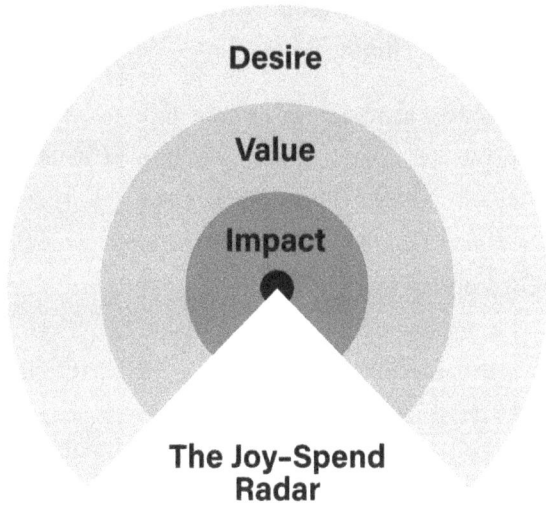

At the edges of this radar screen are hundreds of spending possibilities flickering. As each moves inwards, it must pass through three rings:

1. **Desire** filters out the false wants.
2. **Value** keeps only what aligns with your deeper self.
3. **Impact** ensures the final choice adds to your life without subtracting from your plan.

Anything reaching the centre is clear for guilt-free spending.

Step 1: Set your Joy-Spend budget

Decide how much you'll spend guilt-free each month (5–20% of your discretionary income works well). Transfer this into a separate account or digital wallet; this is your outer boundary.

Step 2: Run every potential purchase through the three rings

Think of each purchase as a 'blip' moving from the outer edge of the radar towards the target in the centre. It must pass through all three rings:

1. **Desire check:** 'Do I really want this or is it just a passing impulse or social pressure?'
   If it's an impulse or not truly your desire, stop here.
2. **Value assessment:** 'Does this match my top three life values and will it bring joy beyond today?' If it's not aligned with who you are and what matters most, drop it.
3. **Impact analysis:** 'What's the ripple effect, financially, emotionally and relationally, over the next week, month or year?' Only if it adds value without sabotaging your future does it make the target.

Step 3: Reflect monthly

At the end of each month, review your Joy-Spend purchases. Which ones still bring a smile? Which faded quickly or caused regret? This feedback refines your radar, so every month your discretionary spending gets sharper and more satisfying.

The Joy-Spend Radar replaces the guilt loop with a permission loop. You spend without guilt, knowing that every pound or dollar that hits the target has passed through your deepest priorities and your future is already protected.

PAUSE FOR REFLECTION

In the last 30 days, which purchases gave you lasting joy and which felt hollow? Write down three ways you'll shift next month's spending to better reflect your values.

> *Small action step*
> Open a Joy-Spend account today. Automate a monthly transfer into it. Spend from this pot without second guessing, your essentials and future are already covered.

Money isn't a scoreboard, it's a story you're writing with your life. A story with no joy is half told. The Guilt-Free Spending Habit lets you live richly now, while building the kind of future you can step into with pride.

When you spend with intention, there's no tension between pleasure and progress. You can have both and, when you do, your wealth becomes more than numbers. It becomes a life worth living.

Joy isn't the opposite of discipline, it's the fuel that makes discipline last a lifetime.

Chapter summary

- Eliminating all luxuries is unsustainable; planned joy keeps motivation high.
- The joy–value filter is a fast, lightweight mental tool to help you decide if a discretionary purchase fits your values and goals. Use it in everyday moments when you need a snap decision, e.g. standing in a shop or scrolling online.
- The Joy-Spend Radar is a visual, guilt-free decision model that filters spending ideas more systematically, with clear 'gates' – desire, value and impact – to pass through. Use it for intentional planning, e.g. deciding which 'Joy-Spend' items to keep in your monthly budget or evaluating bigger, less frequent purchases.
- Automate essentials before discretionary spending to protect your future.
- Mindful, aligned spending replaces guilt with freedom and flow.

Chapter 10

YOUR FUTURE-SELF FUND

The small habit that guarantees
financial security

> **Theme: Security**
> You layer in a habit that builds a dedicated safety net, automatically funding long-term stability so emergencies never derail you.

The greatest gift you can give yourself isn't money today, it's money your future self can count on when life blindsides you.

Auckland, New Zealand, April 2020. The world had gone quiet. Planes grounded. Streets empty. Olivia, a 42-year-old hotel receptionist, sat at her kitchen table staring at the email no one wants: 'Your position has been made redundant.'

The first emotion should have been panic. Mortgage payments, bills, her daughter's school fees; they didn't care about pandemics. But instead, she felt something surprising: calm.

Seven years earlier, Olivia had made a decision most people might think was too small to matter. Every Friday morning, before she bought her weekend groceries, she had an automated transfer move $30 a week, about the cost of two lunches, into an account she nicknamed her 'Future-Self Fund'. No exceptions. No, 'I'll catch up next week.' Just quiet consistency.

When COVID-19 turned her life upside down, that tiny weekly habit had grown into a cushion big enough to cover six months of her essential expenses. She could pay her bills, cover the necessary costs related to her daughter's homeschooling and even help her brother with groceries when he lost work.

'I realized,' she later told us, 'that I was living in the safety net I'd built for myself years before. My past self was my hero.'

When we heard Olivia's story, we felt like she was describing our own. Back in 2012, after we bought our home, we set our sights on our North Star goal: financial independence. We prioritized contributions to our workplace pensions, but we also made a deliberate choice to invest in our Stocks and Shares ISA every month. We thought of it as our 'future tax-free me' fund, a quiet, long-term commitment to the people we were becoming. At first, it was £250 a month. Over time, as we found more margin in our budget, we increased it. We didn't know then that a global pandemic was coming, but we kept the habit.

By early 2020, we'd both transitioned out of corporate jobs and were running our own business. When COVID-19 struck, our business took a significant hit overnight. We weren't eligible for furlough support because of how our income was structured. No salary. No government payments. But we weren't panicking. That 'future tax-free me' fund had grown into years' worth of essential expenses. It became the bridge that carried us through months of uncertainty without needing to take on debt or make desperate decisions.

Looking back, it's clear: the habit wasn't just about growing an investment. It was about buying ourselves time, freedom and peace of mind when we needed them most.

> **The Wealth Habit Mantra 10:**
> Every pound or dollar you save for your future self is a thank-you note you'll one day cash.

Your Future-Self Fund is the financial equivalent of planting an orchard; you may not need the fruit today, but when the season changes, you'll be grateful for the harvest. It's a habit of making deposits into a part of your life you can't yet see but will one day depend on. This isn't about hoarding for a rainy day, it's about engineering security, options and peace of mind for the future version of you.

Whether it's a job loss, a medical emergency or a once-in-a-lifetime opportunity, the reality is the same: if you haven't prepared in advance, you'll be forced to make reactive decisions. The Future-Self Fund replaces reaction with readiness. A plan made in calm will always outperform a decision made in crisis.

THE IMPORTANCE OF PRIORITIZING LONG-TERM SECURITY OVER SHORT-TERM GRATIFICATION

We live in a culture designed to make you trade tomorrow for today. Social media feeds push flash sales. Streaming platforms offer instant entertainment. The coffee shop remembers your order before you've opened your mouth. This is present bias in action – the tendency to give stronger weight to rewards we can have right now over those in the future. Behavioural economists have studied this extensively; research from Princeton shows that scarcity of time or money narrows focus, leading us to undervalue the future.[54]

The Future-Self Fund is the antidote. It's a tangible reminder that future you is just as real as present you, and often far more vulnerable.

Think of it as a contract between two people: the 'you' today, who controls the decisions, and the 'you' tomorrow, who lives with the consequences. The challenge is that 'tomorrow' feels abstract, so we dismiss it. That's why visualization matters. Olympic athletes rehearse their performance in their minds before they compete; you can do the same financially. Picture yourself ten years from now. What will you be grateful to have in place? What emergencies will you be protected from? What opportunities will you be ready to seize? Short-term pleasure spends your money once; long-term preparation spends it twice: first for peace of mind, then for freedom.

Olivia's story shows the payoff in a crisis, but it's not just about disasters. Long-term security means being able to take a career break without panic, move cities for a better quality of life or start a business without begging a bank for permission. When your basic needs are covered by your own foresight, you're free to think bigger.

In our own life, the Future-Self Fund meant that, when the pandemic hit, we didn't need to scramble. The money was already there. But even if you never face a pandemic-level disruption, you will face moments when preparation equals power and the habit you've built will make those moments yours to navigate on your terms.

In Cape Town, South Africa, Samuel, a 29-year-old graphic designer, once spent every spare rand on weekends out. Then his company announced potential redundancies. The fear jolted him into action. He started a Future-Self Fund with just R300 a month. Two years later, when his department was cut, Samuel had enough to cover three months' rent and pivot into freelance work without desperation. 'That fund,' he told us, 'bought me time and time is freedom.'

In Melbourne, Australia, Amelia had been quietly building her Future-Self Fund for years, aiming for 12 months of expenses. When her dream photography course in Paris, France, opened unexpectedly, with only a month to apply, she didn't hesitate. The money was there, waiting. 'I realized my fund wasn't just for emergencies,' she said. 'It was for life-changing yeses.'

Consider Warren Buffett. For decades, he's famously kept billions in cash or cash-equivalents, not because he's trying to guess the perfect market moment, but because he wants the freedom to act instantly when a clear, high-value opportunity appears. The amounts may differ, but the principle is identical: build your security first, so that when life whispers 'now', you can say 'yes' without hesitation.

Your Future-Self Fund is the difference between watching opportunities pass and running to meet them.

HOW TO SET UP A FUTURE-PROOF SAVINGS AND INVESTMENT PLAN

A Future-Self Fund is not just a pile of cash in a jar. It's a system that balances liquidity (quick access when needed) and growth (to outpace inflation). Think of it as two layers:

- **Layer 1: The safety net:** Accessible cash savings covering 3–12 months of essential expenses. This sits in a high-interest savings account or money market fund, so it earns something but isn't at risk. Support this with insurance such as critical illness and income protection.
- **Layer 2: The growth engine:** Investments in vehicles like index funds, Exchange Traded Funds (ETFs) or retirement accounts that you won't touch for years. These work quietly in the background, compounding over time.

The exact balance depends on your circumstances. A freelancer with variable income might keep a larger cash buffer than someone in a stable job. Someone in a high-inflation economy might tilt more towards growth assets.

Start small. When Mary and I began our Stocks and Shares ISA, £250 a month felt like a stretch. But we treated it as non-negotiable, as essential as the mortgage. Over the years, increasing it became easier, not harder, because we built the habit first and adjusted the amount later.

To make your plan future-proof:

1. **Set a clear target:** For example, 'One year of essential expenses plus an investment fund that grows at least 5% annually.'
2. **Choose the right accounts:** Use tax-advantaged accounts where possible such as Individual Savings Accounts (ISAs) in the UK, Roth

Individual Retirement Arrangements (Roth IRAs) in the US, Tax-Free Savings Account (TFSA) in Canada or equivalent.
3. **Diversify simply:** Global index funds or ETFs are cost-efficient and resilient; you don't need to chase trends.
4. **Review annually:** Adjust contributions as income changes, but keep the habit intact.

Your Future-Self Fund is not a rainy-day jar, it's a runway to the life you want.

AUTOMATING CONTRIBUTIONS TO BUILD LASTING FINANCIAL STABILITY

The fastest way to fail at funding your future is to leave it to willpower. Willpower is finite; automation is infinite. Once your contributions are automated, they happen whether you're disciplined or distracted, whether life is calm or chaotic.

Behavioural finance research shows that people are far more likely to stick to savings plans when the money is moved before they see it. This is the 'out of sight, out of spend' principle in action.

A recent study published in *Stress & Health*[55] analysed 20 years of data from over 20,000 Australians and found that, at all income levels, just a 1% increase in saving behaviour was linked to a 0.475% improvement in mental health scores, while a 1% improvement in consistent credit card payments led to a 0.507% boost in wellbeing. Crucially, these benefits persisted even through major economic disruptions such as the 2008 financial crisis and the COVID-19 pandemic, proving that small, consistent habits don't just protect your bank balance, they protect your peace of mind.

Automation is the bridge between good intentions and actual results. Here's how to automate effectively:

- **Pay your future self first:** Schedule the transfer the day after income lands, not at the end of the month when 'leftovers' may never materialize. More on this in Chapter 12.
- **Start where you are:** Even $10 a week matters when it's consistent. Olivia proved that. We've seen Financial Joy Academy (FJA) members start with as little as $5 and grow to thousands over time.
- **Use multiple automations for multiple goals:** One standing order for your cash buffer, another for your investment account.
- **Make it hard to stop:** Keep your Future-Self Fund in an account you don't see daily, ideally at a different bank from your spending account.
- **Increase automatically:** Many banks let you set annual percentage increases in standing orders. Even a 5% boost each year compounds over time.

Automation is not just about removing friction, it's about removing choice. The truth is, on any given day, most of us will choose the short-term treat over the long-term gain. By setting up systems that act on your behalf, you make sure future you always gets paid, even when present you is tempted.

Once automated, the Future-Self Fund stops feeling like a sacrifice. It becomes background noise, quietly growing until one day, in a moment you can't yet foresee, it steps forwards and changes everything.

Small, consistent deposits are quiet today but loud tomorrow.

FRAMEWORK: THE FUTURE-YOU FILTER

At the heart of this habit is a simple decision tool: The Future-You Filter. Whenever you're about to spend, save or invest money, you run it through three steps: visualize, filter decision, confirm action.

In Chapter 9, you learned the Joy-Spend Radar, a visual, guilt-free decision-making model for filtering discretionary spending ideas, from small treats to larger, less frequent purchases. The Future-You Filter works alongside it but focuses on all money decisions, not just joy spending. Use the Joy-Spend Radar for intentional planning around discretionary spending and the Future-You Filter for deciding whether any financial choice will serve your long-term security.

This isn't just about avoiding bad spending. It's about actively steering resources towards the version of you who will need them most – whether that's the parent paying for their child's university fees, the retiree travelling without debt or the entrepreneur launching a business without a bank loan.

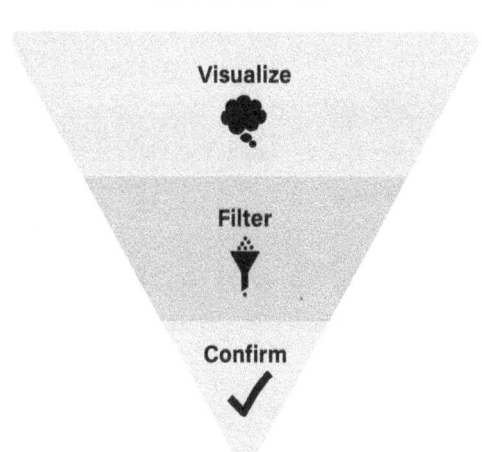

Future-You Filter Funnel

Here is what the Future-You-Filter looks like. At the top, you drop in any financial decision – for example, a purchase, a saving opportunity, an investment choice – and that decision filters down through the three stages:

1. **Visualize:** Close your eyes and place yourself in a vivid, specific moment five, ten or twenty years from now. Imagine yourself as an old man or woman. Where are you living? Who's with you? What does a typical day look like? Most importantly, how secure and free do you feel – financially, emotionally and in your choices?
2. **Filter decision:** Holding that image in your mind, ask: 'Will future me thank me for this?' If the answer is yes, move forwards. If not, reconsider or find an alternative that future you will appreciate.
3. **Confirm action:** Turn the decision into movement immediately, whether that's making the transfer, skipping the purchase or adjusting the plan so the choice becomes reality before the moment (and your resolve) passes.

How it works

The funnel narrows, not to restrict you, but to concentrate your resources where they matter most. The Future-You Filter works because it does three psychological things at once:

- **Bridges the empathy gap:** We're wired to treat our future selves like strangers. Visualization builds emotional connection, making it harder to neglect them.
- **Adds friction to bad decisions:** The question, 'Will future me thank me?' slows down impulse choices just enough to reconsider.

- **Creates instant feedback loops:** Acting right after filtering makes the habit rewarding in the present as well as the future.

It might feel a bit overwhelming to start applying this to every purchasing decision, so here are some step-by-step instructions for slowly starting to apply the Future-You Filter to your everyday life:

- **Step 1:** Identify one regular decision where money slips away, e.g. daily coffee, impulse online buys at night, last-minute travel upgrades.
- **Step 2:** For one month, apply the filter to that category only. Don't try to overhaul your entire financial life overnight.
- **Step 3:** Keep a 'thank me later' log; jot down each filtered decision and the amount redirected to your Future-Self Fund.
- **Step 4:** At the end of the month, review the total. Seeing a lump sum that would have been gone is deeply motivating.
- **Step 5:** Expand to other categories over time, until the filter becomes your default for all financial choices.

Global examples in action

A boda boda (motorbike taxi) rider in Mombasa, Kenya, applies the filter to his daily fuel cash. By topping up slightly less and avoiding unnecessary detours, he sets aside 200KES a day into a Savings and Credit Cooperative (SACCO). Over two years, it funds the down payment for a second bike to rent out, creating a passive income stream.

A nurse in Toronto, Canada, applies the filter to clothing purchases. She decides to buy fewer but higher-quality pieces and redirects the rest into her TFSA. After three years, the balance covers a three-month sabbatical to travel across the country.

No matter your currency, the exchange rate on preparation is always priceless.

PAUSE FOR REFLECTION

Think about a time in the past when you wished you'd been more prepared financially. Now picture your life five years from today, fully funded. What would it feel like to open that account and see the number you've been building?

Give your future self a name such as 'retired me', 'debt-free me', 'world-traveller me'. Write them a one-sentence promise for how you'll protect and provide for them from this day forwards.

> *Small action step*
>
> Within the next hour:
>
> 1. Open a separate savings or investment account if you don't already have one.
> 2. Set up an automatic transfer, even if it's just £5 or $10 a week, from your main account into this new Future-Self Fund.
> 3. Give it a name that excites you, e.g. 'freedom fund', 'future me', 'no worries account'.
>
> The amount matters less than the act of starting. Once the system is in place, you can increase it over time.

One day, something will happen that you didn't see coming — a challenge, an opportunity or both at once. When that day arrives, you'll either scramble or smile with relief. The difference will be the habit you start today: a few pounds or dollars a week, one automatic transfer, one small, consistent choice in favour of the person you're becoming.

Your future self is counting on you. Become their hero now, so that one day you can look back, as Olivia did, and say, 'My past self saved me.'

Chapter summary

- The Future-Self Fund is your personal financial time machine, moving resources from today to the moment you'll need them most.
- Prioritize long-term security over short-term gratification by reframing money choices through your future self's eyes.
- Build a two-layer plan: a liquid safety net (supported by insurance), plus long-term growth investments.
- Automate contributions to remove willpower from the equation.
- Use the Future-You Filter – visualize, filter decision, confirm action – to ensure every financial choice benefits the future version of you.
- Start small, grow steadily and protect the habit above all else.
- When you consistently choose for the person you'll be tomorrow, you guarantee that tomorrow will thank you.

Chapter 11

THE 24-HOUR PAUSE BUTTON

Mastering your built-in brake

> **Theme: Impulse guard**
> Arm yourself with a simple, fool-proof pause that transforms reactive spending into mindful choice.

THE WEALTH HABIT

Wealth doesn't slip through your fingers because of one big mistake. It leaks out through the thousand tiny decisions you didn't pause to question.

Picture the African savanna at dawn: sun spilling through golden grasses, a lion crouched low in the shade. Its muscles twitch with the urge to pounce, but the old lion, unlike the impatient young, waits. Still. Watching. Nearby, a chameleon turns its head slowly, scanning each direction before taking the smallest, cautious step.

In wildlife films narrated by David Attenborough, these moments look like theatre. But they're more than spectacle, they are a masterclass in the power of the pause. The reckless lunge and miss; the patient choose their moment and feast.

The Ashanti Kingdom of West Africa practised this wisdom in human affairs long before the camera lens arrived. Disputes in the village square were never judged in the heat of anger. If tempers flared, chiefs would raise a hand and declare: 'Let the moon cool the head.' Decisions were postponed until the following day. By morning, emotions had ebbed and judgements carried the weight of wisdom rather than the rashness of impulse. Along the Swahili coast, the same truth was passed down in the proverb, '*Haraka haraka haina baraka*', which means, 'Haste has no blessing.' In every age and culture, the truth endures: wealth and wisdom flow not to the fastest mover, but to the one who waits.

That wisdom is just as relevant on the savanna and in the village square as it is today in our digital lives. Yet modern culture trains us to do the opposite. Algorithms reward speed. One-click checkouts erase hesitation. Sale timers pressure us into acting now. We live in a world where hesitation is framed as weakness, yet hesitation may be the very thing that saves us.

In 2017, Clara, a 29-year-old professional living in Singapore, found herself in a spiral that felt impossible to escape. Her workdays stretched long into the night and her primary outlet for stress was online shopping. The glow of her phone became both a comfort and a trap. Each click promised a rush of relief: new shoes, skincare, the latest tech gadgets. It didn't feel like spending money. It felt like numbing the edges of exhaustion.

The illusion shattered when her credit card bill overtook her rent. What had started as the occasional treat had become a quiet drain – hundreds each month flowing to items she barely remembered ordering. 'It was like waking up to find someone else had spent my money,' she later admitted.

A financial coach gave her a deceptively simple rule: pause for 24 hours before buying anything non-essential. At first, it felt unbearable. She would load her cart, finger hovering over 'buy now', before forcing herself to close the app. But something unexpected happened in the pause. By the next day, the urgency had dulled. What seemed irresistible at midnight looked irrelevant by morning.

Clara began keeping a 'pause list' in her notes app, logging every temptation. Weeks later, she scrolled back and laughed at items she no longer wanted. Within months, her spending dropped by 40%. Within three years, she was debt-free and saving towards her first home.

Behavioural scientists would recognize Clara's journey as a classic example of the cooling-off effect, a period of deliberate delay that weakens emotional impulses and strengthens rational decision making.[56] It's the same principle behind mandatory cooling-off periods in financial contracts and property purchases across the UK, US, Australia and around the world.

What saved Clara wasn't earning more money. It was discovering a brake system for her impulses. In her case, the 24-Hour Pause Button became not just a financial rule but a new identity: she was no longer someone who 'couldn't control herself'. She was someone who paused, reflected and chose deliberately.

> **The Wealth Habit Mantra 11:**
> Pause before you purchase. In 24 hours, temptation weakens, clarity strengthens and wealth compounds through choices you no longer regret.

FRAMEWORK: 24-HOUR PAUSE BUTTON

The 24-Hour Pause Button framework follows four deliberate steps: **trigger, pause, reflect, decide**.

- **Trigger:** The spark of temptation, e.g. a '50% off' email, an advert, a shop window.
- **Pause:** Delay the purchase for 24 hours. No decision, no transaction.
- **Reflect:** Use the pause to ask: does this align with my values, goals and financial reality?
- **Decide:** After 24 hours, choose with clarity. Buy it, delay further or drop it entirely.

This framework works because it inserts time between urge and action. Psychologists call this the 'intention–action gap'.[57] Left unchecked, the gap collapses into impulse. With the 24-Hour Pause Button, you stretch the gap and allow your rational mind to regain control.

Think of it as a traffic light for your finances: green is the urge, amber is the pause, red is reflection and only after that comes the decision. Like traffic lights, this sequence prevents crashes, only here the crash is financial regret.

ACTIVATE YOUR PAUSE BUTTON

Impulse buys often happen in seconds. The key is to slow the moment down just enough to re-engage your rational mind. That's where activation comes in: the immediate tools and scripts that stop the transaction before it takes root.

Think of this as installing a circuit breaker in your financial system. Without it, the current of desire runs unchecked and burns through your resources. With it, you create space for deliberate choice.

Here are a couple of examples of how to create a circuit breaker, whether you're out in town with a friend or scrolling through social media in the evening.

When tempted in a shop

'I'll decide tomorrow.' This one sentence is surprisingly powerful. It gives you a socially acceptable excuse while signalling to your brain that the pause rule is non-negotiable.

When tempted online

'Into the pause list you go.' Keep a dedicated note on your phone. Every item goes there for 24 hours. The act of writing it down tricks your brain into believing you've acknowledged the desire, relieving the urge to act immediately.

Accountability hacks

Studies demonstrate that introducing social accountability — for example, telling a partner or peer about your spending decisions — reliably reduces impulsive purchases and helps people stick to their financial goals. Pair up with a trusted friend or family member. Agree that before you buy anything non-essential, you send them a screenshot. Just the thought of explaining yourself is often enough to pause.

Digital tools

If you'd rather remove the factor of willpower out of the equation, there are some amazing digital tools which can help you to block the urge:

- Apps like Qapital or YNAB allow you to set 'waiting rules' for categories, so you can't spend from discretionary pots without a delay.
- Browser extensions such as Impulse Blocker or StayFocusd can be set to temporarily block access to online shops.
- Some fintechs (like Monzo in the UK) allow you to 'lock' savings pots. Transferring money there during temptation gives you a digital barrier.

Real-life scenario

Now let's try out the 24-Hour Pause Button in a real-life scenario. Imagine you're scrolling Instagram and see an ad for noise-cancelling headphones. They're 'today only' discounted. Normally you'd click 'buy now'. Instead, you activate your button. You add the headphones to your pause list. You also text your accountability partner: 'Headphones on the list, I'll check tomorrow.' Activation complete. The purchase urge, once hot, begins to cool.

This is where the magic begins, not because you've decided against the purchase, but because you've reclaimed the power to decide later. And once the fire of urgency fades, you can use the gap intentionally.

FILL THE GAP WITH PURPOSE

A pause without purpose feels like deprivation. That's why most people fail at 'spending bans'. They rely on raw willpower, without creating meaningful alternatives. The 24-Hour Pause Button is different. The 24 hours aren't just empty space, they're a laboratory for reflection and growth. Here's how to transform waiting into wealth.

Journal prompts for clarity

During the pause, ask yourself:

- What problem am I asking this purchase to solve? (Boredom? Stress? Image?)
- Will this matter to me in 12 months?
- What am I giving up by choosing this instead of saving or investing?

These prompts move your thinking from the emotional present into the rational future. Research on 'temporal discounting' shows that when people visualize their future selves – for example, interacting with age-progressed renderings of themselves via AI – they make more prudent financial decisions. In one landmark Stanford study, participants who saw digitally aged avatars of themselves chose to allocate more than twice as much money towards retirement compared to those who didn't.[58]

Micro-habit alternatives to spending

Replace the urge with a small rewarding activity. For example, go for a 15-minute walk, brew a favourite tea or coffee, or spend five minutes on a gratitude list.

Each of these boosts dopamine naturally without spending money. Over time, your brain begins to associate urges not with buying, but with healthier resets.

'If–then' plans

An implementation intention is a simple pre-set plan: 'If I feel urge X, then I will do Y.' It's a great idea to spend some time thinking of the scenarios you might encounter and how you would prefer to react. For example:

- If I see a 'limited time only' sale, then I'll screenshot it and add it to my pause list.
- If I feel stressed and want to shop, then I'll text my accountability partner first.
- If I crave coffee, then I'll make a herbal tea and review my savings app.

These tiny rules automate your response, so you're not relying on willpower in the heat of the moment. This will help you change the habit, not through force, but through a purposeful swap.

A purposeful pause turns into more than just 'not spending'. It becomes a signal to practice gratitude, reconnect with goals or engage in small joys that compound far more than a fleeting purchase ever could.

TROUBLESHOOT, ITERATE AND LOCK IT IN

No habit is flawless. There will be days when you break the rule, when you click 'buy now' before your rational brain shows up. The difference between success and failure is how you handle these slip-ups.

Reframe failure as feedback

Instead of guilt, treat mistakes as data. Ask:

- What triggered me?
- What was I feeling?
- What could I tweak in my pause system?

For example, if you notice you always cave late at night, set a new boundary: no online shopping after 9pm. I (Ken) noticed that I sometimes struggled with impulse buying around 11pm at night after a long day or once our children had gone to bed, so I set a custom mode on my phone that disabled all my apps from 9pm, making it harder for me to fall into the same patterns.

Reflection exercises

Every week, look at your pause list. Circle the items you never bought. Add up their total cost. This gives you a tangible sense of 'money saved' by waiting. Seeing a figure, for example, £300 or $400 not spent in one month, is deeply motivating. It reframes the pause as a profit generator.

Linked cues

To make the pause automatic, attach it to routines. Connect it with banking app check-ins: each morning when you check your balance, follow it by reviewing your pause list. Pair it with evening journalling: jot down one temptation you paused that day and how it felt. Link it to future-self reminders: keep a photo of your financial goal (like a house or retirement trip) as your phone background, so every time you open it, you're cued to pause before spending.

Build in celebrations

Each time you successfully pause, celebrate it, even if it's just saying aloud, 'Yes, I did it!' As we established in earlier chapters, emotion, not discipline, wires habits in place. Small celebrations make the pause feel rewarding, not punishing.

For example, let's say David slipped up during Black Friday, buying three unnecessary gadgets. Instead of spiralling, he analysed: 'The time pressure was the trigger. Next year, I'll unsubscribe from promotional emails in November.' By adjusting the system, he prevented future repeats.

Over time, this iterative process makes the 24-Hour Pause Button less of a conscious effort and more of an instinct. It becomes your default brake, so natural you don't even notice you're using it.

And once the 24-Hour Pause Button is automatic, you're not just avoiding waste, you're preserving capital to channel into habits that accelerate wealth, like paying yourself first (the very next chapter).

PAUSE FOR REFLECTION

Think of the last purchase you regretted. Rewind to the moment just before you bought it. What triggered you? The advert, the stress, the boredom? Now imagine pressing the 24-Hour Pause Button in that exact moment. How would the story have changed?

Write down three scenarios:

1. You paused, then bought it the next day.
2. You paused and the desire faded.
3. You paused and replaced it with something purposeful.

Which version of you ends up wealthier, not just in money, but in peace of mind?

> *Small action step*
> Right now, create a pause list in your phone's notes app. The next time you feel the urge to buy something non-essential, don't check out, add it to the list. Commit to reviewing it in 24 hours. If the desire remains, you can decide with clarity. If not, celebrate the money you've just saved. This list will quickly become a record of temptations resisted, regrets avoided and wealth preserved.

The 24-Hour Pause Button isn't about denying yourself. It's about protecting yourself. Every time you wait, you're proving that you are stronger than the algorithm, wiser than the countdown clock and more committed to your future than to your fleeting impulses.

Every pause you press is an act of power. It's your way of declaring: I decide the pace of my wealth journey, not the adverts, not the pressure, not the world around me.

Chapter summary

- Pause before you purchase. In 24 hours, temptation weakens, clarity strengthens and wealth compounds through choices you no longer regret.
- Use the trigger, pause, reflect, decide framework.
- The pause inserts time between desire and decision, cooling emotional impulses and strengthening rational clarity.
- Use scripts, digital tools and accountability partners to activate your pause.
- Fill the 24-hour gap with journalling, micro-habits and 'if–then' plans.
- Review, reflect and link cues until pausing becomes your default reflex.
- Impulse spending isn't just wasted money, it erodes self-trust. The 24-Hour Pause Button rewires your reflexes, turning temptations into opportunities for growth. Over time, it preserves not just your wealth but your confidence, making every financial choice intentional.

Chapter 12

THE PAY-YOURSELF-FIRST HABIT

Why this is the golden rule for wealth building

> **Theme: Priority**
> Having mastered pause, you now ensure savings always come before spending, turning Pay Yourself First into an unbreakable default.

THE WEALTH HABIT

Most people don't fail to build wealth because they're bad with money — they fail because they keep paying everyone but themselves.

The Pharaoh of Egypt was restless. Night after night, strange dreams tormented him — seven sleek, fat cows grazing peacefully on the Nile's banks, suddenly devoured by seven gaunt and ugly ones. Then seven full heads of grain, healthy and golden, swallowed by seven thin and scorched. None of his wise men could explain it.

Enter Joseph. Once a prisoner, forgotten and falsely accused, he was summoned to the palace. With humility and clarity, he told Pharaoh: the dreams were one. Egypt would see seven years of extraordinary abundance, followed by seven years of devastating famine.

But Joseph didn't stop with interpretation. He gave Pharaoh a strategy: 'Take a fifth of the harvest during the years of plenty and store it under guard. When famine comes, the country will not be ruined and will eat from its own savings.'[59]

Pharaoh was astonished. He put Joseph in charge of the entire land. For seven years, Joseph oversaw vast storehouses filling with grain. And when the famine struck: Egypt didn't starve, it prospered. Neighbouring peoples, unprepared, travelled far and wide to buy from Joseph's reserves. Egypt became the breadbasket of the world.

Joseph's life revealed a deeper truth: his wisdom wasn't self-made. He named his first son Manasseh, which means 'God has made me forget my trouble', and his second Ephraim, which means 'God has made me fruitful'. He knew his plan was more than smart economics; it was stewardship of God's gifts, applied with diligence and discipline.

But Joseph's plan didn't just save Egypt. Years later, when famine reached his homeland, his own brothers, the very ones who had sold him into slavery, travelled to Egypt seeking food. They bowed before the governor of the land, not realizing it was Joseph, and found their survival in the storehouses he had built.

What began as a 20% savings rule in a foreign land became the means of preserving his family line, reconciling old wounds and ensuring that generations after him could flourish.

His strategy was simple but profound: save before you spend and your future will never go hungry. Whether stewarding a household or a nation, the principle is the same. Wealth isn't built by chance. It begins with discipline in seasons of plenty and grows through systems that protect you in seasons of need.

> **The Wealth Habit Mantra 12:**
> Save in plenty, so you prosper in lean years.

PAY YOURSELF FIRST

The Pay-Yourself-First Habit is the golden rule of wealth building because every other principle depends on it. Automation has no effect without it. Investing has no fuel without it. Generosity has no overflow without it.

The act itself is simple: a percentage of every income is first allocated straight into your storehouses. But its impact is profound: it rewires your relationship with money, transforms your sense of control and creates a buffer that makes every financial season survivable.

The psychology behind paying yourself first

Why does this work so powerfully? Because it flips the script of human behaviour.

- **It counters present bias:** Most people prioritize today's desires over tomorrow's security. Paying yourself first locks in tomorrow before today gets a vote.
- **It reduces decision fatigue:** Once automated, you don't have to think about saving, it's already done. You only manage what's left.
- **It builds identity:** Each time you save first, you reinforce: 'I am a wealth builder.' That identity compounds as much as your money.
- **It creates resilience:** Like Joseph's Egypt, your storehouses prepare you for famine seasons, such as job loss, illness, recessions, caring for a loved one, etc. You don't panic; you pivot.

Pay yourself first or you will always pay others first.

> ### A note for people of faith
> For many people of faith, giving to God comes first. Christians, for example, often practise this through a tithe, the first tenth of their income. Others give to their place of worship or to causes that reflect their values.
>
> The principle of paying yourself first does not replace that. It complements it. Think of it this way: giving honours your values, while saving honours your future. Both are acts of stewardship.
>
> Joseph's example shows this balance beautifully. His plan wasn't about hoarding, it was about provision for his household, for Egypt and for the nations beyond it. In the same way, when you prioritize

giving and saving before lifestyle spending, you secure the freedom to live generously without fear of running dry.

Whether your first slice flows to God, to a cause or to your own storehouse, the order matters: values first, future second, lifestyle last. This sequence ensures your money reflects both who you are and who you are becoming.

THE 80/20/7 RULE: YOUR MOMENTUM CYCLE

Joseph's wisdom wasn't just a survival tactic, it was a timeless wealth principle. He taught us the power of setting aside a portion during seasons of plenty, before anything else was touched. In modern terms, we can call this the 80/20/7 rule: live on 80% of your income, save and invest 20% and commit to this for seven years.

Why seven? Because seven is long enough to transform your financial foundation, yet short enough to feel achievable. You're building a system that continues to work long after you stop. A system that ensures you'll never face your own 'seven years of famine' unprepared.

The 80/20/7 Rule

80% Lifestyle	20% Saving

Commit for 7 years

Here's what this looks like in practice.

- If you earn $30,000 a year after tax, setting aside 20% ($6,000) for seven years builds contributions of $42,000. Invested wisely at 7% average return, it grows to around $56,000 by year seven. Stop saving at that point and let compounding take over and by year 30 (if you have the time horizon), that same money could be worth $264,000.
- On $60,000 a year after tax, you'd save $12,000 annually. After seven years, that grows to over $111,000. Leave it invested at 7% average return and in 30 years it could grow to more than $526,000.
- At $100,000 a year after tax, the same habit grows your seven-year savings into $185,000, compounding to around $877,000 by year 30, even if you never add another penny.

FRAMEWORK: THE GOLDEN-FLOW MODEL

Picture a river. At its source is your income, every pound or dollar flowing in. Most people let that river rush straight downstream to bills, lifestyle and expenses. By the time it reaches their future, the riverbed is dry.

The Golden-Flow Model changes the order of the river. The first channel diverts a fixed share, say 20%, into your 'storehouses': savings, pensions and investments. Only after that is secured does the river continue downstream to cover essentials and lifestyle.

This flow mirrors Joseph's wisdom: fill the silos first, then feed the people. In practice, your 'silos' might be a tax-free savings account (e.g. an Individual Savings Account (ISA) / Roth Individual Retirement Arrangements (Roth IRAs) / Tax-Free Savings Account (TFSA) or equivalent), a pension or a high-interest savings account. By re-routing the flow at the source, you guarantee that your future self is always fed before your present consumes it.

And with enough consistency, that flow doesn't just secure your own future, it creates a surplus that can one day spill outwards to bless your family, community and generations after you.

The Golden-Flow Model has three steps: allocate, adjust, monitor.

Step 1: Allocate

The first step prioritises saving before spending. This is simple in principle but revolutionary in practice: when money comes in, the first slice goes to you. Not your landlord. Not your energy provider. Not your favourite restaurant. You.

Joseph's brilliance was not just in predicting famine, it was in reallocating abundance. Whether the harvest was good or better, the system stayed the same.

Modern wealth builders must do the same. Choose a percentage, for example, 10%, 15% or Joseph's 20%. Automate it so that every month, without fail, that percentage diverts into your 'storehouses'. These can be:

- A pension (long-term storehouse).
- An ISA or brokerage account (growth storehouse).
- A savings account (short-term buffer storehouse).

What matters is the order. If you save first, you guarantee growth. If you wait to see what's left, you guarantee disappointment.

Step 2: Adjust

Life is dynamic. Children arrive, mortgages increase, careers shift, health changes. The Pay-Yourself-First Habit isn't rigid, it's adaptive.

Joseph adjusted distribution during famine depending on what people needed. He bartered livestock, redistributed land and tailored food supply systems for priests. He never stopped stewarding the flow, but he flexed its shape.

We recommend doing the same. During high-earning years, you may be able to save 25% or more. During tighter seasons, you may drop to 10%. The percentage may flex, but the principle never breaks: always pay yourself first, no matter how small the amount.

Think of this as 'wealth muscle memory'. Even in lean times, you maintain the habit. Because once broken, it's hard to rebuild.

This is the secret the wealthy live by: they don't stop the flow. They keep it alive through abundance and famine alike. That's why their money never runs out, it's always feeding the future before fuelling the present.

Step 3: Monitor

Pharaoh trusted Joseph because he monitored everything: grain silos, bartering systems, compliance with laws. Without monitoring, Egypt's abundance would have vanished into corruption or chaos.

In your financial life, monitoring doesn't mean obsessing, it means staying aware. A simple ten-minute check-in each month is enough. Did my savings transfer happen automatically? Are my accounts aligned with my goals? Am I leaking money into lifestyle creep or unnecessary expenses? Tools can help, as we covered previously in Chapter 7. The goal isn't micromanagement, it's assurance that the flow is working, and building guardrails so that wealth accumulates by default.

CASE STUDY: FROM NO PENSION AT 40 TO £200,000 IN 5 YEARS

When Eleanor Harrington turned 40, she faced a sobering reality: despite owning a home and having a stable family life, she had no pension of her own. 'I had no pension at this point because I'd prioritized buying a house. The gap was glaring. It was a huge concern.'

Eleanor, now 48, lives in London, UK, with her husband and their 11-year-old daughter. She works as an IT manager, but the road to her current stability was anything but smooth.

After her daughter was born, Eleanor spent five years out of the workforce. That break meant she had lived without an income, a period that left her feeling financially vulnerable despite her husband's support.

> Being at home unable to work made me feel exposed. My mum was left in a poor financial position after my parents' late divorce and she'd been a stay-at-home parent for 12 years. That shaped my mindset. I knew I never wanted to rely on someone else for my security.

That sense of vulnerability became the turning point. Eleanor committed to saving and investing at least 20% of her income, treating it not as an afterthought, but as the first call on her money. Because she had already learned to live without an income during her career break, the discipline came surprisingly easily. 'It felt natural. I automated it and treated it as non-negotiable.'

Five years later, Eleanor has built roughly £200,000 across her ISA and pension, split almost equally. The number is significant, but what it represents matters even more.

I feel secure. I have the option not to work if my health or my husband's health becomes an issue. That peace of mind is priceless. Being financially independent is very important to me.

Her discipline has also lifted a weight from her husband's shoulders.

It would have been expensive for him to fund both our retirements. By taking responsibility for my own, we're both better off – and he won't have to work many more years just to cover for me.

Eleanor sees her 20% savings habit as a legacy, not just a safety net. She invests for her daughter and makes a point of teaching her about money.

Especially for girls, it's vital. Childcare is rarely split equally and women can lose so much ground in those years. I want my daughter to start ahead, not behind.

When asked how she stays motivated to keep saving even though the future is uncertain, Eleanor is clear-eyed:

I'm nearly eight years away from being able to access a pension, so that doesn't feel far. What keeps me motivated is seeing friends go through devastating life changes – a sudden cancer diagnosis, a child becoming disabled. These things happen and savings give you security and choice when they do. If I died tomorrow, at least my family would have financial security. That matters to me.

For younger people, her advice is equally direct:

If I was 25, I'd be maxing out a Stocks & Shares ISA, because it's accessible along the way. I understand pensions feel distant, but if there's one certainty, it's that taxes are going up, not down. My advice to young people is: take advantage now.

Her advice for anyone wanting to save and invest 20% is simple but powerful:

Automate it, then you don't have to think about it. Budget for everything, including fun and holidays. Learn as much as you can about investing. Make the most of employer pensions.

For Eleanor, paying herself first has done more than build wealth. It's given her freedom, lifted a weight from her marriage and set an example for her daughter. What began as a response to financial vulnerability has become a framework for independence, one that echoes Joseph's wisdom: store a fifth today and your future will never go hungry.

COMMON OBSTACLES
(AND HOW TO OVERCOME THEM)

Overcoming these challenges matters because paying yourself first doesn't stop with you, it multiplies your ability to step in when others need help, just as Joseph once did.

- **'I don't earn enough to save 20%'**: Start with 5%. Build the habit, then increase. The percentage matters less than consistency.

- **'Emergencies keep wiping out my savings':** That's exactly why you must save first. Build an emergency fund alongside long-term investments.
- **'I'll start when I earn more':** If you can't save $50 on $1,000, you won't save $500 on $10,000. Habits scale, excuses don't.
- **'I feel guilty saving when my family needs help':** Joseph's saving wasn't selfish, it fed nations. Your savings today will create future capacity to help others tomorrow.

WHY THIS HABIT IS NON-NEGOTIABLE

Every wealthy person, whether a millionaire in London, an entrepreneur in Lagos or a retiree in Singapore, has this principle embedded: they pay themselves first. Without it, everything else collapses. With it, everything else compounds.

The Pay-Yourself-First Habit is not about greed. It's about stewardship. It's about acknowledging that your future self deserves protection as much as your present self demands gratification. It's about aligning with the wisdom of Joseph, who knew that foresight and discipline were as sacred as faith. This is the habit that turns income into wealth and wealth into legacy.

PAUSE FOR REFLECTION

Take a quiet moment to reflect on Joseph's story. Imagine your own 'seven years of famine', for example, a job loss, an illness, an unexpected downturn or simply the day you retire.

The Pay-Yourself-First Habit

- If those years started tomorrow, would your storehouses be full enough to carry you through?
- What percentage of your income do you currently save before you spend?
- How would your life look if, for the next seven years, you lived on 80% and saved 20%?

Write your answers down. Notice any resistance that surfaces such as fear, guilt or doubt. Ask yourself: what would it cost me if I never built this habit?

> *Small action step*
>
> Set up your Golden Flow today.
>
> 1. Log in to your bank account online.
> 2. Create one automatic transfer that moves at least 10% (aim for 20%) of your income into a dedicated 'storehouse' account, e.g. savings, pension or investment.
> 3. Label it clearly: Pay Yourself First.
> 4. Lock it in so it happens before bills or spending.

Don't wait until you feel ready. Start with what you can, even 5%. The power isn't in the amount, it's in the order. Once the flow begins, you move from living on leftovers to living with foresight.

Joseph didn't wait for famine to strike. In years of plenty, he made choices that protected the years of scarcity, choices that preserved nations and reconciled him with the family who once betrayed him. His foresight blessed generations.

Your decision to pay yourself first carries the same power. It may look small – a standing order, a fraction set aside before bills – but it's no less life-changing. It's the discipline that ensures your future self will never be left begging. It's the habit that turns income into wealth and wealth into freedom.

Chapter summary

- Wealth isn't built by chance, it begins with discipline in seasons of plenty and grows through systems that protect you in seasons of need.
- Pay yourself first or you'll always pay others first.
- Use the 80/20/7 rule: live on 80% of your income, save and invest 20% and commit for at least 7 years to build unstoppable financial momentum.
- Like Joseph's seven years of saving, your disciplined contributions can multiply into abundance that lasts for decades.
- The Golden-Flow Model is a practical system that ensures you always pay yourself first and secure your future: allocate, adjust, monitor.
- This habit ripples outwards, e.g. blessing your family, relieving pressure on loved ones and shaping the financial wellbeing of generations you may never meet.

Building The Wealth Habit

Pillar 2: Build the Habit
Principle lens: Keep it automatic

You've moved from intention to repeatable action.

The habits in this Pillar work best when they no longer depend on effort, memory, or motivation.

Ask yourself: *Which wealth habit now happens without me needing to think about it?*

PILLAR 3
BUILD THE SYSTEM

Chapter 13

THE EFFORTLESS-INVESTING HABIT

How to make investing automatic, stress-free and a lifelong habit

> **Theme: Lifelong investing**
> Building on automated buffers and micro-investing, you design a tiered funnel that keeps you diversified yet hands-off.

Wealth is built in your sleep when your money is working harder than you are. The secret is making investing so simple and automatic that compounding carries on night after night, without your permission or attention, while your other wealth habits quietly accelerate the journey.

Everywhere you look, people are working harder, longer and with more stress than ever, yet many still feel behind. The uncomfortable truth is that effort alone doesn't make you wealthy. Hard work pays the bills; it's investing that buys your freedom.

That's where effortless investing changes the game. Imagine if every pound or dollar you earned brought along a twin that never slept, never took holidays and quietly worked 24/7 on your behalf. That's what automation and compounding do together. They build a workforce of money that multiplies in the background while you live your life. The wealthy aren't always the smartest in the room, they're the ones who put their money to work automatically, without fuss.

JOHN ARRILLAGA: WEALTH WITH THE TWO-MILE PRINCIPLE

John Arrillaga grew up as one of five children in a working-class family in Inglewood, California, eating bread-and-lettuce sandwiches because money was always tight. On a basketball scholarship to Stanford, he washed dishes, did gardening jobs and delivered mail just to cover living costs. That discipline never left him.

In the 1960s, having worked as a commercial real-estate broker, Arrillaga met his business partner, Richard Peery, and they began buying

The Effortless-Investing Habit

thousands of acres of fruit orchards around Palo Alto, California, where they saw colossal potential, turning them into simple, low-rise office parks. This coincided with the semi-conductor industry taking off, with companies like Intel expanding rapidly. [60]

They started with just $2,000 of their own cash and financing assistance from others and began developing before they had tenants. They didn't spread themselves thin across the state. They focused on a two-mile radius around Stanford, knowing every plot, every permit, every potential tenant. That narrow circle of competence became their edge, a perfect example of what we call the 'two-mile principle': true wealth doesn't come from knowing everything, it comes from going deep on a small patch and letting compounding do the heavy lifting. Over the ensuing decades, they built more than 12 million square feet of office space in Silicon Valley and made tens of billions of dollars from selling and leasing property.[61]

And here's where his story speaks directly to the mindset of investing and the overwhelm that many experience:

- **Circle of competence shrinks the universe:** Overwhelm says, 'I need to know every stock, every fund, every sector.' Arrillaga says, 'No. Focus on one patch, one strategy, one habit.' His two-mile radius is a metaphor for your own tax-free investing habit: automate into a global index fund instead of chasing dozens of 'hot' ideas.
- **Boring beats brilliant:** Overwhelm is fuelled by flashy headlines, e.g. 'Meme coins!' Arrillaga started building with dull concrete tilt-ups, the equivalent of boring index funds. His fortune proves that steady, boring compounding is enough.
- **Simplicity over complexity:** Overwhelm thrives on spreadsheets, endless analysis and FOMO. Arrillaga made things effortless by

avoiding unnecessary debt and focusing on cash flow. Likewise, you can keep investing simple: automate, reinvest and hold.
- **Integrity over cleverness:** Overwhelm tempts us with shortcuts and secret strategies. Arrillaga's fairness in negotiations, e.g. sometimes insisting the other side keep more, is a reminder that clarity, not complexity, compounds best.

But Arrillaga's edge wasn't just simplicity. Like Warren Buffett, he instinctively asked the most powerful investing question: 'And then what?' Where others saw orchards, he saw the next order of demand – Stanford's industrial park already too small, tech headcounts rising, engineers pouring into Silicon Valley. He built boring tilt-ups ahead of the curve and demand caught up.

The lesson isn't to become a Silicon Valley tycoon. It's that these habits scale to any level: stay within your circle of competence, keep things simple, value steady cash flow over flashy bets and always ask, 'And then what?' Effortless investing isn't about knowing more, it's about needing less and letting compounding work quietly in the background while your other wealth habits do the rest.

> **Why 'And then what?'**
> **is the most powerful investing question**
>
> Most investing mistakes come from stopping at first-order thinking. First-order thinking looks only at what's obvious: 'The market's down, so it must be bad.' Second-order thinking asks: 'And then what?' 'If markets fall now, what happens next? Will this create better buying opportunities? Will compounding eventually erase this dip?'
>
> Warren Buffett calls, 'And then what?' the most important

question in investing because it forces you to zoom out from the noise and see the long-term consequences.

You can use the same lens with your tax-free investing or pension habit:

- 'The markets have dipped . . . and then what?' History suggests they recover and your automated contributions buy more shares at lower prices.
- 'Dividends are being reinvested . . . and then what?' Over years, those reinvested dividends become a snowball larger than your original contributions.
- 'I've set up £300/month or $500/month . . . and then what?' In a decade, it's worth tens of thousands. In 30 years, potentially hundreds of thousands, tax-free.

The 'And then what?' question is a simple habit of thought that turns short-term overwhelm into long-term clarity.

> **The Wealth Habit Mantra 13:**
> Set it. Spread it. Let it grow. Freedom for life.

WHY INVESTING IS ESSENTIAL FOR LONG-TERM FINANCIAL SECURITY

Inflation continues to nibble away at savings left in cash and even the hardest-working professionals often find they're running on a treadmill, faster, but not further.

Most of us won't sing like Adele, play football like Mbappé or invent the next iPhone. And that's okay. You don't need extraordinary talent to build wealth. What you do need is access to the extraordinary engine of businesses that grow, adapt and thrive over time. That's what equities give you: a way to share in the success of thousands of companies serving millions of people every day.

If you lack rare talents, as most of us do, your edge isn't genius, it's ownership. Equities let you own a slice of the world's progress. That's why long-term investing is the closest thing to a universal wealth habit: it converts ordinary earnings into extraordinary freedom.

Over long periods, broad equity markets have historically outperformed cash and inflation. The FTSE All-Share, the S&P 500 and other broad indexes,[62] have delivered positive real returns to patient investors.

Yet most actively managed funds fail to outperform simple market benchmarks after fees. The S&P Indices versus Active (SPIVA) scorecards show a consistent pattern: most active funds underperform their benchmarks over time in the UK and globally (with occasional exceptions in bonds).

Research shows that among GBP-denominated international active equity funds, 78% of global equity funds underperformed the S&P World Index, 76% of US equity funds underperformed the S&P 500 and 78% of European equity funds underperformed the S&P Europe 350.[63] In fact, the majority of global equity funds domiciled in the US, Europe, Japan, Canada and Australia underperformed the S&P World Index, with underperformance rates all falling within the range of 70%–85%.[64]

So, for most people, the base case should be low-cost, passive index investing that they can hold for decades.

The real threat to long-term security isn't lack of cleverness, it's human behaviour. The DALBAR study,[65] which has tracked real investor returns for decades, finds that investors routinely underperform the very funds they invest in because they chase performance, sell after falls and sit out recoveries.

Automation counters those impulses: steady contributions at set intervals remove the temptation to time the market.

Finally, time is the ultimate multiplier. A simple mental shortcut called the 'rule of 72' shows you how: divide 72 by your annual rate of return to estimate how long it takes for your money to double. At around 10% annual growth, money doubles roughly every seven years. For illustration, let's say you start with a single $10,000 investment with no extra contributions and let it double seven times over 49 years. You'd end up with about $1.28 million. That's a 128-fold increase without stock-picking genius.

But you don't need half a century for this principle to matter. In your twenties or thirties, you still have decades of doubling ahead. In your forties, fifties or later, a few doubles can still turn $10,000 into $40,000 or $80,000 within your lifetime. The point isn't 'wait forever'; it's that compounding multiplies whatever time you give it. Tax-efficient accounts like Individual Savings Account (ISA) / Roth Individual Retirement Arrangements (Roth IRAs) or pensions protect that growth, so every extra year you stay invested does more of the work for you.

You cannot save your way to freedom on cash alone. You need an engine that grows faster than inflation, doesn't rely on your mood and keeps working when you're busy living. That's what disciplined, automated investing delivers.

BEWARE OF THESE MENTAL TRAPS

Even with the best intentions, your brain will try to sabotage you. Watch out for the following nine types of behaviour that plague investors.

- **Loss aversion:** Chasing investments that look like they'll give big returns without much risk.
- **Narrow framing:** Making a decision in isolation without thinking through the bigger picture.
- **Mental accounting:** Taking on too much risk in one pocket of money while being overly cautious with another.
- **False diversification:** Thinking you're spreading risk, when in reality you're just picking different flavours of the same thing.
- **Anchoring:** Clinging to a past reference point or familiar experience, even when it's no longer relevant.
- **Media reaction:** Jumping at headlines without pausing to examine the facts.
- **Regret:** Beating yourself up more for actions you took that went wrong than for opportunities you missed.
- **Herd behaviour:** Following the crowd even when the outcome looks poor.
- **Optimism bias:** Assuming the good stuff will happen to you, while the bad stuff only happens to other people.

HOW TO MAKE INVESTING HANDS-OFF AND AUTOMATIC

The fastest way to make investing effortless is to put the system on rails. Once the rules are set, the habit runs without willpower. Here's how to build it:

Pick your platform and account

Choose a provider that supports automated monthly contributions into your preferred investment or retirement account – ISA or SIPP (UK), 401(k) or IRA (US), TFSA or RRSP (Canada), Superannuation (Australia) or a local equivalent. Look for low fees and access to global equity or multi-asset funds. DIY platforms let you choose funds directly. The best platform is the one you'll use consistently.

Decide your 'always' amount

Pick a percentage you'll invest every month (e.g. 10–20% of net income). Fixed percentages scale with your earnings and keep lifestyle creep in check.

Automate contributions on payday

Set up an automatic transfer from your main bank account straight into your investing, brokerage or retirement account. Paying your future self first turns intention into inevitability and removes the monthly willpower test that trips up most people.

Use dollar or pound-cost averaging

Drip-feeding buys more units when prices are low and fewer when they're high, smoothing the experience and reducing the urge to time the market. While lump sums often win on maths (markets go up more than down), dollar or pound-cost averaging wins on behaviour and behaviour is where most investors lose.

Pre-choose a low-cost, diversified core

A global equity index fund or multi-asset fund with automatic rebalancing handles diversification without constant oversight. Your job is to fund it; the fund's job is to diversify.

This is where overwhelm creeps in. Many people think they need to pick individual stocks as their main strategy. But the truth is, the heavy lifting comes from owning the whole market.

Warren Buffett captured this well in his shareholder letter:

> Charlie and I are not stock-pickers; we are business-pickers. We own publicly-traded stocks based on their long-term business performance, not because we see them as vehicles for clever trades or short-term moves.[66]

Automating into a global index fund means you're quietly buying hundreds or even thousands of businesses at once, without fussing over share prices. If you want to pick the occasional stock later, fine, but your core should already be compounding for you automatically.

Put rebalancing on rails

Rebalancing means bringing your portfolio back to its original mix of stocks and bonds. Choose a fund that rebalances automatically or set an annual calendar reminder to top up laggards. No ad-hoc tinkering.

Default rules for windfalls and raises

Decide today: '50% of any pay rise or windfall goes straight into my investment or retirement account.' The rest you enjoy guilt-free. That way, your wealth habit grows alongside your lifestyle.

Use a 'too-hard' filter

If you can't explain an investment to a ten-year-old in five sentences, pass and keep the idea in the 'too-hard' pile. Warren Buffett credits just about a dozen 'truly good decisions' across nearly six decades for Berkshire's results, roughly one exceptional idea every five years.[67] Your habit should not depend on being exceptional every month.

Protect the habit

Keep an emergency fund accessible so market dips don't force sales. Automate and forget. Review annually, not daily.

Embrace boring brilliance and celebrate progress

Your job isn't to feel clever, it's to be consistent. Each year, celebrate the real milestones: the contributions you made, the dividends reinvested and the fact you stayed the course. Progress comes from habits repeated, not headlines read.

This is the heart of effortless investing. It isn't about clever moves or perfect timing, it's about systems that run without you. Once the rails are in place, you're already ahead of most investors who chase news, tips and trends. Your money compounds quietly in the background, freeing your mind for better things.

THE ROLE OF ROBO-ADVISORS, AI-DRIVEN PORTFOLIO MANAGEMENT AND DIGITAL TOOLS

A generation ago, investing required spreadsheets, manual rebalancing and hours of monitoring. Today, technology does the heavy lifting for you. Most platforms now offer automatic deposits, dividend reinvestment, portfolio rebalancing and simple goal tracking – all designed to remove friction and help you stay consistent.

The real value isn't complexity, it's behaviour. Automation protects you from the two biggest investment killers: emotion and interruption. When the right actions happen by default, you're no longer relying on discipline, mood or memory, your system keeps going whether you're busy, tired or distracted.

AI and robo-advisors are improving risk controls, nudges and long-term planning, but the power comes from simplicity, not sophistication. You don't need advanced algorithms or perfect timing. You just need a platform that automates the basics so you can stay invested for decades. Refer back to Chapter 7 for examples of automation tools by region and their key features.

ISA MILLIONAIRES: HOW ORDINARY PEOPLE BUILT £1M TAX-FREE AND HOW YOU CAN TOO

What if I told you there are now thousands of everyday people in the UK who've quietly become ISA millionaires – no lottery wins, no inheritances, no secret tricks? Just legal tax shelters, consistent investing and time.

Not long ago, ISA millionaires were rare – only a few hundred existed.

The Effortless-Investing Habit

Today, that number is approaching 5,000[68] and tens of thousands more are on track, sitting between £500,000 and £1 million. The pipeline is large and rising.

How long does it take? On average, around 22 years of steady contributions. Someone who starts at 30 could reach the milestone by 52, well before traditional retirement. The average ISA millionaire is older (around 73), but younger millionaires do exist – including some in their thirties – often helped by strong long-term stock performance. The point is: this isn't fantasy, it's habit.

And how do they invest? They favour global, growth-oriented portfolios. Most of their money sits in stocks, funds and Exchage Traded Funds (ETFs),[69] with very little left in cash or bonds. Older investors often hold investment trusts because, for much of their investing lifetime, index funds and ETFs weren't widely available. If the same journey began today, the core would almost certainly lean towards low-cost index funds.

Their traits and habits are remarkably consistent:

- They start early and let time do the heavy lifting.
- They set clear goals, often with a specific target and deadline.
- They automate contributions the moment they're paid.
- They invest in global index or multi-asset funds as a core and reinvest dividends so the 'snowball' grows faster.
- They increase contributions as their income rises (a great rule of thumb: put 50% of every pay rise into your ISA or local tax-free equivalent).
- They avoid panic. ISA millionaires aren't the ones who guessed the bottom, they're the ones who stayed in their seats.
- They tend to be DIY investors rather than relying on advisers who often underperform. That said, advisers are useful if your situation is complex.

Let's make this concrete. Take Joanne, 25. On payday she automates £300 a month into a global equity index fund inside her Stocks & Shares ISA. She ignores headlines, keeps buying through dips and reinvests every dividend. Over 40 years, at a 7% long-term return, that could grow to more than £750,000 tax-free. If she increases contributions with pay rises – say towards £500 a month in her thirties – reaching £1 million becomes entirely realistic.

The power here isn't in Joanne's maths, it's in her habit. By automating, she removes emotion from the process. By staying invested, she lets compounding do its quiet, exponential work. ISA millionaires aren't the lucky few, they are the consistent few.

And here's why this matters now more than ever: while AI and automation is creating new opportunities for some, it is also reshaping up to 30% of existing jobs globally, which means your career income is less secure than it once was. Professional occupations normally requiring a degree or equivalent period of relevant work experience are more exposed to AI than other occupations.[70]

A well-funded ISA or local equivalent provides not just financial wealth, but freedom, liquidity and resilience. Even if you move abroad for new opportunities, your existing ISA keeps compounding tax-free. It's a portable safety net, anchoring your financial independence no matter where life takes you.

FRAMEWORK: THE EFFORTLESS-INVESTING FUNNEL

Imagine your investing system as three taps feeding into a clear tank labelled 'your future wealth'. The taps are: core index, thematic ETFs and opportunistic picks. We've created a visual to show how to create an effortless and reliable investment strategy, using these three taps. This mental picture reinforces the habit: most of your wealth comes from the steady, boring flow, while only a tiny portion ever depends on judgement calls.

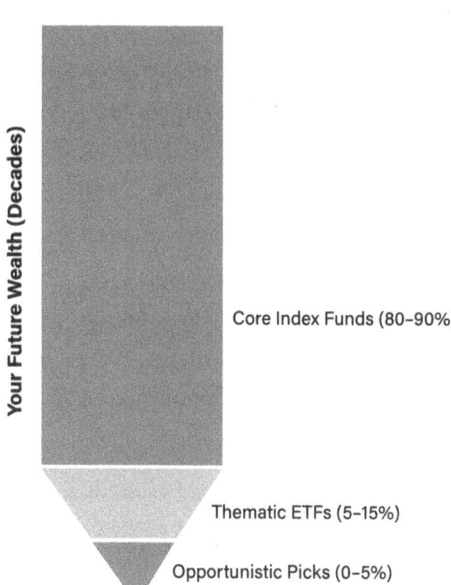

Let's dive into the ratios of each funnel into your tank and what they are:

Funnel 1: Core index (80-90%)

This is your engine and the largest tap — it is your automated standing order into a global index fund or diversified multi-asset fund inside a tax-advantaged account (like an ISA or SIPP in the UK, a 401(k) or Roth

IRA in the US, a TFSA in Canada or superannuation in Australia, etc.). It drips steadily every payday, forming the base of your wealth. Broad, boring and breathtakingly effective over decades.

Funnel 2: Thematic ETFs (5–15%)

A smaller tap represents modest 'tilts' or ETF investments into themes you believe in, such as renewable energy, AI, healthcare or sustainability. These tilts keep investing engaging without jeopardizing your long-term compounding. They're optional, capped and deliberately modest.

For some, this is also where values meet wealth. Thematic ETFs can align your portfolio with what matters to you, whether that's ethical investing, climate-conscious funds or supporting innovation in sectors you care about. The key is keeping it small enough to reflect your values without risking your future.

This layer can also include alternative assets, such as gold, which act as a hedge against inflation, currency devaluation or systemic risk and can sit here alongside other commodities or precious-metal ETFs. You might include 2–5% exposure through a gold ETF or diversified commodity fund as an alternative to holding physical bars or coins.

Funnel 3: Opportunistic picks (0–5%)

At the top, a tiny tap represents your opportunity bucket. Most of the time it stays off. But occasionally, when a rare and obvious idea passes the five-sentence test (you can explain it to a ten-year-old in plain language), it switches on briefly, adding a short surge before shutting off again. These bets should be small, temporary and always flow back into your core. A few examples:

- **Pandemic Crash (2020):** Global markets fell ~30% in weeks. Calm investors who bought broad-market ETFs or index funds at the bottom locked in long-term gains.
- **American Express (1960s):** After the 'Salad Oil Scandal', the stock collapsed, even though the business fundamentals were sound. Buffett, following his investment philosophy of buying when others are fearful, bought American Express shares at a low price and later profited greatly when the company recovered.
- **Individual stocks:** Sometimes a single company with strong fundamentals is temporarily mispriced, whether it's a household name hit by short-term headlines or a clear long-term winner the market has overlooked. A small stake can pay off, but only if it passes the five-sentence rule. Remember, investments can go up as well as down and with individual stocks you must be prepared for the possibility of losing money.

The key takeaway here is that these opportunistic picks are not the cake, they are the sprinkles. Keep them tiny, keep them rare and don't confuse luck with habit.

All three funnels flow into a single tank labelled 'your future wealth'. Inscribed on the tank is this important message: 'Automate the core. Keep tilts modest. Let rare ideas stay rare.' The outcome of the Effortless-Investing Funnel is a system that builds wealth while you sleep, without endless tinkering.

PAUSE FOR REFLECTION

Write down your investment approach in five sentences or less. Imagine you're explaining it to a bright ten-year-old. If you can't, it's too complicated.

- What is your core?
- Do you have any tilts and why?
- Under what conditions would you make an opportunistic investment?
- How are contributions automated?
- How long will you hold before you touch it?

Read it back. Does it feel simple enough to stick with potentially for decades? If not, simplify until it does.

> *Small action step*
>
> Today, log in to your investment platform or open an account if you haven't yet.
>
> - Set (or increase) your monthly tax-free investing contribution to an amount you can stick with for at least 12 months without fail.
> - Choose a low-cost global equity index fund or ETF as your core holding after some research.
> - Turn on auto-dividend reinvestment or choose an 'accumulation' fund so your money compounds automatically.
> - Enable auto-rebalancing (or pick a fund that does it for you).
> - Add a recurring calendar reminder for the same date every year to review your contributions and allocations.
> - Create a one-page 'too-hard list'. Anything you can't explain in five sentences goes straight on that list, no exceptions.

The Effortless-Investing Habit

This step takes less than 30 minutes, but it can quietly shift the entire trajectory of your financial future.

The wealthy don't get there by predicting every twist in the market. They get there by doing what most people can't: making investing so simple and automatic that nothing interrupts it.

You don't need to be a genius. You need a funnel that keeps flowing, year after year, no matter what the headlines say.

Every dollar, pound, euro or yen you invest today is a worker you send out into the world. Some will toil quietly, a few will strike gold. Together, they'll create a workforce of money that outlives your job, outpaces inflation and outlasts uncertainty.

Start it. Automate it. Trust it. Then get on with your life while your money works for you.

Chapter summary

- Hard work alone rarely builds wealth. Only your invested income buys tomorrow's freedom.
- Effortless beats extraordinary. Investing doesn't require brilliance, it requires simplicity, automation and patience.
- Automation is your superpower. Standing orders, auto-dividend reinvestment and annual check-ins turn intention into inevitability.
- Avoid effortful traps. If it requires spreadsheets, leverage or endless tinkering, it's not effortless.
- Runway matters more than brilliance. The earlier you start, the more compounding does the heavy lifting.
- Always ask 'And then what?' to go beyond first order thinking.
- Technology helps. Robo-advisors, digital platforms and AI tools make it easier than ever to automate, diversify and hold for the long term.
- ISA millionaires are real. You, too, can work towards tax-free wealth wherever you are in the world through consistency, not speculation.
- The Effortless-Investing Funnel is made of 80–90% core index funds, 5–15% thematic Index funds or ETFs and up to 5% opportunistic picks.
- Five-sentence test. If you can't explain your investing plan simply, it's too complex.

Chapter 14

THE SIDE-HUSTLE HABIT

From invisible ownership to simple experiments: the smart way to stack income streams

> **Theme: Additional streams**
> You don't build wealth with one stream or by waiting for permission. This habit is about stacking smart, repeatable income streams: from negotiating invisible ownership, to monetizing rare skills, to launching simple cash flow experiments on the side. One stream pays the bills. Several buy your freedom.

THE WEALTH HABIT

Most people are chasing income. The wealthy are negotiating ownership.

At 17 Dean was homeless. No roof over his head, no job and no savings. Just sofa surfing, with his dream fading fast in south London's grey sky. The dream? Football. It had been his future, his identity, until injury closed that door. What followed wasn't just disappointment, it was debt. At just 18, Dean was £89,000 ($118,000) in the red, a mix of overdrafts, credit cards and car loans, all racked up trying to maintain the image of a footballer's lifestyle, surrounded by friends still in the game.

His schoolmates had moved on to university or full-time work and he was stuck, crushed between survival and shame. The kind of shame that makes you disappear from people's lives because you can't afford the bus fare, let alone a conversation about the future.

Here's the twist. He didn't stay stuck or wait for a lottery ticket or a knight in shining armour. Instead, he found his first real job, cold calling in tech sales for a small American software company expanding into the UK. It was entry level and commission based. Nothing glamorous, just work.

Around the same time, something else happened. He met Danielle, his future wife, and she welcomed him into her life and home. It was the first step out of homelessness and the first building block of the life they would go on to build together. Dean showed up, listened and learned. He grew and, slowly, opportunity started to notice him back.

Over the next two decades, that same young man, Dean Forbes, would rise to become the CEO of multiple tech companies. But not just any CEO, a multi-exit CEO and leader who built companies, including one valued at €1bn ($1.2bn), which got acquired. And, with each acquisition, he walked away, not with a thank-you bonus, but with millions.

Not because he was the founder or that he got lucky, but because he had developed a rare and invisible side hustle: he negotiated equity inside the companies he worked for. He didn't just trade hours for income, he traded value for ownership. At every step of his career, Dean asked one question most employees never think to ask: 'Can I own a piece of what I'm helping to build?' That one habit, negotiating equity as a condition of contribution, quietly transformed his financial future. While others were climbing the corporate ladder, Dean was quietly collecting keys to the vault. It didn't matter that he hadn't founded the companies. What mattered was that he'd learned to play the game that actually builds wealth: ownership > hours.

Dean's story isn't about being extraordinary, it's about having an extraordinary habit: thinking like an investor, even while being an employee. He didn't work outside his job to build wealth, instead he turned his job into his wealth-building machine.

You may never be a CEO, and you don't have to be. But what if you stopped seeing your job as just income and started seeing it as leverage? What if your biggest side hustle isn't a business you start after work, but a decision you make during work? This chapter isn't just about freelancing or creating and selling online. It's about rethinking how you earn, how you own and how you multiply, because in the wealth game, side hustles aren't just about effort, they're about access.

OWNERSHIP OVER HOURS: HOW THE WEALTHY THINK ABOUT WORK

The wealthy don't think in terms of pay grades, they think in terms of equity stakes. They don't just ask, 'How much will I earn this year?' They ask, 'What part of this value do I own?' That's the shift. Most people are stuck in what we call the 'hourly trap': you trade time for money. The company grows and the founders win. You get a pay slip and they get an exit.

Ownership isn't just smart – it's strategic. It's a wealth habit hiding in plain sight. Most people are never taught that the right type of employment can be a wealth-building vehicle, if you know how to structure it. They see jobs as cages, not vehicles, and negotiate for comfort, not upside.

Here's the uncomfortable truth: if you're helping a business grow its revenue, acquire users, expand into new markets or build proprietary systems, you're building value and value deserves compensation, not just through salary, but through equity, performance-based bonuses or profit-sharing. That's how the wealthy think and how you need to start thinking.

Reflecting on this in our personal lives, we've worked across different types of employers and seen this hidden wealth habit unfold. I (Ken) started with manual cash-in-hand jobs like cleaning, moved to salary-only roles, then progressed to salary plus bonus and pension, and later to a senior role with share options. Over time – and after much struggle – I secured employment as a CFO in a venture capital business where I negotiated a seven-figure share of profits if the companies we backed succeeded. That role gave me the potential to create more wealth than I ever could in a salary-only job.

How to apply this wealth habit

With every opportunity you take – be it a job, freelance gig, joining a startup, or starting a collaboration – ask yourself: 'How could I share in the success I help create?' The real shift is mental and isn't a one-time tactic. It's a habitual mindset. Here's how to apply this mindset wherever you work.

Know your value

Make a simple list: how does your role help the business grow revenue, reduce cost or increase efficiency? You can't negotiate ownership if you can't define your impact.

Time your ask strategically

The best moment to negotiate equity or profit-sharing isn't during your job interview. It's after you've made a measurable difference or when your employer is motivated to keep you during a critical moment.

Start the conversation

Ask the question most people never ask: 'As I continue helping grow this business, what opportunities are there for me to share in that upside through equity, options or profit-sharing?' Even if the answer is no, you've reframed how you're seen from employee to strategic contributor.

Explore alternatives

If shares aren't available, look for other ways to share in success. It could be a result-driven agreement, a creative side project or a custom incentive.

EQUITY THINKING:
THE INVISIBLE SIDE HUSTLE OF THE WEALTHY

Equity thinking is the habit of approaching your work like a builder, not just a contributor. It's a mindset, a posture and a quiet inner voice that asks: 'If I'm helping build this, why don't I own a piece of it?'

It shows up long before a formal negotiation in the problems you solve, the gaps you fill and the conversations you're willing to have.

How Dean stumbled into equity, then mastered it

Dean's first experience of equity wasn't about title or salary, it was about spotting gaps and stepping up. When colleagues left the small and expanding tech firm he worked at, he quietly took on their workload, becoming the de facto lead for international growth. That initiative led to his first stake in a company that eventually sold for $550 million. He didn't start by asking, he started by creating value no one could ignore. That's equity thinking in action.

The habit behind the outcome

You don't wake up one day and land a life-changing payout. You build the muscle through micro-habits like:

- **Tracking your measurable impact:** For example, 'I grew customer retention by 30%.'
- **Learning the language of commercial value:** For example, profit, margin, customer lifetime value, ROI (return on investment).
- **Volunteering for high-impact projects that drive growth:** Not just high-visibility ones.

- **Asking the right question at the right time:** 'If I help deliver X, could we discuss profit share, a bonus or even equity participation?'

Every time you do this, you're building the equity habit, elevating the conversation and positioning yourself not just as labour, but as leverage.

Equity isn't just for CEOs

Don't count yourself out. Equity comes in many forms – from share options and performance-based bonuses to licensing deals, revenue-sharing or even matched pension contributions. The key is this: if you're helping build something valuable there are often creative ways to share in that upside, even without a formal equity package. You don't need a fancy title to benefit. You just need to think like someone who belongs at the table.

In our own careers, we've benefitted the most from negotiated annual bonuses (always investing at least 50% in the stock markets), taking up matched pension contributions and profit shares. Thinking this way in our places of employment, over a number of years, gave us the confidence to start our own side hustles with 100% equity, begin joint ventures and create products with royalty arrangements and licensing plans.

Equity is earned through strategic value

Equity isn't given because you ask, although asking already puts you ahead of most people. It's earned because you add something no one else can.

That's exactly what Dean did. When a venture-backed firm tried to bring him on as CEO, they offered the standard 4–6% equity package.[71] But Dean pushed back, not with ego, but with evidence: 'Based on what I'm walking away from and the scale of what I'll build, it needs to be more.' That's not entitlement, that's leverage. They agreed because he had receipts.

Whether it's sales, growth, turnarounds or exits, Dean didn't just ask for more, he showed why it made sense and that's the takeaway: before you negotiate upside, make your upside undeniable.

Dean once shared the biggest risk he ever took. He said:

> We were negotiating a deal to sell the company and I took all of the money me and my wife had – every pound that we had – and we bought all of the shares and stock options that were available to us. Like, literally using all of our cash. And then the deal broke down.
>
> So, we were kind of living without money for a long period of time, until we were able to get that deal back on track and exit that company for €125 million.
>
> We went all in. Bet on yourself.[72]

That's not luck, that's leverage and ownership.

It didn't start there, it started with a mindset: 'What do I own here?' It started with small equity conversations, value logs and positioning, but it led to a moment where Dean wasn't just working inside a company, he was risking like a founder. That's what equity thinking makes possible.

But here's the catch: equity only works if you have something valuable to negotiate with. Dean could ask for ownership because he consistently brought unique value to the table. And that brings us to another overlooked Side-Hustle Habit, one that's less about contracts and more about you. If you want to multiply your earning power, you don't just need more hours or even more opportunities. You need a skill stack so rare and complementary that people can't ignore you. That's what we call the 'Ronaldo effect'.

> **The Wealth Habit Mantra 14:**
> Wealth flows to those who stack skills others can't easily combine.

STACKING RARE AND COMPLEMENTARY SKILLS: THE RONALDO EFFECT

Cristiano Ronaldo is known not just as one of the greatest footballers in history, but as one of the most valuable athletes of all time. His brilliance isn't down to a single ability. Thousands of professional players can strike a ball, sprint at speed or head with power. Ronaldo's true advantage lies in how he stacks rare and complementary skills. He mastered discipline like an Olympian, honed his fitness until he was leaner at 38 than most at 22, developed a fearsome aerial game, nurtured unshakable mental toughness and built a global brand that extended far beyond the pitch.

Individually, none of these skills are unique. Together, they form a combination almost impossible to replicate. And that is why he not only earned millions in salary, but multiplied it many times through endorsements, sponsorships and his own ventures, ultimately becoming the world's first football (soccer) billionaire. His success demonstrates a critical wealth lesson: skills compound just like money.

Why skills compound like money

Most people stop at mastering one 'base skill', usually their profession. But in a noisy, competitive world, especially one being disrupted by AI, being good at only one thing makes you easily replaceable. The truth is, wealth doesn't just reward mastery, it rewards uniqueness. And uniqueness comes from the ability to combine complementary skills in a way others don't.

Take two examples:

- An accountant who also learns storytelling and camera confidence can build an online audience, becoming a trusted educator rather than just another number cruncher.
- A schoolteacher who learns video editing and social media marketing can transform classroom techniques into a thriving digital membership business.

In both cases, the stack of skills creates a new playing field. Each additional layer multiplies the value of the first. Just like compound interest turns pennies into pounds, complementary skills turn ordinary careers into extraordinary opportunities.

THE SKILL-STACK LADDER

To make this principle practical, think of skills as rungs on a ladder:

- **Base skill:** Your primary craft or profession. It's your starting point, but on its own it rarely builds lasting wealth.
- **Complementary skill:** An adjacent ability that enhances the base. For example, a lawyer who learns negotiation psychology or a software developer who learns UX design.
- **Rare edge:** The differentiator. This is the skill most people in your field avoid or overlook, e.g. branding, networking, AI tools, salesmanship. It's the piece that makes you not just useful but irreplaceable.

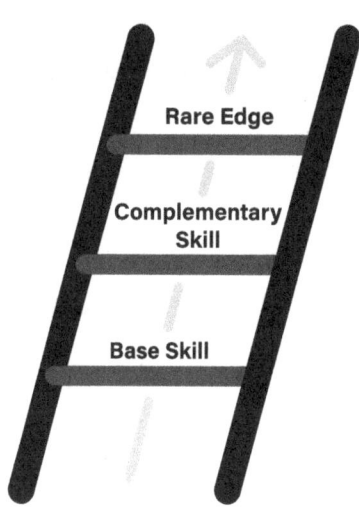

It's this combination, not perfection in one, that creates wealth multipliers and exponential value.

Here are some examples of how the Skill-Stack Ladder plays out in real life:

- **Engineer + communication = leadership:** Most engineers build solutions; the one who can explain ideas simply becomes a project lead, consultant or founder.
- **Writer + traditional and AI Search Engine Optimization (SEO) = content entrepreneur:** The internet is full of writers. But the one who understands digital visibility builds blogs, books and businesses that print money while they sleep.
- **Musician + digital marketing = global reach:** A talented pianist may play to a hundred people a night. The one who stacks music with marketing reaches millions online – teaching, performing and licensing compositions worldwide.

None of these examples demand overnight reinvention. They're built through small, deliberate layering of habits, just like wealth itself.

HOW TO BUILD YOUR SKILL-STACK HABIT

Stacking rare and complementary skills creates leverage. It makes you irreplaceable — and opens the door to equity, unique side hustles and income streams others can't replicate. The more distinct your value, the more opportunities you unlock. Here's how to build yours:

- **Audit your base skill:** Write down your current profession or strongest ability. That's your foundation.
- **Identify complementary skills:** Ask: 'What skill would make my base two times more valuable?' For example: public speaking, negotiation, sales or AI literacy.
- **Choose your rare edge:** This is where wealth hides. Pick a skill that very few in your industry bother with. It could be brand building, storytelling or mastering new tech.
- **Commit to micro-habits:** You don't need to be world-class overnight. Start small: ten minutes learning, one post, one coffee. Over time, the stack compounds.
- **Monetize the attack:** Test your stack in the real world. Teach, share or build. Let the market show you where your value lies.

This is how we started The Humble Penny and the Financial Joy Academy (FJA), built a global audience and even became *Sunday Times* bestselling authors, having more positive impact than we ever thought was possible. It took stepping outside our base skills (a.k.a. our comfort zones), to create a growing skill stack with exponential value.

HOW TO START A SIDE HUSTLE WITH MINIMAL TIME AND EFFORT

Not everyone will be able to negotiate equity today and that's okay. While you build your long game, you can start the short game immediately. What matters is getting in motion. Every income stream you build, no matter how small, trains your brain to stop depending on a single source. Here's how to start fast, lean and smart.

The $1 to $1,000 challenge: a 30-day income experiment

Imagine this: it's the end of the month and your salary doesn't land. No warning. No explanation. You need $1,000 (or £1,000) in the next 30 days. You can't rely on your salary and maybe you don't even have savings to fall back on. What do you do?

It's a test of creativity, courage and value. And it's the exact challenge members of our community have taken with real results. To get started, forget the word 'business' or 'side hustle' for a minute. Think of this as a fun, time-bound experiment with a real reward at the end. You're about to prove to yourself that you can create income anytime, from scratch.

Your hypothesis: 'If I focus on solving problems with simple skills, I can generate income outside my job within 30 days.'

Your mission:

- Make $1 (or £1) this weekend.
- Make $1,000 (or £1,000) this month.

But here's the catch: you must put something at stake, something that will make not acting feel more uncomfortable than trying.

Lock in your social contract

Before you begin, tell one person what you're doing (friend, partner, sibling). Text them: 'I'm doing a $1 to $1,000 challenge this month. If I don't follow through, I owe you $50.' Or, if you're feeling brave, post your commitment on Instagram and tag @thehumblepenny, because commitment + social pressure = follow through.

Making it public makes it real. Why? Because we take action when there's skin in the game, not just information. The thought of losing $50 is called 'loss aversion', a cornerstone of behavioural psychology. It's the idea that we feel the pain of loss twice as strongly as the joy of a gain. In experiments, people will work harder to avoid losing $50 than to gain $100.

By putting something at stake (e.g. 'I owe you $50 if I don't complete this') or making a social contract (e.g. 'Tell a friend or post online that you're committing to this challenge'), you introduce consequences for not taking action, which increases follow-through dramatically. Without stakes, it's a nice idea. With stakes, it's a real decision.

You also see this in action when you write something down or say it out loud, it dramatically increase their chances of following through because you're creating a subtle but effective 'accountability loop'.

Stage 1: Make your first $1 (£1) this weekend

Don't wait for a perfect idea, name or website. You have 48 hours to make money outside your job. Because that first $1? It rewires your brain. It says, 'I can make money anytime I choose. I don't need permission.'

You're no longer just an employee. You're a value-creator. You go from consumer to producer. This taps into self-perception theory, where people infer their identity from their behaviour. You think, 'If I just made

$1 by solving a problem, then I must be capable of creating income, not just earning it.' That's why the first $1 is worth more psychologically than financially.

Try one of these by Sunday night:

- Ask three friends or family: 'What small task would you happily pay $5–10 for?' Do one.
- Sell one unused item on Facebook Marketplace or Vinted.
- Share a useful affiliate link (book, budgeting app) and earn a commission.
- Create a super simple digital product (e.g. monthly meal planner, revision checklist) and post it on Gumroad.
- Offer a mini-service in your WhatsApp group or church: CV help, design, budgeting.

No branding, no perfection, just solve a problem and get paid.

The result? Confidence, momentum and a new neural pathway that says: 'I can create income, anytime I choose.'

Track your result. How much did you make? What did you learn? How did it feel to earn money this way?

Made your first $1 or £1? Create a story or post and tag us on Instagram @thehumblepenny and use #FirstDollarWithoutPermission – let's celebrate your new income superpower, because small wins build big momentum.

Stage 2: Make Your First $1,000 (£1,000) in 30 days

Now that you've made $1 or £1, you've crossed the threshold. You've proved it's possible. Let's scale it to four figures, not by working harder, but by being intentional.

Instead of 'Start a business' (which feels heavy, permanent and risky), you reframe the journey as, 'Let's run a 30-day experiment with a specific goal and a defined endpoint.'

This taps into experimental framing, reducing fear of failure by making action feel temporary, low-risk and curiosity-driven. And that reduces perfectionism. You are more likely to act when it feels like a test than a commitment

Step A: Pick one skill and one audience

Choose something you can do using your existing skills (or learn quickly) and someone specific to serve.

For example:

- Help overworked families declutter their homes for $100/hour. No qualification required.
- Cook and deliver healthy meals for busy professionals tailored to their dietary requirements. For example, we often have certain Nigerian dishes cooked and delivered to us during busy months.
- Tutor secondary-school students via platforms like Tutorful, Superprof or independently).
- Manage social media for a creator or startup.
- Create and sell digital templates (resumes, planners, trackers).
- Optimize CVs or LinkedIn profiles for $50–100.
- Teach someone how to use ChatGPT for work or freelancing.

Step B: Craft one offer

Avoid saying, 'I do coaching' or 'I do design'. Be specific and outcome-focused, for example, 'I'll help you declutter one room in three hours and create a system to keep it tidy for $400' or 'I'll teach your child five maths hacks to boost their GCSE grade for £70.'

The clearer your offer and the more tangible the result, the faster the sale.

Step C: Repeat and refine

Once you've made $100 or £100, ask:

- Can I offer this again tomorrow?
- Can I turn it into a monthly service?
- Can I use Stripe, Calendly, Notion or Airtable to automate delivery?
- Can I serve ten clients instead of one?

Your job isn't to build an empire, it's to learn, earn and systemize. The money doesn't come from effort alone, it comes from building repeatable value. You've got 30 days to prove it to yourself.

Every Sunday night, ask: what worked? What didn't? What will I try next week? This is how you turn effort into data and data into growth. Remember: experiments never fail. They just reveal what works faster.

The other reason this experimental approach works is because: gamification + progress tracking = motivation. The 30-day challenge structure adds a sense of gamified progress:

- $1 = Level 1 unlocked (you proved it's possible).
- $100 = System working (you validated your skill and offer).
- $1,000 = First real financial breakthrough (you created leverage).

Stage 3: Make $10,000 (£10,000)

Now it gets really exciting. To make $10,000 (£10,000) use the same system, repeated and refined. Each stage builds your skills, systems and identity. $1,000 proved it works. $10,000 proves it's repeatable.

The moment you earn money from your own effort, something shifts. You're no longer just a consumer of opportunities. You're a creator. One dollar becomes ten. Ten becomes a hundred. A hundred becomes a thousand and so on. That's how freedom starts with a tiny moment of belief, backed by action.

Your wealth hour

Commit to two 60-minute blocks every week. No distractions or overthinking. Just one clear intention: 'Move something forwards that could make me money.' Use that time to research demand, build your offer, reach out to people, deliver value, collect testimonials or refine your next version. It's never about having more time, it's about defending one hour that builds your future.

You now have a plan. First $1? This weekend. First $1,000? This month. Real freedom begins the moment you stop waiting and start doing. No pressure, just possibility. No hype, just habits. That's the real side-hustle game, and now you're in it. Even if things don't go fully to plan in these first 30 days, you will have learned lots and can refine the experiment and keep testing.

> *Real talk from the $1,000 (£1,000) challenge*

While writing this book, we ran the '$1,000 (£1,000) in 30 days challenge' with 30 people with nine-to-five jobs in our FJA community, with weekly check-ins and reviews. Here's what we learned:

People didn't wait for perfect. They:

- Took photos of items to sell on Vinted and eBay.
- Updated LinkedIn profiles to reflect new services.
- Made daily business calls and sent cold messages.
- Secured freelance contracts within days.
- Explored local markets, meal prep services and digital training ideas.
- Set daily accountability goals like: 'By this time tomorrow, I will have…'

Some felt resistance. One member said, 'We've been programmed, so we need to unlearn some of the things that are limiting us from excelling.'

But week by week, through our 'lunch time club' learning and accountability calls, mindsets shifted from passive to proactive. Even ten-minute micro-action sprints to take one small money-making action there and then on the live calls created the environment for people to take immediate action.

The lesson? Starting small doesn't mean thinking small. Action rewires identity and identity fuels results.

FRAMEWORK: THE INCOME STACK

Don't underestimate the power of multiple income streams in achieving financial freedom. Here's a truth very few people are taught: most millionaires have more than one income stream. Most non-millionaires rely on only one, their job.

This doesn't mean you need seven streams today. It means you build one at a time, like scaffolding. Here is how to approach it, using the Income Stack Framework: **primary job, side hustle, digital asset, royalties**.

Layer	Description	Example
Primary Job	Your main income	Employment or contract work
Side hustle	Time-for-skill exchange	Coaching, freelancing, tutoring
Digital asset	Built once, sold repeatedly	Ebooks, templates, online courses, memberships
Royalties	Long-tail passive income	Affiliate income, licensing, brand deals, intellectual property royalties

Your journey might begin with coaching on the side, but over time, you build assets that earn while you sleep. That's how ordinary people create extraordinary options.

USING AI-DRIVEN TOOLS AND AUTOMATION TO SCALE SIDE BUSINESSES AND MAXIMIZE EFFICIENCY

AI isn't replacing doers; it's replacing friction. It removes the technical, time-consuming or expensive barriers that used to slow people down. In other words, if you're a doer, AI makes you faster. If you're waiting for permission, AI won't save you, it'll just widen the gap between you and those taking action.

You don't need to know how to code: AI can build your website. You don't need to be a designer: AI can create your logo and carousel. You don't need to hire a marketer: AI can write your sales copy, emails and product descriptions. You don't need weeks to test a business idea: AI can help you launch in hours.

The 'I don't know how' excuse is disappearing. That's friction, gone. Here's how to use it to your advantage:

Content and admin:

- **ChatGPT:** Write landing pages, social posts or course scripts
- **Notion AI / Claude:** Organize your offer, plan launches, summarize content
- **Zapier / Make.com:** Automate email delivery, payments and product access

Design and branding:

- **Canva Magic:** Instant graphics, social templates, eBooks
- **Midjourney / DALL·E:** Generate product mockups or unique art

Strategy:

- Ask AI to act like your business coach: 'I have 2 hours/week. What side hustle could I launch using my skill in [X]?' It won't do the work for you, but it will remove 90% of the friction.

> *Small action step*
>
> Pick one of these to act on this week:
>
> - Map your current income stack. Where are you now and what's your next level?
> - Write down one skill someone would pay you to solve a problem with, then outline a $10–100 offer.
> - Practice one 'equity thinking' habit this month: track your value, speak your worth or ask a bigger question.
> - Schedule two 60-minute 'wealth hours' to build or ship your first/next income stream.
>
> The Wealth Habit isn't about working harder. It's about earning wider, owning more and building leverage over time.

Chapter summary

- Dean Forbes' story reveals that the most powerful side hustle may not be outside your job, but inside it, through equity thinking.
- Equity thinking is the habit of asking, 'What do I own here?' and using strategic value to negotiate ownership, not just salary.
- This isn't just for CEOs. It can mean bonuses, share options, royalties, profit-share or commissions, if you deliver value.
- To negotiate well, you need leverage and that starts with a rare and complementary skill stack ('the Ronaldo effect').
- Try a low-barrier income experiment that runs alongside your main income and build future freedom.
- Whether you're leveraging ownership, skills or systems, this habit is about stacking income streams that work for you. One stream pays the bills. Several buy your freedom.

Chapter 15

THE GLOBAL-WEALTH HABIT

How moving can accelerate your wealth

> **Theme: Strategic mobility**
> You stop treating your location as fate and start using it as a financial strategy – moving, adapting and designing your environment to multiply freedom.

Most people never realize that their postal code may be their most expensive financial decision.

You can change jobs, switch banks, even invest in the global stock market, but if your environment is draining more wealth than it gives back, you'll always feel one step behind.

We remember that feeling vividly – boxes lined the hallway, but this time they represented progress, not panic; a move made with intention, not reaction.

For us, the wake-up moment came when we realized that staying in London no longer made financial or lifestyle sense. London's already inflated property prices kept climbing and the extra hundreds of thousands in mortgage borrowing would have meant working at least a decade longer, robbing us of precious years of financial freedom. We wanted more space to start a family, a garden and greenery for wellbeing, cleaner air, greater safety and an overall lower cost of living.

When we mapped the numbers, the truth was simple: everything we wanted, financial breathing room and a better quality of life, was possible less than 30 miles from where we lived. That short move bought us time, space and peace of mind. Others we know have gone further, moving 100 miles or more and seen even greater net gains in cost and lifestyle.

Across the world, millions are realizing the same thing. From San Francisco to Austin, Johannesburg to Cape Town, London to Manchester, people are discovering that geography can be one of the most powerful wealth levers of all. This is not about escaping; it's about optimizing.

And for those whose work or family ties mean staying put – such as teachers, nurses, small-business owners or tradespeople – the same principle applies. You can still leverage geography by optimizing within your current radius: living just a few miles farther from a city centre, moving one transport zone out or even renegotiating housing or workspace costs.

The Global-Wealth Habit isn't about relocation alone; it's about location awareness, knowing how where you live and work shapes your freedom and making that dynamic work for you. It teaches you to use location itself as an engine for freedom because where you live shouldn't strangle your wealth, it should serve it.

Every generation faces a different kind of mobility. For our parents, it meant leaving everything and bravely moving across continents in search of opportunity and stability. For us, it might mean changing postal codes for peace of mind or even starting a new chapter in a new country where the cost of living is lower, the sun shines longer and the pace of life feels more human. The Global-Wealth Habit is about realizing that where you live is as powerful a wealth choice as what you earn, and that moving with intention can unlock years of freedom and wellbeing you didn't know were hidden in your map.

Most people invest globally through index funds without thinking twice, yet live as if their world ends at the edge of their postal codes. Many people think of 'mobility' as something physical, for example, moving house, city or country. But in the context of wealth, mobility begins as a mindset shift: the decision to stop accepting your environment as fixed and start treating it as fluid.

When you master the Global-Wealth Habit, you're not just changing postal codes; you're learning to see cost, tax and quality-of-life differences as tools to build freedom faster. Whether you stay within your country or look abroad, the goal is the same: to live where your money and values stretch furthest and to design a life that compounds peace, not pressure. In this chapter, we'll show you how to do that using what we call the Location-Leverage Loop, a framework for turning geography into one of your greatest financial advantages.

THE WEALTH HABIT

In 2019, we met a couple, James and Tolu, through our community. Both worked in tech. They loved London but felt trapped by monthly costs: £2,300 ($3,100) rent, £300 ($400) commute each, £1,800 ($2,400) nursery fees and other lifestyle costs. By the end of the month, they ended up saving almost nothing.

Then lockdown reshaped work. Their companies went fully remote and they asked a simple question: 'What if we could earn London salaries but live elsewhere?' Within six months, they relocated to Coventry. Their housing costs halved overnight, childcare fell by a third and they could walk to the park rather than squeeze into the Tube. Their quality of life improved, yet their income stayed the same. They used the savings to overpay their mortgage and invest monthly in index funds.

We've seen the same with friends who earn an income in London, but quietly live and work remotely in Ghana, Thailand or Colombia, where the cost of living is a fraction of what they were used to.

Across the Atlantic, our friend Michael left Manhattan, New York, for Houston, Texas. His living costs dropped 40% while his business income rose. And in Portugal's Algarve region, families from across Europe are quietly thriving with lower living costs and favourable taxes without lowering standards of living.

What links them isn't privilege, it's curiosity. They questioned an assumption few ever do – that you must live where you work or run a business or that success only lives in expensive postal codes.

Their moves were small experiments, not dramatic escapes. Yet each gained time, savings and peace of mind. Their decisions illustrate the Global-Wealth Habit: learning to view where you live as an active wealth variable, not a fixed background condition.

> **The Wealth Habit Mantra 15:**
> Where you live should serve your wealth, not strangle it.

UNDERSTANDING GEOGRAPHIC ARBITRAGE: UNLOCKING WEALTH THROUGH LOCATION

Most people already understand financial arbitrage, buying something undervalued in one market and profiting from the difference in another. Geographic arbitrage is the same principle applied to life. It's the art of earning in one economy and spending in another, or simply relocating to where your cost of living, taxes and lifestyle all work harder for you. And it doesn't require global wealth, only global thinking.

For example, when a family earning £70,000 moves from London to Manchester, their income remains the same, but their rent may drop by nearly 50%.[73] When a UK remote worker relocates to Lisbon, Portugal, or Valencia, Spain, their lifestyle costs can fall by 30–40%,[74] while the quality of food, weather and healthcare often improves. According to the OECD Better Life Index and Eurostat data,[75] many southern European cities offer safety and healthcare standards similar to northern Europe, yet everyday costs, such as housing and groceries, are typically 20–40% lower. Even within the same city, shifting from a high-cost borough to a more affordable one can buy back hundreds each month, money that can compound towards financial independence.

What makes this powerful is not the move itself but the mindset behind it. Once you see location as a variable, not a constant, you start unlocking opportunities most people never notice.

In short, geographic-arbitrage is not about chasing the cheapest place, it's about finding where your money and values go furthest together.

STRATEGIES FOR MAXIMIZING WEALTH AT HOME AND ABROAD

Start small. Examine your current region. Could moving one hour away reduce the net of housing and transport by 25% while keeping the same salary? Are there emerging 'secondary cities' like Birmingham, Nottingham or Leeds in the UK; Austin and Charlotte in the US; Porto and Valencia in Europe; Kigali and Nairobi in Africa; and Kuala Lumpur in Asia, where property prices, rents and childcare costs are far lower, yet opportunities are rising? Would a smaller town with good transport links allow you to own rather than rent?

For instance, in the UK a £500,000 two-bed flat in London can be swapped for a £250,000 four-bed home in Nottingham. With a 20% deposit (£100,000), your mortgage would fall from £400,000 to £150,000. At today's rates, that shift alone could cut your mortgage term by 10–12 years or free up £1,000 a month to invest or overpay debt.

Let's think deeper about the second-order effect of this and how it compounds into decades of additional wealth, freedom and time. Imagine that you invest that £1,000 monthly for the next 20 years at a 7% annual return: you'd build roughly £520,000, nearly another home or a fully funded freedom fund. If you invested for 30 years, that becomes £1.2 million.

And that's before you add in lower council tax, childcare and transport costs. The ripple effect of one relocation could be the difference between retiring at 65 or 55, between part-time freedom at 50 or working full-time into your seventies.

This is why Plan B living isn't about running away. It's about redeploying your life capital, i.e. your time, income and energy, into environments that multiply their impact instead of draining it. When you layer these, the outcome isn't a smaller life, it's a larger margin for freedom.

The Global-Wealth Habit

Lever	Typical saving or gain	Potential long-term effect
Housing	£1,000/month	£520k–1.2m invested value over 20–30 years.
Commuting (working remotely)	£300/month saved, plus time	5–7 hours/week back for family or side income.
Childcare /schooling	£400–800/month	Savings can total £100k–200k over childhood years.
Tax/local costs	5–10% net gain	Adds years of financial breathing room.

Your postal code can accelerate or delay financial independence by a decade or more. The earlier you re-optimize your geography, the faster compounding starts working for you instead of against you.

Now let's take a look at cross-border moves. Remote work and global mobility have opened the map. Some options you might want to investigate include:

- **Digital-nomad visas:** Over 60 countries now offer them these,[76] from Portugal and Spain to Barbados and Thailand. They usually require proof of income and health insurance.
- **Golden-visa and startup programmes:** For those seeking residency through investment, countries like Greece, Italy and the UAE provide clear pathways.
- **Remote-work passports:** Programmes such as Estonia's and Malta's cater to salaried employees who can work online.

These are not only for digital elites. Teachers, consultants, creators and healthcare professionals increasingly use them for lifestyle and savings gains.

KEY CONSIDERATIONS AND LASTING BENEFITS OF GEOGRAPHIC ARBITRAGE

Moving location isn't only about saving money; it's about designing a life with flexibility built in. The most resilient families today think beyond postal codes, they think in plans.

While the ultra-wealthy have long diversified across countries through what's known as 'flag theory', holding citizenship, assets and business interests in multiple jurisdictions, you don't need five flags to build freedom. You just need one intentional move that gives you more breathing room.

We call this idea the 'everyday Plan B'. It's about creating a small but powerful form of location diversification that fits ordinary lives:

- **Plan B income:** A remote job, a freelance contract or a side online business that can move with you.
- **Plan B location:** A city, region or country where the cost of living and pace of life align better with your values.
- **Plan B network:** Friends, colleagues or family abroad who can help you test a new environment.

Even if you never leave your home country, simply exploring a Plan B option broadens your sense of control. It changes the mental frame from 'I have to stay' to 'I get to choose'.

If you decide to relocate, begin with a three-month trial. Rent before buying, join local groups, learn how people live day to day. Building community early turns relocation from a financial move into a life upgrade. A few of the key considerations to keep in mind when choosing a new location are:

Financial trade-offs

Each country has its own tax and healthcare rules. Research double-tax treaties, possible exit taxes and local registration requirements carefully. If you work remotely, confirm where your income is taxed and where you can access healthcare. Tools such as Wise or Revolut Business simplify international payments and multi-currency accounts, making it easier to manage cross-border income efficiently and compliantly.

Long-term resilience

A single postal code ties you to one economy, one tax regime and one job market. A Plan B mindset builds resilience and optionality into your life, like a backup generator for your freedom. If one economy slows, another may be rising; if one currency weakens, your savings or income elsewhere provide balance.

Psychological benefits

Exploring new environments resets habits. Different surroundings often lead to simpler living, richer relationships and less stress-driven spending. Many people find that moving, even locally, breaks emotional inertia and revives creativity.

The lesson is simple: you don't need offshore empires or multiple passports to live strategically. For a few, a second passport or residency expands their options. But for most, the real passport that matters is the one to flexibility – earning, living and investing across borders when life calls for it. Geography is a lever, not a limit.

THE EVERYDAY PLAN B LIFE WHEEL

A simple reminder that freedom expands when at least one of these areas becomes flexible.

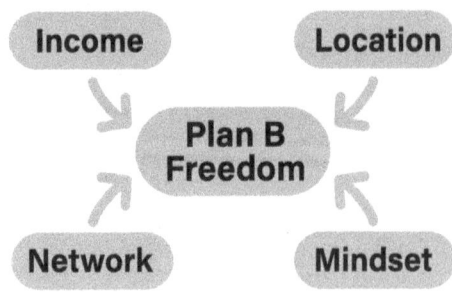

DO YOU NEED A PLAN B? THE FREEDOM CHECK-IN

If you're like many individuals and families we meet, you can feel the tension rising. Life in much of the Western world feels heavier: higher bills, shrinking privacy, longer hours, shorter patience. You're earning, but not advancing. You might be comfortable, yet feel restless.

So, pause and scan this QR code to take a quiz we created, not to judge your life, but to re-evaluate where it's heading to see if you need a Plan B.

The quiz will reveal one of three options: i) optimize where you are, ii) explore your options and start scanning, iii) begin designing your Plan B life now.

If the idea of moving feels impossible right now, you're not alone. For most people, the barriers are real, for example, children in school, ageing parents, familiar routines, limited savings or the fear of losing community. But progress doesn't always mean relocation; it can start with exploration. Visit for a week, research remote roles, build savings with intention. Each small step builds confidence and options. Freedom grows from curiosity, not certainty.

Remember, a Plan B doesn't always mean emigrating. For some, it's relocating to a smaller city where money stretches further and community still runs deep. For others, it's securing remote work, exploring Africa, the Caribbean, the Middle East or Asia for a season, or building assets that buy time freedom. The point isn't to flee, it's to reclaim choice.

Your Location-Leverage Loop will help you explore that choice systematically, so your next move, whether across town or across continents, expands both your wealth and your wellbeing.

FRAMEWORK: THE LOCATION-LEVERAGE LOOP

The Location-Leverage Loop is a four-stage system that transforms geography from a constraint into a wealth-building ally: **scan, select, shift, synergize**.

- **Scan:** Gather data on the cost of living, regulation, safety, healthcare and lifestyle. Use Numbeo, Organisation for Economic Co-operation and Development (OECD) indices or local forums.
- **Select:** Choose optimal destinations, domestic or international,

aligned with your financial, lifestyle and family priorities, e.g. schools, community, career.
- **Shift:** Relocate in phases: first domestic move, then temporary relocation via digital-nomad visa, then residency or citizenship, if desired or possible.
- **Synergize:** Align banking, tax and lifestyle systems for ongoing arbitrage: remote income, plus local cost savings, plus global investment access.

It's a simple loop: awareness leads to choice, choice to movement, movement to integration and integration feeds back into awareness as your life evolves.

Continuous Learning and Lifestyle Optimization

One lesson many movers learn the hard way is to keep your plans private until they're real. Moving, whether ten miles or ten time zones, can stir strong emotions in others. People often project their own fears or feel left behind. Protect your peace, plan quietly and share only when decisions are made. It's easier to move forwards when you're not defending your choices.

Let's now look at how you can apply each stage of the Location-Leverage Loop to your own life.

Scan your map

Start with your current reality. List major expenses: housing, transport, childcare, taxes. Use public databases to compare other regions or countries. Quantify, don't romanticize.

Don't rely on glossy blogs or hearsay. The best research comes from people already living the life you're considering. Join private Facebook or Reddit groups for your target city, listen to their challenges and ask what they wish they'd known before moving. You'll get unfiltered insights that no relocation guide will ever show you. In addition, you can find recommended relocation experts and advisers in such groups to guide you on any complexities.

Select with values and seasons

Wealth isn't just numbers, it's alignment. Ask, 'Does this location support our long-term goals – financial, educational, spiritual and social?' The best choice is the one that maximizes freedom and fulfilment.

Your ideal location also often depends on your season of life. If you're still building income or a business, you need proximity to networks, clients and opportunity, not a remote village with patchy Wi-Fi. If you're well established, the equation changes: you might trade noise for nature, speed for space or meetings for meaning.

Pick the wrong setting for your season and you risk either burning out or stagnating. The right move aligns your geography with your goals, not just your cost of living.

Shift in phases

Relocation works best in phases. Treat it as an experiment. Start with a short domestic trial, perhaps a six-month rent in Manchester or Nottingham to test costs, schools and community fit. Keep core income stable (remote work or freelance) while testing the new environment.

Once confident, explore international options, such as Portugal's Lisbon or Valencia, Spain, where digital-nomad visas and quality-of-life metrics align. Each phase reduces risk while building experience.

No residency or tax regime lasts forever. Governments change rules faster than families can adapt. Portugal's Non-Habitual Residency (NHR) scheme closed to new applicants after a decade; Spain's 'Beckham Law' has tightened over time; digital-nomad visas come with expiry dates and renewal uncertainty. What looks safe today may be gone tomorrow. That's why flexibility, not perfection, is the real asset. Your goal isn't to find one forever place but to build optionality into your plan.

Synergize your systems

Once you've made a move, the goal is to align your financial, legal and lifestyle systems so they work together rather than against you. This is the stage where your new environment stops feeling temporary and starts operating like a long-term asset.

Begin with the basics. Set up local accounts for daily expenses, automate savings and investments and use tools such as Wise, Revolut or Monzo to move money efficiently across borders. These multi-currency platforms let you hold and send funds in different currencies with minimal fees, protecting you from exchange-rate losses and delays.

It's also wise to open at least one international or secondary bank account outside your primary country of residence. This isn't about secrecy, it's about continuity and control. In recent years, thousands of UK residents have had accounts restricted or closed due to tightening compliance rules. A second account, whether in another country or through a regulated digital bank, acts as a safety valve. If one door closes, your life and business don't grind to a halt.

Governments don't need your permission to change the rules. Banks can freeze accounts, residency laws can flip and the push for digital ID systems can alter access overnight. Structure protects you.

Keeping at least one international bank account, a digital wallet or dual-currency setup provides peace of mind. It's not about distrust, it's about design. When one system stalls, another keeps you moving.

Everyone chases the same global cities like, London, New York and Dubai, yet outsized returns and better lifestyles are often found in undervalued places quietly rising.

Cities like Valencia in Spain, Kraków in Poland, Nairobi in Kenya and Ho Chi Minh City in Vietnam combine strong infrastructure, low living costs and an entrepreneurial heartbeat. The future rarely starts in the world's most established capitals; it grows on the edges, where ambition meets affordability.

When your finances, paperwork and lifestyle flow together across trusted platforms, you unlock genuine location leverage, the flexibility to live, earn and bank with confidence wherever life takes you, without being dependent on a single system or postal code.

THE LOOP IN ACTION: FROM LONDON, UK, TO SHARJAH, UAE

Amina Yonis, a 30-something millennial and mother of two, was born and raised in east London to Ethiopian parents. She built an impressive academic career, earning a PhD in cancer research before founding a growing online education business, The Page Doctor. Life was good, but by the time her children reached nursery age, she and her husband began to feel squeezed.

Nursery fees rivalled their mortgage, taxes kept rising and the quality of family life was slipping. 'We weren't running away from London,' she said. 'We were asking where our family could grow better.'

They began to scan new possibilities, exploring Malaysia, Singapore and the United Arab Emirates. The UAE stood out for its safety, warm climate and forward-thinking attitude to entrepreneurship and technology. 'The mentality here is: we want the next generation to be better than the one before,' Amina explained. 'You can feel that belief in possibility everywhere, not just among Emiratis, but in everyone who moves here.'

They selected Sharjah, a quieter, greener emirate just 20 minutes from Dubai, where housing and schooling costs were lower and the lifestyle more family oriented. 'Dubai is exciting, but Sharjah felt right for this season,' she told us. 'It's safe, community-focused and grounded. The children can play outside freely and our day-to-day costs are far lower.'

The family shifted using a one-year remote work visa, keeping their UK business running while testing life in the UAE. Within months, their outgoings dropped sharply: utility bills were a fraction of what they'd paid in London and their children's nursery fees and rent halved, though upfront payments were structured differently, for example, rent was typically paid six months in advance. 'Once you've made that payment, you can breathe,' Amina explained. 'Our monthly bills are low and the extra space makes it worth it.'

Amina's synergy came from rethinking how and where she worked. Her UK company continued operating, but she set up a second business licence in the UAE, opened a local account and began collaborating with universities and education bodies there, opportunities that had been harder to access in the UK. 'In the UK, it often felt like there was a ceiling. Here, it feels like anything is possible.'

Beyond the numbers, what struck her most was the sense of safety and freedom. 'I can leave my laptop in a public library for an hour and it'll still be there when I return,' she said. 'That peace of mind alone has changed how I live.'

She also noticed a different kind of value, one rooted in accountability. 'I don't mind paying tax,' Amina said. 'I just like to see where it's going. Here, things work. When something breaks, it's fixed. You can see your contribution in the quality of life around you.'

For Amina, the move wasn't permanent, it was a one-year experiment that turned into a new chapter. Her family still visits the UK each summer and may return one day, but for now, she calls Sharjah home – not as an escape, but as an evolution.

Her story embodies the Location-Leverage Loop in motion: scanning, selecting, shifting and synergizing until her environment worked for her family, not against them.

PAUSE FOR REFLECTION

Take ten minutes to journal the following:

- If I could work from anywhere in the world for the same income, where would I choose to live and why?
- What three things stop me from moving or even exploring that option?
- Which cost of living or quality-of-life factor is hurting my financial progress most right now?

Awareness creates momentum. Sometimes the only thing keeping you stuck is assuming you have to stay put.

> *Small action step*
> Open Numbeo.com.[77] Compare your current city with two alternatives,[78] one domestic and one international. Note the difference in housing, utilities, transport, childcare, restaurants and groceries. Next, calculate what a 20% reduction in expenses would mean for your savings or investment rate. Even if you never move, the exercise reveals how much geography affects wealth. The first step to location leverage is data.

Relocation is a one-off action; wealth habits make it sustainable. Track your savings rate monthly, re-evaluate annually and stay open to the next iteration of the loop. Your goal is not constant movement but continuous optimization.

The ultimate wealth habit is sovereignty; the ability to live and earn on your own terms. That doesn't mean isolation, it means independence. When you're no longer bound to one employer, one postal code or one government's permission, you experience a quieter kind of freedom, the freedom to choose, adapt and breathe.

Every generation faces a different form of mobility. For our parents, it was leaving their home countries for opportunity. For us, it might be shifting postal code or continent to preserve freedom. The Global-Wealth Habit is not about restlessness or escape. It is about choice, the freedom to decide where your money and values can coexist best.

When you see geography as a variable, not a given, you take control of one of the largest levers in your financial life. And with remote work, digital businesses and rising global connectivity, this lever is more accessible than ever.

We moved once and felt its impact, not because our income changed, but because our environment did. Freedom isn't just earned, sometimes it's found on a new street, in a new city or under a different sky.

Chapter summary

- Challenge location complacency – your postal code is a financial decision.
- Use cost-of-living, tax and quality-of-life differences to expand wealth and freedom.
- Use the Location-Leverage Loop Framework – scan, select, shift, synergize, then repeat for continuous optimization – to make the most of where you live.
- Compare data, test moves in phases and automate savings from any cost gains.
- Geographic arbitrage is not a trend; it's a mindset of mobility and resilience, living where your money and values stretch furthest.

Chapter 16

THE FINANCIAL-FREEDOM CALENDAR

The power of weekly, monthly and yearly money rituals

> **Theme: Rhythmic reinforcement**
> With multiple habits humming, you set up a calendar of check-ins and reviews that keeps your entire system healthy over years.

> 'Now Joshua was old, advanced in years. And the Lord said to him: "You are old, advanced in years and there remains very much land yet to be possessed."'[79]

There's an ancient story about a leader named Joshua who, even after a lifetime of victories, was told there was still more land to claim – a reminder that life's work is rarely complete. The message wasn't about endless conquest, it was about faithful stewardship. Even after seasons of achievement, there is always purpose beyond accumulation – work that refines us, impacts others and keeps what we've built alive.

The same is true of our financial lives. Working until retirement and then stopping isn't the goal. Freedom isn't about chasing more; it's about managing well what you already have and continuing to live with purpose, whether that purpose earns money or not. The Financial-Freedom Calendar helps you do just that. By building weekly, monthly and yearly rituals into your life, it turns money from a one-off project into a living rhythm, one that keeps your financial life meaningful, balanced and sustainable long after the world says you should stop.

Wealth is not built in one dramatic moment. It is built in rhythms. Think about it: every athlete has a training calendar. Every successful business has a reporting cycle. Every strong marriage has regular check-ins. Yet most people treat their finances like a 'once in a while' event, only facing them when forced to – after a bill, a crisis or a tax letter. The result? Drift. Missed opportunities. Slow leaks that compound into financial stress.

The truth is: your money needs a calendar just as much as your body needs meals and rest. A Financial-Freedom Calendar is not about more complexity, it's about setting simple weekly, monthly and yearly rituals that keep your wealth habits alive. Done right, it takes less than an hour a week but rewires the trajectory of your financial life.

WEALTH RHYTHMS AROUND THE WORLD

Around the world, people have long understood that rhythm is the quiet engine of progress, each culture expressing it in its own way.

KAKEIBO, THE ART OF MINDFUL SPENDING

In Japan, the practice of *kakeibo*, often called the 'art of mindful spending', goes back over a century.[80] Families would keep handwritten journals of their daily purchases, but the power of the practice lies in reflection. Putting pen to paper forces the brain to process more detail than digital tracking ever could. You don't just note the amount, you consider why you spent it, how it made you feel and whether it aligned with your priorities.

Practitioners often dedicate five minutes at a set time each week to this ritual. Some even advocate using cash, since the act of handing over physical notes makes spending more accountable. The mantra is simple: 'Spend well to save well.' Over time, this mindfulness transforms not just spending but life itself.

Esusu and *stokvel,* wealth through rhythm

Across West Africa, there is a centuries-old financial practice called *esusu* (sometimes called *ajo* in Nigeria and *susu* in Ghana). In South Africa, a similar system is known as a *stokvel*. At its core, the idea is simple: a group of people commit to contributing a fixed sum on a regular basis (weekly or monthly) and the pooled money is given to one member in turn. The cycle repeats until everyone has had their share.

On paper, it looks like nothing more than a rotating savings plan. But in practice, it is so much more. Each contribution date becomes a ritual. Members gather, share food or stories and hand over their contribution. It's not just about money, it's about accountability, trust and rhythm. By keeping to the calendar, members not only build financial resilience but also strengthen community ties.

We once spoke with a woman in Lagos, Nigeria, who has used *esusu* groups for over 20 years. Every Friday, she and a circle of ten women contributed a fixed sum. Her turn to receive the lump sum often fell near school term time, allowing her to pay fees in one go. Others used their turn to buy bulk goods,[81] start side businesses or fund weddings. Without access to formal loans, this rhythm was their financial lifeline.

In South Africa, *stokvels* have grown into a national force. Research by Ipsos estimates that nearly 11 million South Africans participate in over 800,000 *stokvel* groups, collectively saving over R50 billion ($2.8 billion) annually.[82] And these arrangements have evolved. Today, many *stokvels* aren't just saving for groceries or school fees, they're pooling resources for big-ticket purchases like homes and even long-term investments in shares and other assets.

These aren't fringe practices, they are mainstream systems powered by rhythm, proving that disciplined rituals can scale from daily survival to serious wealth building.

What makes them powerful is not just the money exchanged but the predictability of the ritual. Everyone knows when the contribution is due. Everyone knows when their turn is coming. This structure prevents drift, enforces discipline, builds accountability and transforms scattered intentions into collective progress.

The lesson? Whether it's handwritten *kakeibo* journals in Japan or *esusu* gatherings in Africa, the principle is the same: money grows stronger when it follows a rhythm.

> **Wealth Habit Mantra 16:**
> Financial freedom isn't built in one-off decisions – it's sustained through weekly, monthly and yearly rituals that keep your money aligned with your vision.

WHY FINANCIAL CHECK-INS ARE CRITICAL TO LONG-TERM SUCCESS

Most people fail with money not because they lack income, but because they lack rhythm. Research consistently shows that people who review their finances regularly are far more likely to reach their goals. Morningstar's renowned *Mind the Gap* studies reveal that the average investor captures 1.7% less[83] than their funds' returns each year because of poorly timed trades – buying high during optimism and selling low in panic. Regular check-ins don't magically boost returns; they build the disciplined behaviours that prevent these costly mistakes.

When individuals review their finances consistently – weekly, monthly or quarterly – they're more likely to stay invested, automate contributions and resist reacting emotionally to market swings. This rhythm of engagement, backed by decades of behavioural finance research, encourages people to stick with long-term plans, make thoughtful adjustments and stay grounded in reason rather than headlines. Across studies and economies, the same pattern holds true: financial resilience grows not from income or luck, but from consistency and adaptability over time.

Some argue that investors might be better off not checking their portfolios at all, with less temptation to sell and fewer emotional swings. There's truth to that. Behavioural economists call it 'myopic loss aversion'[84] – the more often we look, the more likely we are to overreact to short-term fluctuations or losses. But the answer isn't to look away, it's to look with purpose. Intentional, rhythmic reviews – done monthly or quarterly, not daily – shift you from emotional reaction to mindful stewardship. Over time, this discipline strengthens confidence and detachment, allowing you to stay invested while still staying in control.

Hot tips spread fast – WhatsApp groups, X threads, YouTube shorts. The danger isn't information, it's impulse. That's where your 24-Hour Pause Button from Chapter 11 comes in. Use it here: wait, reflect, then act only at your next scheduled review. Rhythm beats rush.

Money decisions compound in silence. Small leaks, such as an unused subscription, a creeping lifestyle cost or a forgotten direct debit, seem trivial on their own. Left unchecked for months, they quietly erode progress. A weekly review catches the leak early. A monthly review realigns goals. An annual review ensures your trajectory matches your life's vision.

Think about your health. Fitness requires regular check-ins, for example, daily steps, monthly weigh-ins and annual health checks. Money works the same way.

Check-ins also nurture self-control and accountability. Many people admit they avoid looking at their finances because they 'don't want to know the damage'. Yet predictability reduces fear. Like shining a torch in a dark room, check-ins reveal the truth and the truth is always easier to manage than the unknown. Scheduled reviews create feedback loops that rebuild confidence after setbacks, help spot small deviations before they spiral and encourage shared responsibility within families. Money moves from secrecy to teamwork, replacing tension with trust.

Ultimately, financial check-ins aren't about chasing higher returns, they're about reinforcing the behaviours that create them. Each review strengthens patience, discipline and automation. Over time, those habits close the gap between what your investments could earn and what you actually keep. In volatile markets and through life's changes, rhythm – not reaction – is what separates those who drift from those who build lasting wealth.

THE KEY MONEY HABITS TO IMPLEMENT ON A REGULAR SCHEDULE

So, what belongs on your Financial-Freedom Calendar? Think of it in three layers: weekly tune-ups, monthly deep dives and annual reviews.

Weekly (15–20 minutes)

- Check bank balances and credit cards.
- Review upcoming bills and income.
- Cancel one unused subscription or unnecessary expense.
- Discuss one financial decision with your spouse/partner, if applicable.

This weekly rhythm keeps you present. It's like brushing your teeth – you prevent cavities before they form.

Example in our lives: We like to go for a walk of up to 45-minute to discuss how we feel as the world around us changes or gets more expensive, plus what we are doing about any unexpected or planned expenses in the week.

Monthly (60–120 minutes)

- Review full spending categories.
- Track progress towards savings or debt-reduction goals.
- Adjust automatic transfers if income/expenses have shifted.
- Schedule a 'money date' or family dinner conversation.

The monthly review is where you zoom out. Think of it as your 'financial health check'.

Examples in our lives: We have a monthly 'money day', either at home or out in a different environment, like a cafe or restaurant. This meeting usually lasts for two to three hours and begins with an agenda. We typically discuss:

- How we're doing as a couple and as a family, emotionally, physically, financially and spiritually, and what we've done to grow as individuals.
- Top five financial highlights for the month.
- Our key incomes and expenses against our goals for the year.
- We discuss our net worth (mainly investments) for us and our children.
- Assess liquidity and flexibility in our investments and how that's growing.
- Any noteworthy news or trends and how they might affect our family plans.
- We repeat this for our business.
- Finally, we discuss any expectations for the upcoming month in terms of key events or cash flow.

Yearly (half-day to a full day)

- Review investment performance versus goals.
- Rebalance portfolios where necessary.
- Plan for tax allowances: Individual Savings Accounts (ISA), Self-Invested Personal Pension (SIPP), Tax-Free Savings Account (TFSA), Roth Individual Retirement Accounts (Roth IRA) or local equivalent.
- Set financial goals for the next 12 months, with a focus on aligning money with life priorities.

This annual ritual is about resetting the compass. It's when you ensure your money serves your bigger mission: family, freedom, legacy.

Some people add seasonal reviews, like quarterly check-ins to adjust budgets or savings based on life rhythms (e.g. school terms, bonus cycles). The point isn't rigidity but rhythm. Money habits, like exercise, only stick when tied to predictable moments in your life.

Examples in our lives: Every other quarter, we have a 'baecation' (a trip without children) to reconnect and reimagine life. These trips are often local, for example, one night in a local hotel or a budget weekend away to a European city. Annually, we like to have a major life review tied-in with our planned family holiday, so that we're inspired in a new environment and free of our usual routines. Our most recent one was a trip to Singapore, to explore opportunities there, but also to create our 'ten-year plan'. Creating this plan took about five hours, with big conversations about our life's vision, asking: where do we want to live and why? What quality of life do we want? How do we further prioritize our health as we get older? What travel adventures do we want to experience? What stage of life will our children be in and what are the costs? Where are we now financially and how will that change with these plans? What do we need to start doing today and annually to make sure we are heading in the direction of our life's vision? Then, every year, we review how we're doing against this vision, make adjustments, while also considering whether it still serves us as the world around us changes. The goal with these annual reviews is to keep it fun and to dream big.

HOW TO CREATE A ROUTINE THAT KEEPS YOU FINANCIALLY FIT

The key is not just what you do, but how you structure it. Here are four principles to make your Financial-Freedom Calendar stick:

1: Anchor it to existing routines

Pick a day and time already associated with reflection. For example, Sunday evenings before the work week begins. Habits are more likely to stick when attached to existing cues, as you learned in Chapter 1.

2: Make it visible

Post your Financial-Freedom Calendar on the fridge, in your planner or as recurring events on Google Calendar. Visibility creates accountability and you're far more likely to achieve your aims. We use Google Calendar for recurring events, colour-coded for different themes, for example, weekly 'family events' in yellow, 'baecations' in coral, 'annual reviews' in green, etc.

3: Keep it short and consistent

Don't overcomplicate. Start with a 15-minute weekly check-in. Add monthly and yearly layers once the rhythm sticks. Progress, not perfection, is the goal.

4: Make it enjoyable

In Japan, *kakeibo* journals often become personal keepsakes. In Africa, *esusu* meetings are social gatherings. In your home, make it a money dinner, add music or light a candle. Ritual sustains rhythm.

Over time, these rituals become identity. You are no longer 'someone trying to manage money'. You become a household that stewards wealth. The same way a runner doesn't ask, 'Should I train today?' – they just run – you'll no longer ask, 'Should we check our finances?' You'll just do it.

This is how ordinary families become financially extraordinary.

FRAMEWORK: THE FINANCIAL-RHYTHM METHOD

This framework rests on four beats: **daily awareness, weekly tune-up, monthly deep dive, yearly rest**. Visualize it like a heartbeat. Each beat matters. Miss one and health declines. Together, they sustain life.

- **Daily awareness:** A quick glance at balances or transactions, keeping you connected to reality.
- **Weekly tune-up:** A 15-minute review of spending, bills and small course corrections. This can be enhanced by *kakeibo*'s five-minute handwritten reflection.

- **Monthly deep dive:** A fuller review of budgets, goals and allocations.
- **Yearly reset:** A half-day ritual for vision setting, tax planning and portfolio review.

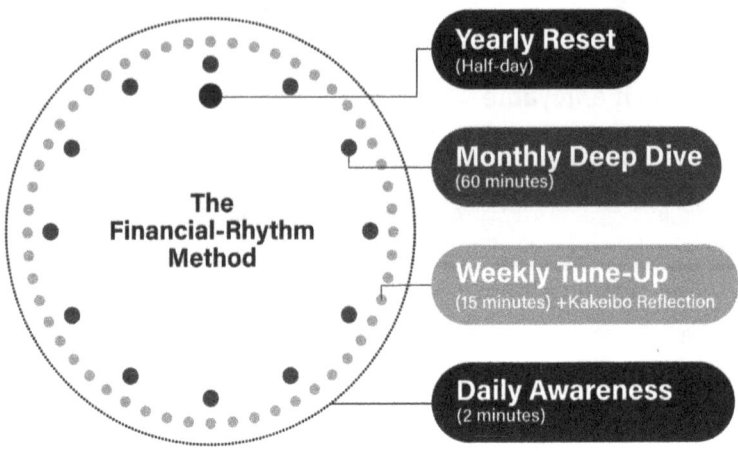

How it works

The Financial-Rhythm Method works because it replaces willpower with rhythm. Willpower fades; rhythm sustains. By combining systems (automation, reviews) with reflection (*kakeibo*) and accountability (*esusu*), you build financial fitness.

It adapts across life stages:

- **Singles:** Weekly check-ins prevent drift.
- **Couples:** Money dinners build trust.
- **Families:** Annual vision days align generations.
- **Communities:** *Esusu* and *stokvels* prove rhythm works collectively.

Behavioural finance confirms that consistent reviews reduce impulsivity and increase long-term goal success. Neuroscience shows handwriting deepens processing. Social sciences show group accountability strengthens discipline. Together, they prove the Financial-Rhythm Method isn't just theory, it's a global, proven rhythm.

PAUSE FOR REFLECTION

When was the last time you reviewed your finances – not in panic, but in peace? What would shift if you and your household set aside 15 minutes each week, one hour each month and one day each year to align money with vision? Write down three reasons you've avoided regular check-ins in the past. Now, write down three ways you could make them enjoyable and consistent going forwards.

> *Small action step*
>
> Open your calendar app right now. Block out three recurring events:
>
> - 15 minutes weekly (choose a fixed day and time).
> - 1 hour monthly (same day each month).
> - Half a day yearly (pick a date tied to a meaningful moment, like your birthday or new year).
>
> Label it 'Financial-Freedom Calendar'. That's it. You don't need a perfect system yet, just the rhythm. Every rhythm you set is an act of stewardship – a small declaration that your time and money will serve a greater purpose.

I, Ken, live by a philosophy I call 'take your place'. I haven't always believed in myself, but I've always believed in taking my place in the world. Even when I don't feel good enough, I keep showing up.

Years ago, I applied and got accepted to Cambridge University, unsure I belonged there. Later, when we wrote our first book *Financial Joy*, I questioned whether anyone would read it, but it went on to become a *Sunday Times* bestseller. Those moments taught me something simple: you don't need to feel ready to take your place.

That same philosophy guides me today. I've taken my place as a bestselling author, international speaker, creator, award-winning entrepreneur and, most importantly, a loving husband and father. First, I believe I have a place. Next, I take my place.

In the same way, financial freedom is never given to you – you have to take it by showing up, again and again. Setting up your Financial-Freedom Calendar is how you take your place in your financial life – a quiet act of courage and stewardship. It's your way of saying, 'I belong here. My future matters.' That's where true freedom begins.

Joshua was told there was still land to possess, even in his later years. That truth is just as real for us. No matter your age, income or stage of life, there is always more ground waiting to be claimed, not only in wealth, but in freedom, impact and legacy.

Your Financial-Freedom Calendar is how you take possession of that land. It's not a frantic sprint or a one-off victory. It's a rhythm – steady, repeatable steps that cover ground week by week, month by month, year by year.

So, do not think of retirement as the end. Do not think of age as disqualification. And do not think of freedom as a far-off dream. With each small ritual, you reclaim more of the land that belongs to you. Keep walking the calendar and you'll find the territory of financial freedom unfolding beneath your feet.

Chapter summary

- Joshua's reminder of 'unfinished land' shows freedom isn't a finish line but an ongoing journey.
- Wealth is built in rhythms, not one-off events.
- Financial check-ins prevent drift, reduce anxiety and build accountability.
- The Financial-Rhythm Method includes: daily awareness, weekly tune-ups (with *kakeibo*), monthly deep dives, yearly resets.
- Weekly rituals are for: checking balances and bills, reflection, cancellations.
- Monthly rituals are for: full review of spending and saving, goals, making adjustments.
- Yearly resets are for: reviewing investments, tax planning, vision setting.
- *Kakeibo* adds mindfulness. Handwriting reflections deepen awareness.
- *Esusu/stokvel* adds community rhythm. Collective check-ins build trust and resilience.
- The Financial-Freedom Calendar transforms money into stewardship. It keeps finances purposeful beyond retirement.
- Take your place. Financial freedom is never given to you; you have to take it by showing up, one rhythm at a time.

> ### Building The Wealth Habit
>
> ## Pillar 3: Build the System
> **Principle lens: Keep it compounding**
>
> You've connected habits into systems that grow beyond individual effort.
>
> This is where time becomes an ally, not a pressure.
>
> Ask yourself: *Where is time now doing more of the work than I am?*

PILLAR 4
BUILD THE LIFE

Chapter 17

THE GENEROSITY HABIT

Why giving makes you wealthier

> **Theme: Purpose**
> Having built and automated wealth, you now embed giving as a daily micro-habit – closing the loop from self-growth to community impact.

Generosity isn't subtraction, it's ignition.

Wealth multiplies the moment you open your hand, sparking abundance in your mindset, your community and your future. We don't get poorer by giving away good things; we get richer – in mind, relationships and legacy.

Across every faith, philosophy and field of research, one truth stands firm: those who give, receive. By spending on others' wellbeing, we strengthen our own. By letting go of some of what we own, we secure what truly matters.

THE NEAPOLITAN *CAFFÈ SOSPESO* – GENEROSITY IN AN ESPRESSO CUP

In a small café tucked in a Naples side street, a regular orders his morning espresso. But instead of paying for one, he pays for two – leaving one *sospeso* or 'suspended', for someone he'll never meet. Later that day, a jobless street poet walks in and quietly asks the barista, 'Is there a *sospeso?*' A smile follows; a free espresso slides across the counter – hot, strong and served not with pity, but dignity.

This ritual began during the hardships of early-20th-century Naples and surged again in the post-war years. Even as money grew scarce, generosity became routine: café patrons saw giving not as charity, but as community. The gesture cost less than a euro back then, yet created a culture of daily kindness. As a Neapolitan writer wrote:

> When a Neapolitan is happy, for some reason he decides to offer a coffee to a stranger, because it is like offering a coffee to the rest of the world.[85]

Today, cafés across Italy, and even abroad, honour *Caffè Sospeso* Day every 10 December, celebrating an idea that turns a simple purchase into a shared act of abundance. The same spirit now lives on in 'pay it forward' moments around the world – from Naples to Starbucks drive-throughs, where customers quietly cover the order of the person behind them. What began as a humble Neapolitan gesture has become a global ritual of everyday generosity.

From a single espresso in Naples to acts of compassion unfolding in the world's quietest corners, the law of generosity doesn't change – only its scale.

Globally, the World Giving Index[86] reveals a pattern that defies logic, but confirms humanity. The most generous nations aren't always the richest – Indonesia, Kenya and Nigeria all rank in the world's top five, each proving that generosity travels on spirit, not surplus.

Even in a world of uncertainty, giving hasn't retreated, it's resurged. In 2023, more than 4.3 billion people gave time, money or help to strangers, matching the highest level of global generosity ever recorded. Africa is now the only continent where generosity is rising across all three measures – giving money, volunteering time and helping a stranger. In Kenya and Nigeria, more than eight in ten adults helped a stranger last year, while The Gambia also ranks among the world's top five for overall generosity. It's a reminder that abundance is a mindset before it's a bank balance.

And in Singapore, one of the wealthiest nations on earth, generosity has been designed into the system through tax incentives, volunteer leave and matched-giving schemes, helping it rise to third place globally. It shows that when generosity is systemized, it multiplies.

Across continents, generosity and happiness move together. Communities that give most also trust most and thrive longest. The data tells one story, but humanity tells the same one louder: wherever generosity becomes habit, prosperity endures.

> **The Wealth Habit Mantra 17:**
> Wealth grows best in open hands, not closed fists.

HOW GENEROSITY SHIFTS YOUR FINANCIAL MINDSET FROM SCARCITY TO ABUNDANCE

Scarcity begins in the mind, not the wallet. It whispers: 'If I give, I'll have less.' Generosity replies: 'If I give, I'll have enough and more will flow through me.'

Behavioural research from the University of British Columbia found that even small acts of giving can lift our happiness.[87] In one series of studies, participants who spent a modest windfall, as little as $5 or $20, on others reported feeling happier than those who spent the same amount on themselves. The researchers went further: across a nationally representative survey, people who devoted a greater share of their income to others consistently reported higher wellbeing and, in follow-up field studies, those randomly assigned to spend money on others became happier than those told to spend it on themselves.

Neuroscience studies – including brain-imaging research from the University of Zurich[88] and the University of British Columbia – confirm why giving feels good: it activates the same reward circuits (known as the mesolimbic reward system[89]) that light up with food, love or connection, while calming the fear-based amygdala. This biological design is no accident; when generosity feels rewarding, we're wired to repeat it. Each act of release tells your body, 'I am safe.' Over time, repeated generosity rewires those neural pathways, training both brain and heart towards a stable, abundant identity.

The generosity paradox is ancient and universal: those who give, receive; those who grasp, lose. Across time and tradition, the message is clear – what you release returns, multiplied.

THE CONNECTION BETWEEN GIVING, PURPOSE AND LONG-TERM WEALTH

True wealth isn't just measured in assets and numbers; it's the lasting impact you create and the meaning you experience through life. Generosity anchors you to a purpose beyond consumption, a clear pathway to building 'wealth that lasts', both financially and emotionally.

Thinking back to my own personal journey, generosity didn't come naturally to me (Ken). However, my mum is the most successful person I know and the most generous. I have often wondered whether her giving spirit is something she was born with or something she learned. I believe it's more of the latter and when I began modelling her ways, everything changed.

Years ago, I started volunteering at City St George's, University of London, as a professional mentor. I'd give up my lunch breaks to meet a stranger and talk about their journey. After seven years, I had gained friends, life lessons and joy that money can't buy. Seeing the results of my giving kept me going year after year and created the foundation for the work we do at The Humble Penny and the Financial Joy Academy (FJA), without which this book would never have been written. That hour a week that I sowed looked like subtraction, but it multiplied my purpose and eventually gave me a new career. Although it has taken me a while, generosity now comes more naturally and remains an active journey. It's the purest form of joy that I experience, especially when done quietly and unexpectedly.

What's true in one life is echoed across communities everywhere. Across cultures, giving with purpose transforms both giver and community. Purpose anchors patience. It turns generosity into a feedback loop where meaning fuels money and money fuels meaning.

MAKING GENEROSITY A CORE WEALTH HABIT

Wealth leaks without structure; generosity channels it. Generosity isn't an occasional reaction – it's a repeatable habit that builds and sustains wealth. Regular giving systems are the keystone of every legacy-building framework, from the practice of tithing to modern tools like donor-advised funds.

Neuroscientists call this the reinforcement loop: each act of generosity activates the brain's reward pathways, strengthening the habit and lowering the emotional friction of giving again. Behavioural economists see the same pattern – pre-committing to generosity dramatically increases follow-through. Just as automatic investing compounds wealth, automatic giving compounds impact.

Across cultures the rhythm repeats. In Japan, the *furusato nozei* (hometown tax) programme lets residents redirect part of their taxes to support rural communities. In return, they receive a local thank-you gift, turning taxation into a gesture of connection between urban earners and the countryside. In Kenya, *harambee* gatherings raise collective funds for education and healthcare. In faith traditions, structured giving is both worship and wealth management – generosity ritualized as shared prosperity.

The science is clear: consistent generosity not only boosts wellbeing and life satisfaction, it correlates with lower stress and greater longevity. Each gift is a quiet act of trust that rewires scarcity into sufficiency.

Sociologists Christian Smith and Hilary Davidson, in *The Paradox of Generosity*, found that people who live generously score higher across five wellbeing metrics – happiness, health, purpose, lower depression and personal growth – with a causal loop: generosity breeds wellbeing, which in turn breeds generosity. When giving becomes rhythmic, gratitude has room to grow.

So, how do you make that rhythm sustainable? Build structure around it – simple, repeatable cues that keep generosity flowing even when motivation fades. Initiate the flow, pause to notice the impact, then reinforce it through celebration and small increases over time. Once generosity becomes scheduled, it stops competing with mood or memory, it becomes part of who you are.

Yet even the most generous hearts need balance. Giving without guardrails can slip into depletion or resentment. To sustain abundance, the open hand must also know when to rest.

Guardrails: Generosity with boundaries

Don't give to the point of leaving yourself broke, exhausted or in debt. We've seen people we've coached playing the rescuer or the people pleaser to the point where they give everything they have in disposable income and end up stuck themselves. Debt-fuelled giving breeds resentment.

- Don't enable people by giving too much, because it feeds the wrong habits. Help in ways that build capacity, not dependence.
- Set limits you can honour and don't get caught in the moment by overpromising. Specific promises protect both sides.

- Give what's useful, not just abundant, for example – time, attention and connections often matter more than cash.

The logic of gift

Across cultures, wise societies have recognized a logic of gift – the understanding that healthy economies depend not only on exchange but on grace. A world run purely on transaction loses its soul; generosity restores balance. When we give without expectation, we strengthen the social trust that allows prosperity to endure. The open hand doesn't weaken the market, it humanizes it.

The logic of gift reveals the deeper truth: giving isn't loss, it's circulation – the movement that keeps both wealth and wellbeing alive.

But insight alone isn't transformation. To live this truth, generosity needs a rhythm, a simple, repeatable flow that turns good intentions into embodied habit.

That rhythm is captured in what we call the Open-Hand Wealth Principle, the framework that transforms generosity from a moment into a lifestyle.

FRAMEWORK: THE OPEN-HAND WEALTH PRINCIPLE

At its core, this principle has five stages: **give, reflect, reinforce, repeat, legacy**. A closed fist hoards; an open hand circulates. The wider you open it, the stronger the return flow.

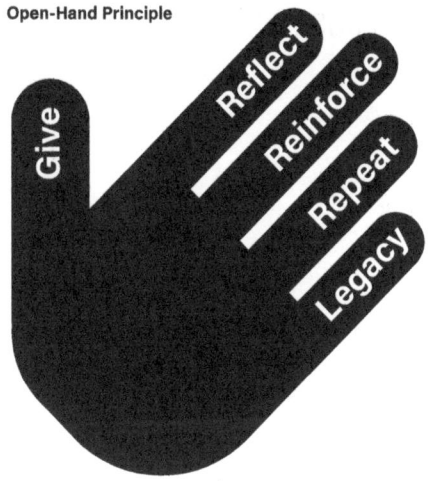

How it works

- **Give:** Spark movement; release resources or time.
- **Reflect:** Notice impact; internalize gratitude. Observe non-monetary returns, such as peace, creativity, relationships. Track the ripple. Keep an impact ledger to note how giving affects mindset and opportunities.
- **Reinforce:** Celebrate, record and scale the habit with rituals. End each week recalling one moment of giving and gratitude – what psychologists call savouring.[90]
- **Repeat:** Automate generosity with standing orders and donation apps. But be sure to prevent compassion fatigue by planning and budgeting generosity in a sustainable way.
- **Legacy:** Mentor, share credit and let kindness set the tone. Recognize the leadership dividends. Generosity builds stronger teams and boosts morale and loyalty. Lastly, consider family integration – if you have children, let them choose a cause each quarter, training empathy early.

PAUSE FOR REFLECTION

When did a small, quiet act of generosity change the course of your day or someone else's? Write the scene. What did that moment reveal about who you're becoming?

> *Small action step*
> To kick-start your generosity habit, try these:
>
> - **The generosity jot:** Each week, record one thing you gave, e.g. time, advice or money, and how it felt. Reflection hard-codes abundance.
> - **Micro-rituals:** Buy a stranger's coffee, check in on a friend, gift your seat, volunteer an hour. Each act trains the reflex of release.
> - **Practise the give first rule for 30 days:** Each time money or time enters your life, release 1% to someone or something that lifts others. After a month, you'll hold written proof that generosity compounds mood, motivation and opportunity.

Generosity is the final test of wealth. It asks: can you possess money without becoming possessed by it?

Each act of giving is a quiet declaration of freedom – proof that fear no longer commands you. It aligns you with an ancient rhythm older than any economy: the rhythm of sowing and reaping.

Keep your hand open long enough and you'll see: generosity isn't the end of abundance, it's where true wealth begins.

Chapter summary

- Generosity transforms scarcity into abundance and turns wealth from ownership into stewardship.
- Across cultures and centuries, it remains the universal law of increase: the more you release, the more life returns.
- Purpose-driven giving anchors meaning through every season and rewires your mind toward security and joy.
- The Open-Hand Wealth Principle – give, reflect, reinforce, repeat, legacy – turns generosity from an act into identity.
- Structured, reflective, joyful giving compounds trust, fulfilment and opportunity across generations.
- True wealth isn't measured by what you hold but by what flows through you.

Chapter 18

THE NETWORK EFFECT

How relationships build wealth

> **Theme: Leverage**
> With generosity in place, you harness relationships, building accountability circles and opportunity networks that amplify every habit.

THE WEALTH HABIT

Your relationships are your highest-leverage asset and the compound interest of human connections far outpaces any bank account.

If you stripped away your job title, income and possessions, what would remain? Your relationships – the invisible infrastructure of your future. Across every culture and economy, wealth has always travelled through human connection. Someone introduces you to a mentor who changes your trajectory. A friend recommends your business. A partner believes in you and your potential before the world does. Behind almost every success story, there's a quiet web of relationships amplifying that success. Yet, in our hyper-digital age, many of us have mistaken followers for friends and contacts for connections. We scroll more but connect less. This chapter is your reminder that money flows where trust and character go, and both live in relationships. Trust gets you in the room; character keeps you there. The wealthy don't just invest in stocks, they invest in people.

Across every field, from marketplaces around the world to offices in New York and startups in London, relationships remain the unseen accelerator of progress. Whether you're an employee seeking your next opportunity, a creative shaping ideas or a founder building a vision, your network determines the doors that open. The right relationships can shift a career, spark a business or change a life.

One story that captures this truth began in the UK, but its lessons travel anywhere people aspire to grow. It's the story of how trust, character and connection turned one man's idea into a movement.

HOW THREE RELATIONSHIPS LAUNCHED A MOVEMENT

When Dr Raphael 'Raph' Sofoluke launched the UK Black Business Show in 2017, the idea was small, but the relationships behind it were mighty. He credits three key relationships that turned a personal vision into a movement – providing emotional support, strategic access and a team culture strong enough to scale.

The foundation: his wife

Before he became known for building platforms and partnerships, Raph was a rapper. 'My life could have gone in a very different direction,' he says, 'but faith and my wife, Opeyemi, kept me grounded.' They met in 2009, married in 2016 and he calls her 'number one' in shaping his journey.

While she worked at J.P. Morgan, he moved through sales roles and early entrepreneurial experiments. There was never insecurity about income – only partnership. When a probationary job ended unfairly just as his side project gained press, he was devastated. 'She didn't shame me or panic. She said simply: "I've got you. I've got us. Find your feet".'

She helped him refine pitch decks, polish wording and level up his presentation. 'When someone believes you can do more,' he says, 'it gives you permission to aim higher.'

The game-changer: Sam Jennings and Clarion Events

During the pandemic, while working at Clarion Events, Raph entered a company-wide competition for a £15,000 ($20,000) innovation prize, submitting his idea just two minutes before the midnight deadline. The pitch earned applause but not the award.

'At the end, something told me to say what I actually do,' he recalls. So, he mentioned the UK Black Business Show to Sam Jennings, Clarion's head of mergers and acquisitions. That single sentence changed everything. Instead of taking his idea, Clarion chose to back him. 'They told me to quit my job and gave me money to build a team, plus an office next door to my old one. That's how the first UK Black Business Week began.'

Raph still had to produce full business plans and growth projections, but once approved, the support was transformative. With funding and mentorship from Jennings and Clarion's CEO, revenue tripled year after year, eventually crossing into seven figures. 'Sometimes you just need money and mentoring to take yourself to the next level.'

The pillars: Melina and Mags

Beyond family and mentors, two team members — now friends — became a part of his support system. 'Melina and Mags hold me up at work,' he says. 'When I'm low, they remind me to be myself and lead the team.' Their commitment goes beyond work: 'We pray and fast for the business. Sometimes when I can't, they fast on my behalf.' This shared spiritual discipline has become part of the culture — loyalty and belief woven into the business DNA.

Raph's story is the Network Effect in motion: connection creating collaboration and collaboration creating commitment. His marriage anchored belief; a mentor multiplied opportunity; a team protected the mission. Each relationship carried both trust and character — the twin currencies of sustainable success.

LESSONS ON RELATIONSHIP CAPITAL

Relationship capital multiplies when you pair belief with boldness.

- **Do the work first:** Relationships open doors only when proof of concept is visible.
- **Be a giver:** Generosity builds trust and draws people who amplify your vision.
- **Take calculated risks:** Whether it's a midnight submission or a bold investment, faith in your work often precedes favour.
- **Speak up:** A last-minute reveal of his idea unlocked a life-changing partnership.
- **Value mentorship as much as money:** Access, guidance and advocacy compound faster than cash.
- **Build a culture that believes:** Colleagues who support you and protect the vision are assets as real as investment.

> **The Wealth Habit Mantra 18:**
> Wealth compounds through connection. Build the bridges before you need them.

WHY FINANCIAL SUCCESS IS DEEPLY TIED TO RELATIONSHIPS AND CONNECTIONS

The Network Effect is the principle that your net worth grows in proportion to your network's depth, diversity and trust.

Economists describe success as a function of talent, effort and opportunity. But opportunity doesn't float randomly, it flows through people. In short, money follows your effort, but your network determines the quality of opportunity those efforts can access. Your network isn't just support; it's an asset class — one that compounds faster than any fund when trust and character fuel it.

In one of the most comprehensive studies of upward mobility, Raj Chetty and his team at Harvard analysed the social networks of over 20 million Americans. They found that children from low-income backgrounds who grew up in neighbourhoods with high 'social capital', i.e. connections to people with diverse incomes and careers, had significantly higher chances of escaping poverty.[91] Most strikingly, the study revealed that if children from poor families lived in neighbourhoods where 70% of their friends were wealthy (i.e. the typical rate of friendship for higher-income children) their incomes in adulthood would increase by about 20%, on average. This underscores how access to wealthier social networks can directly and powerfully shape a child's economic prospects.

In another research paper looking at how social networks affect stock market participation and savings behaviour in the US, they found that in counties where friendships with prosperous individuals were more common, investment and saving rates were noticeably higher.[92] More importantly, these friendships with wealthy individuals play a more important role in shaping people's financial behaviour than two other forms of social capital they studied — having a close circle of friends or living in a civically active community.

Of course, proximity to wealth alone doesn't guarantee financial success. But knowing people who invest can make the idea of investing feel more accessible and less intimidating, especially when those friends become informal guides, examples and sounding boards.

The lesson? Your relationships are ladders.

Strong ties provide stability, for example, the friends, family and mentors who stand by you. Weak ties (e.g. distant or casual friendships or followers on social media), meanwhile, provide new information and access to worlds beyond your own. This was first identified by sociologist Mark Granovetter in *The Strength of Weak Ties*,[93] which showed that people often find better jobs and opportunities through acquaintances than close friends.

The same applies to wealth. A friend-of-a-friend mentions a property deal, an investor connects you to a co-founder, or a former colleague introduces you to a mentor who sees what you can't. Wealth building is never a solo sport.

To make money is to move money, and money moves fastest through networks of trust.

HOW TO CULTIVATE A HIGH-VALUE NETWORK THAT BRINGS OPPORTUNITIES

A high-value network isn't about status, it's about symbiosis. Every person in it grows because of the others. Here's how to build yours intentionally:

Step 1: Map your current network

Start with what you have. Write down everyone in your orbit – friends, colleagues, mentors, acquaintances. Identify your 'circles of proximity':

- **Circle 1:** People you speak to weekly.
- **Circle 2:** People you speak to quarterly.
- **Circle 3:** People you admire but haven't met.

Your goal is to strengthen circle 1, nurture circle 2 and reach into circle 3.

Step 2: Diversify your connections

When everyone you know looks, thinks or earns like you, your network starts to echo itself. In our experience, people with more diverse networks across industries, ages and backgrounds generate better ideas. New voices bring new opportunities.

Step 3: Be in rooms where conversations compound

Certain conversations only happen in certain rooms. A single introduction in such spaces can rewrite your future. Prioritize environments that attract ambitious, values-driven people, for example, conferences, accelerators, mastermind circles or even volunteering initiatives. One well-chosen event can replace a year's worth of surface networking. We'd especially recommend paying to be in such rooms where in-person conversations happen.

Step 4: Lead with generosity and offer value first

People remember who helped them when they didn't have to. Offer introductions, share insights, give meaningful gifts, uplift others publicly. Neuroscience shows that acts of generosity, as we saw in Chapter 17, trigger dopamine in both giver and receiver, cementing stronger social bonds.

The currency of a network is not business cards, it's value given. When you ask, 'What can someone do for me?' you build a brittle network. When you ask, 'What value can I bring?' you become someone others want to connect with, others seek out. This flips the dynamic.

Step 5: Follow up like it matters – because it does

The average person forgets 70% of new connections within a week. Follow-up is where real networking begins. Send a brief, genuine message: 'I enjoyed our chat about X, here's an article I mentioned.' That's it. Authenticity beats eloquence. Over time, your follow-up reputation becomes your network advantage.

PRACTICAL STRATEGIES FOR NETWORKING AND LEVERAGING RELATIONSHIPS FOR FINANCIAL GROWTH

Now let's turn connection into tangible wealth outcomes.

Partner laterally

Find people at your level doing complementary work. If you teach online courses, partner with someone who designs websites or manages email marketing. Together, you can serve clients more holistically and split costs or referrals.

Host small, purposeful gatherings

Dinners and roundtables are timeless wealth accelerators. Keep them small (six to eight people), diverse and theme-focused, for example, 'How AI is changing small business.' When you convene people, you earn relational equity. You become the connector, the person people remember.

Create digital proximity

Use LinkedIn or YouTube posts to share consistent, useful content. Every post acts as a digital handshake and leads to more inbound opportunities than those who don't post. We personally aim to share at least two to three pieces of high-impact content on each platform per week. This could be newly created content or repurposed. The key is to remember it's about them first, before it becomes about you, so offer value always.

Track your Network ROI

Keep a simple log: who you met, what value you gave and what came of it. Review quarterly. Like financial capital, social capital compounds when tracked intentionally.

A practical rule of thumb: every month, reconnect with one person from your past, meet one new person in your field and add value to one person ahead of you. Three acts, infinite returns.

Blend authenticity with ambition

People can sense if they're being 'networked'. Aim to connect, not collect. When your motive is mutual growth, opportunity finds you.

The most important relationship ROI: who you marry

No relationship influences your wealth trajectory more than your partner. Your spouse (or life partner) is not just your emotional counterpart, they are your financial co-founder. They'll either be the making of you or, in time, break you financially.

We've been happily married for 14 years so far and we know with certainty that we've built wealth, reached financial independence, avoided money fights and created a stable environment for our children because we married the right person for the right reasons.

We didn't come from money, but we saw potential in each other and, more importantly, we were aligned on mindset, values, faith and life vision. We also had safeguards around us to help us flourish, for example, our loving parents, siblings whose examples (good and bad) taught us, mentors who shared wisdom from their successful or struggling marriages, and friends who love and support us. Finally, our church community prayed for us and helped us start well through weeks of marriage preparation classes – including one on managing money together.

Long-term studies from the University of Georgia[94] show that financial satisfaction is significantly higher in couples who align on values, spending and saving priorities, and who treat money as a shared household asset rather than separate property. Agreement on spending matters most, since its effects are felt daily, while saving disagreements surface more slowly. The key drivers are trust, communication and a shared sense of 'ours', not 'mine'. In short, financial peace in marriage comes from unity, not uniformity – agreement over control and partnership over possession. With this as a foundation, even if you face financial stress, you're far more likely to tackle it as a unit and come out of it still together.

Consider what a healthy financial partnership brings:

- **Compound ambition:** When you both think long-term, wealth goals double in velocity.
- **Mutual accountability:** You become each other's mirror, reinforcing the right habits – saving, investing and generosity.
- **Network merging:** Two circles merge into one powerful ecosystem of opportunity.

- **Emotional resilience:** A supportive partner amplifies confidence in calculated risks – from changing careers to launching ventures. Such resilience is also priceless during difficult times such as job losses or health problems.

Marriage, when grounded in shared purpose and trust, becomes the most profitable partnership of your life. The reverse is also true – misaligned financial values, lack of commitment and abuse (physical, financial, psychological or coercive control) can quietly erode progress.

Choose and continually invest in the person who multiplies your peace and your potential.

Charlie Munger said this on Mistakes To Avoid In Life:[95]

We all know people who are out-married – their spouses are so much better. Think what a good decision that was for them, way more important than money. Many did it young; they stumbled into it. You don't have to stumble into it, you can be very careful. A lot of people are wearing signs: 'Danger, danger, do not touch,' and people just charge right ahead. That's a mistake.

Choose wisely, grow together and you'll find that love aligned with purpose compounds faster than any investment.

THE HABIT-CHANGING POWER OF COMMUNITY

Communities accelerate what individuals sustain. Psychologists call this 'social contagion' – the phenomenon where habits spread through proximity.

The Network Effect

When you surround yourself with people who discuss investments, growth and purpose, those conversations become your new normal.

Community doesn't just provide encouragement, it rewires what you believe is possible. Here is a story from Bena Nakawuki, a member of the Financial Joy Academy (FJA):

> Growing up in London, UK, in a working-class Ugandan household, financial literacy was never taught to me. My mum, a nurse, worked constantly to raise four children. My money mindset was simple: get a good education, get a stable 9–5, save what you can. I did exactly that through my twenties and thirties because anything beyond that just wasn't in my frame of reference. I never saw wealth or financial freedom modelled in a way that looked like me or made sense to me.
>
> Fast-forward to 2022, when I stumbled across a Humble Penny YouTube video on breaking the cycle of being broke. That video had a profound impact on me. For the first time, I realized the traditional work model wasn't the only path. It stirred something in me and sparked a journey of learning about financial independence and FIRE (Financial Independence, Retire Early).
>
> That search led me to Ken and Mary's community, FJA. It was refreshing – honestly, healing – to finally find a group of like-minded people who looked like me, understood my background and were working towards similar goals. In a short time, my entire attitude towards money shifted. I began investing for wealth, something I would never have attempted without FJA's resources and support.
>
> One of the best things about being in community is knowing you're not alone. Entrepreneurship, investing, property, even

day-to-day finances can feel overwhelming and lonely. Without FJA, I can honestly say I would have either given up or, worse, never started. The opportunity cost of that would have been huge.

A year into the journey, I had completely cleared my debts. For years I'd carried several thousands of pounds, feeling trapped and powerless. Becoming debt-free felt liberating. It gave me options. Since then, I've begun investing consistently, opened Individual Savings Accounts (ISAs) and created new income streams online and in property.

I've learned that many of us don't fail because we lack ambition, we fail because we lack accountability and community. Accountability actually works! I even launched a website, Benalicious.com, after procrastinating for years. Sharing it in the community finally moved it from idea to action.

There's an African proverb that says, 'If you want to go fast, go alone. If you want to go further, go together'. For me, that's exactly what the FJA community represents and why I'm so grateful.

This story illustrates a deeper truth: community compounds consistency. You borrow courage from others until it becomes your own.

Community is the habit keeper. It holds you accountable when motivation fades, celebrates small wins and normalizes wealth building as a lifestyle, not a season.

HOW TO NURTURE A COMMUNITY THAT MULTIPLIES YOUR HABITS

Your goal is not just to join a community, but to contribute to one. The giver becomes the anchor, the connector, the person who multiplies value for everyone else. And wealth, being reciprocal by nature, finds its way back.

- **Show up consistently:** Regular presence builds trust faster than enthusiasm.
- **Add value first:** Share insights, introductions or encouragement before you seek help.
- **Create touchpoints:** Join group calls, host small gatherings or start accountability threads.
- **Be the anchor:** Every thriving community needs connectors; become one.

FRAMEWORK: THE RELATIONSHIP ROI MODEL

Here is a simple framework that shows you how the right relationships yield the highest returns in wealth, wellbeing and opportunity: **connect, collaborate, commit.**

- **Connect:** Reach across boundaries and initiate genuine contact.
- **Collaborate:** Exchange value, ideas and form opportunities.
- **Commit:** Build trust that compounds over time through consistency and contribution, forming lifelong allies.

Each loop through this model strengthens the social fabric that supports your financial growth.

THE WEALTH HABIT

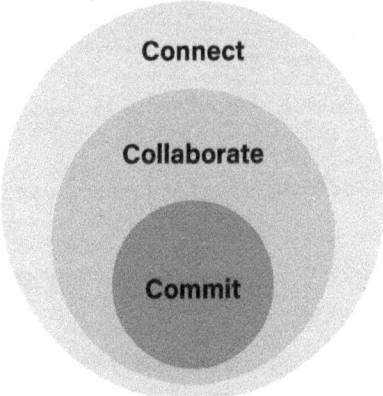

The Relationship ROI Model

Wealth flows inwards through these layers and outwards again through generosity. Allow community to reinforce your habits. Repeat this cycle intentionally and the compounding begins.

PAUSE FOR REFLECTION

Ask yourself:

- Which three people in my network have I unintentionally neglected? What one value I can give them this week?
- When was the last time I helped someone without expecting anything in return?
- Who are my 'five growth allies' – people whose mindset elevates mine?
- Does my partner (if you have one) accelerate or hamper my network-growth efforts? What conversation do I need to have?
- Am I currently in a community that aligns with my ambition and

celebrates progress, not perfection? If not, what group could I join or create?

Write names down for some of these questions. Reach out to one of them today with a simple message: 'I appreciate what you're building. How can I support you?'

You'll be surprised how quickly your next breakthrough travels through that bridge.

> *Small action step*
> This week, invite one person to have coffee – someone outside your immediate circle (a weak tie). Before the meeting, prepare three ways you can add value to them (introduction, insight, resource). After the meeting, schedule a follow-up and send a thank-you note. This one action alone is the gateway to many more. Then, schedule this task quarterly so network building becomes rhythm, not random.

At the start of your wealth journey, you may think you're climbing alone. But the higher you go, the clearer it becomes: no one reaches the summit solo.

Relationships are the ropes that pull you forwards when the climb gets steep. Every mentor, collaborator or supportive partner becomes part of your safety net and your springboard.

As you grow your network, remember: the goal is not to know more people, but to know more deeply. Wealth multiplies through trust, not transactions.

So, keep showing up. Keep connecting authentically. Because every meaningful conversation you have today could be the opportunity that shapes your tomorrow.

Chapter summary

- Wealth flows through relationships – the bridges between opportunity and action.
- Financial success is relational, not just rational.
- Cultivate a high-value, diverse network grounded in generosity, trust and character.
- Turn connections into collaborations and commitments that compound over time.
- Recognize that your most important partnership, your spouse or life partner, carries the highest relational ROI.
- Embed yourself in a community that normalizes accountability and wealth building as a way of life.
- When you invest in people with the same consistency that you invest in markets, you activate the greatest multiplier in the world – trust – and character keeps it compounding.

Chapter 19

THE ANTI-FRAGILE MONEY MINDSET

Thriving financially through chaos and change

> **Theme: Anti-fragility**
> Drawing on every system you've built, you turn fear, volatility and uncertainty into fuel for freedom and long-term advantage.

THE WEALTH HABIT

When the storm hits, the anti-fragile don't brace, they pivot and rise.

Every decade brings a new crisis wearing a different mask: recessions, pandemics, trade wars, AI upheavals, inflation spikes. In each cycle, millions retreat in fear while a small, prepared group advance. They aren't luckier, they're trained to think differently. This chapter is about joining them: learning how to turn economic chaos into your competitive advantage.

When British-Ghanaian entrepreneur and mother of three, Valerie Labi, first returned to Ghana, she wasn't chasing a grand plan. She was searching for purpose. Born in Hertfordshire to Ghanaian parents who came to the UK in the 1970s, Valerie built what looked like a secure path – a degree in economics from Southampton University, a career at a multinational accounting company and a front-row seat in London's financial world. 'The rat race was what I was trained for.'

Then came the 2008 financial crash. Valerie was part of the team handling the administration of a failing bank. One day, she and a partner sat across from a woman, a middle-aged banker who had taken her entire bonus in company shares, and told her that everything she'd worked for was now worthless. 'She'd given her whole life to that place,' Valerie recalls. 'No family, no time, just work. Overnight, it meant nothing. I remember thinking, "That could easily be me in ten years' time."'

That moment changed her trajectory. She realized how fragile even 'stable' systems could be, and that security built only on salary and status could disappear overnight. 'I didn't want to just work for profit,' she says. 'I wanted to build something that solved real problems.'

Years later, during the pandemic, another crisis rewrote her story. Pregnant and stranded in London while the world shut down, she remembers driving through deserted streets to give birth:

The Anti-Fragile Money Mindset

It was the day 10,000 people died from COVID. My husband was stuck in Ghana and my cousin stepped in to support me. As we drove through London, I didn't see a single person. I remember thinking, 'If the world is ending today, I want to be in Ghana.'

That was the moment she knew her heart had crossed over completely. 'If everything stopped tomorrow, I wanted every contribution I made to be on the continent.'

Back in Ghana, Valerie settled in Tamale, the calm heart of northern Ghana. Life there slowed her down and sharpened her eyes. Neighbours often complained about transport – fuel prices rising, motorbikes breaking down and delivery riders barely surviving. 'It hit me that movement itself had become unaffordable,' she says.

Even before the pandemic, Valerie had been experimenting on the side, buying old bicycles and fitting them with small electric conversion kits ordered on Amazon. But when the world shut down, something shifted. 'The pandemic made me go all in,' she recalls. 'What had been a side project suddenly felt urgent – I needed to find resources, build a team and make it real.'

Four years on, Wahu has grown from those prototypes into an assembly plant in Accra employing local engineers and equipping hundreds of delivery riders with affordable electric bikes. Riders pay through flexible plans, spending about $13 a month on power instead of $250 on petrol.

Today, Wahu is closing an $8 million funding round and expanding across Africa, but Valerie still calls the journey 'a work in progress'. *She says*, 'You build through uncertainty, not after it passes.'

Her story is a living definition of the Anti-Fragile Mindset: when fear says 'stop', faith and purpose whisper 'build'. Because real wealth isn't what you hold when life is calm and comfortable, it's who you become in chaos, shaped by courage and fuelled by purpose.

THE FEAR ERA

We're living through what future historians may call 'the fear era'. People fear losing jobs to AI. They fear the systems they once trusted are watching, taxing or restricting them more. They fear retirement slipping further away as pension ages rise. They fear the widening gap between elites and everyone else. In the UK, over one-third of adults now say they feel financially anxious most days.[96]

Many also fear outsiders, believing immigration is stealing opportunity. This wave of anti-immigration sentiment is sweeping much of the West. Yet data tells a fuller story: immigrants have founded over half of the most valuable start-ups in the US.[97] Although fewer than 15% of people in the UK were born abroad, nearly four in ten of the nation's 100 fastest-growing companies were founded by immigrants[98] and diverse economies consistently outperform insular ones. The anti-fragile understand that resentment is a symptom of scarcity thinking, not a solution to it. Real security comes from creating, not excluding.

Fear, however, is information. It points to what people value and where they've surrendered control. The anti-fragile don't dismiss fear, they decode it. They build systems that make them ungovernable by panic. This isn't rebellion, it's responsibility – designing finances so that no employer, government policy or algorithm dictates your wellbeing.

Uncertainty isn't a signal to freeze, it's an invitation to act. Every prior habit you've learned – automation, diversification, generosity, community – has prepared you for this. Now it's time to weave them into the mindset that makes all of them unbreakable.

> **The Wealth Habit Mantra 19:**
> When fear rises, build systems. When systems shake, build skills. When the world retreats, move forwards with purpose.

WHY ECONOMIC DOWNTURNS CREATE WEALTH-BUILDING OPPORTUNITIES

When economies contract, three things happen: prices fall, competition thins and habits reset. Those moments, though painful, are where new fortunes are quietly made.

Historically, half of all companies on today's Fortune 500 list were founded during recessions or bear markets.[99] According to Fidelity, five of the eleven US recessions since 1950 led to positive stock-market returns and, generally, stocks have grown more than they've contracted.[100] Why? Because fear discounts everything – assets, talent, ideas.

Discounted assets

When fear spreads, people rush to sell and that's when real opportunities appear. Good businesses, funds or properties start selling for far less than they're worth. If you've built up some savings or automated investing through your Set-and-Soar System (Chapter 7), this is when you quietly buy what others are too scared to hold. You're not taking wild risks, you're buying quality on sale.

Thinner competition

Hard times clear the field. Many businesses that overborrowed or stretched too thin simply don't make it. That might sound bleak, but it creates space for those ready to move. Research by J.P. Morgan shows fewer new businesses start during recessions, yet the ones that do often grow much faster once recovery begins.[101] If you stay steady and keep learning, you can step into the gaps others leave behind.

Systemic change creates new winners

Every crisis speeds up change. The pandemic accelerated remote work. Climate pressure is fuelling renewable energy. Technology is reshaping money itself through digital finance. If you pay attention to these shifts and position yourself early, you'll find the upside before everyone else does. Anti-fragile people don't just survive the wave, they ride it.

Don't panic, pivot

But the next decade's turbulence won't just come from recessions. The ground is shifting beneath every part of the global economy. Artificial intelligence, automation and cyber threats are already changing the value of skills, jobs and even whole industries. Studies suggest that nearly 40% of the global workforce will need to learn new skills before the end of this decade.[102] At the same time, environmental and resource pressures are reshaping everything from food to finance. One UK study found that nature loss alone could cut national growth by up to 12% by the 2030s.[103]

These aren't random risks, they're part of a larger economic and social reset, shifting the way the world works. And that's exactly where new opportunities begin. Anti-fragile wealth builders don't wait to see what happens, they prepare early. They develop skills that can't be replaced by algorithms, invest in industries built for a sustainable future and look for opportunities in places others overlook.

And remember, downturns never last forever. Research shows the average recession runs for about 11 months, while the recovery that follows can last five years or more.[104] So, the real question isn't if the storm will pass, but who will be ready when it does.

Imagine your household or small business when income suddenly drops by 20%. Most people panic and cut back everything. You do something different – you pivot. You launch a smaller, digital version of what you offer, renegotiate costs so they flex with income and keep investing little by little through your index funds. When the recovery comes, you're not starting again from zero, you're already ahead, stronger and positioned to grow.

HOW TO PREPARE FINANCIALLY FOR UNCERTAIN TIMES

Preparation is the oxygen of anti-fragility. Without it, opportunity suffocates.

Liquidity and buffers

Hold three to six months' worth of expenses in instant access form. Cash reserves are the single best protection during recessions. For families with dependants or self-employment income, aim to extend that to nine to twelve months. If you're already in retirement, aim for a larger cushion, typically twelve to eighteen months of living costs in cash or near-cash accounts. This helps you avoid selling investments at the wrong time and gives your portfolio room to recover when markets fall. Think of it as your 'sleep-well fund' – peace of mind that keeps your long-term strategy intact.

Low leverage and flexible costs

The more fixed your expenses are, the more fragile your life becomes. Review your loans, leases and subscriptions for anything that locks you in and see what can be made flexible. Keep costs that move with you, not against you. Ask yourself, 'If my income dropped by 25%, could I still breathe easily?' If the answer is no, it's time to simplify. Flexibility isn't weakness, it's one of the strongest forms of protection you can build.

Multiple income streams

Whether you're in London, Lagos or Lisbon, dependency on one salary is risky. Layer side hustles, digital assets or royalties aligned with your values and time. During crises, one channel sustains another.

Stay invested, add strategically

Long-term data shows that missing just the ten best days in the market each decade halves your returns.[105] Stay consistent; use downturns to buy discounted, quality investments.

Invest in skills

AI will replace some jobs, but it will also create new ones that need emotional intelligence, creativity and real leadership. The best investment you can ever make is in your own ability to adapt. Every new skill you learn, whether technical or human, becomes a hedge against uncertainty and a magnet for opportunity.

Safeguard financial autonomy

Central Bank Digital Currencies (CBDCs), such as the digital pound and others around the world, are in the works[106] and promise efficiency yet raise privacy and anonymity concerns. Anti-fragile households diversify access, maintaining multiple accounts, reputable, decentralized platforms and, where sensible, non-digital reserves (for example, gold, physical cash and prepaid essentials). This isn't rebellion, it's resilience: ensuring no single gatekeeper can freeze your options.

Protect against major shocks

Insurance isn't exciting, but it's essential. Health, life, income and business-interruption cover act as your invisible safety net when the unexpected happens. In the UK, while 37% of adults have life insurance, only 14% have any form of income protection,[107] yet it's one of the simplest ways to support yourself financially if you're unable to work due to illness or injury. Longer term, life insurance is an easy way to create generational wealth. Across the world, the families who stay steady through tough times usually have one thing in common – they protected themselves before they needed to. They moved their biggest risks off the table while things were still calm.

Personal considerations

In our own lives, as parents raising children entering their teens, we've started asking ourselves new questions. With AI and information more accessible than ever, will going to university still hold the same value by the time they're 18? Or might there be smarter, more strategic paths that avoid crippling student loans, for example, degree apprenticeships, learning a trade or even starting a small business early?

We can already see how technology is transforming the future of work. So, we're thinking long-term: what if their investment accounts, the ones we've funded since they were born, could one day go towards their first homes or even buying them time to explore international opportunities and grow those investments themselves?

That's not reacting to headlines, that's engineering long-term positioning. And that, in essence, is the anti-fragile edge.

FRAMEWORK: THE ANTI-FRAGILE COMPASS

At the core of this chapter lies a simple, circular system: **prepare, adapt, capitalize, reinforce**. Each stage feeds the next. Preparation stabilizes and gives you confidence; adaptation reveals opportunity to pivot; capitalization builds wealth; reinforcement secures the habit and strengthens systems before returning to north. The compass turns endlessly, reminding you that anti-fragility isn't a one-time fix, it's continuous calibration. Here is how it works, step-by-step:

The Anti-Fragile Compass

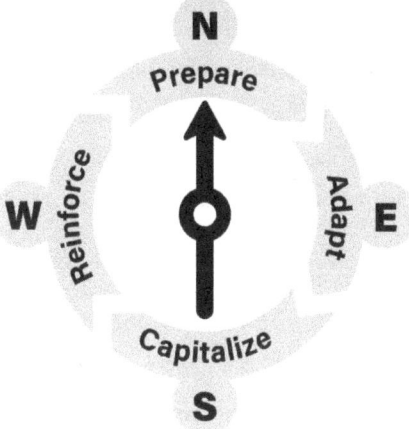

Step 1: Prepare

Audit your exposure and introduce buffers. List every vulnerability, for example, income dependency, high debt, overspending, single-market exposure. Awareness is immunity's first stage. A one-income household with no cash buffer is fragile. A household with multiple flows – salary, side business, investments – is adaptive.

Step 2: Adapt

Build flexibility into fixed costs. Negotiate the things that tie you down, for example, utility plans, mortgages, supplier contracts or rent – so they can move with you. The more flexible your costs are, the easier it is to breathe when things tighten. We saw it during the pandemic: businesses and households that could quickly scale down or renegotiate terms stayed afloat far longer than those locked into rigid commitments. Flexibility isn't a luxury, it's oxygen.

Step 3: Capitalize

Convert information into advantage. Every crisis produces excess information and too little interpretation. Spend 30 minutes weekly scanning for signals in technology, legislation, demographic trends. Then ask: how might this affect my sector, my income, my portfolio? Turning noise into knowledge is anti-fragility in action. Stay informed and move when others hesitate.

Step 4: Reinforce

Document lessons and solidify gains. After every challenge or period of disruption, take time to look back and write down what actually helped you stay steady, for example, your cash levels, the people or suppliers you could rely on, the decisions that paid off. Then update your personal playbook so you're even stronger next time. Anti-fragile families don't just survive disruption, they learn from it and build more freedom with every test.

KINGSLEY IJOMAH: RE-LEARNING THE FUTURE

My (Ken) brother, Kingsley, demonstrates the Anti-Fragile Money Mindset in action.

When Kingsley (43) and his wife set off to travel the world after their wedding, he had no idea that the biggest journey wouldn't be through countries, it would be through change. A seasoned software engineer, he returned three years later to find the world of tech unrecognizable. The tools he once mastered were obsolete, companies were freezing contracts and a new force, artificial intelligence, was rewriting everything.

He describes it simply: 'In software, languages die all the time. But AI didn't evolve slowly, it arrived overnight.' Suddenly, what companies needed wasn't people to code systems, but people who could make those systems think.

For a while, the silence was real. Contracts disappeared, income dropped and the career he'd built felt like it had expired while he was gone. But rather than panic, he chose to rebuild from the ground up. He read obsessively, bought online courses and reached out to experts on LinkedIn. Then he began creating small AI tools to solve his own everyday problems. He shared his work publicly, one post at a time.

Slowly, curiosity turned into opportunity. Companies began contacting him for projects and Kingsley reinvented himself as a machine-learning AI engineer. The work returned, this time with more purpose and control than before.

You don't need to understand code to see yourself in this story, replace 'software engineer' with your own job title and the lesson is the same.

Kingsley's path mirrors what it means to be anti-fragile:

- **Prepare:** Study, experiment and stay curious.
- **Adapt:** Build something small and useful for yourself first.
- **Capitalize:** Share the journey while others hesitate.
- **Reinforce:** Focus on durable skills that outlast every hype cycle.

He says his income has not only recovered but grown, though the journey continues. His story is a reminder that the real security isn't in a job title; it's in the courage to learn again when the world changes faster than you planned.

PAUSE FOR REFLECTION

Take a moment to write down your thoughts to these questions:

- What's the one financial fear that quietly drives your choices right now? (Job loss? Rising costs? Taxes? Feeling like the system's in control?)
- Which direction of the Anti-Fragile Compass do you find hardest right now – preparing, adapting, capitalizing or reinforcing?
- What's one small step you could take this month to turn that fear into focus?

Because reflection turns awareness into agency, and agency is where financial peace begins.

> *Small action step*
>
> Over the next seven days:
>
> - Check your financial safety buffer. Make sure you've got enough to breathe if life wobbles for a bit.
> - Spot one opportunity hiding in fear. It could be a discounted investment, a new partnership or a skill everyone else is too anxious to learn right now.
> - Take one small action. Invest a little. Start learning. Reach out. Move while others freeze.
>
> Because tiny, decisive steps taken in uncertain times don't just protect you, they strengthen your anti-fragile muscle for life.

The Anti-Fragile Money Mindset

You now stand at the point everything in this book has been leading to. The habits, systems and frameworks you've built are your flight instruments, but this mindset is the engine that keeps you steady when the air around you shakes.

It's tempting to see volatility as danger. But look closer: every period of uncertainty is also a reset. It reveals what's weak, rewards what's adaptable and transfers wealth from those who freeze to those who move with wisdom.

You don't control governments, markets or policies, but you do control how you respond. The Anti-Fragile Mindset isn't about predicting the future, it's about positioning yourself to thrive no matter what the future brings.

You now hold every mindset, system and habit needed not just to weather uncertainty, but to grow through it.

Chapter Summary

- We're living through what feels like the 'fear era' – AI disruption, economic uncertainty, rising costs and social tension have made fear the background noise of modern life.
- But fear is information, not destiny. The anti-fragile don't run from it; they read it, decode it and design systems that keep them steady when others shake.
- Downturns don't destroy wealth, they redistribute it. Position yourself where it flows next.
- Build liquidity. Diversify income. Let volatility become your teacher, not your threat.
- Stay curious. Use fear as data to see what's inefficient, undervalued or ready to change.
- Embrace the Anti-Fragile Compass – prepare, adapt, capitalize, reinforce – and let it guide every major decision.
- Look beyond recessions. Anticipate structural shifts in technology, geopolitics and climate – they're where tomorrow's opportunities are born.
- Protect your financial independence. Embrace innovation, but don't hand over your freedom to any one system, employer or platform.
- Because true wealth is freedom with structure – the ability to live well, stay calm and keep growing no matter how the world changes.

Building The Wealth Habit

Pillar 4: Build the Life
Principle lens: Keep it fun

You've shaped wealth to support freedom, meaning, and relationships.

At this stage, progress is measured less by numbers and more by how life feels.

Ask yourself: *Where does my wealth now create joy instead of pressure?*

Chapter 20

CONCLUSION

Live The Wealth Habit

We began this journey with one idea: small changes make you rich. Not just in money, but in peace, progress and purpose.

You've learned how habits become systems and how systems make freedom inevitable. You've built a mindset that multiplies, simplified your money and designed routines that work even when you rest. You've discovered that wealth isn't a finish line – it's a rhythm.

Now the work is to live it.

Start where you are and build the pillars: build the mindset, build the habit, build the system and build the life.

Ignore the noise. Keep it simple. Keep it automatic. Keep it compounding. Keep it fun. The four principles of *The Wealth Habit* will carry you through every season, good or hard, fast or slow.

Let your wealth grow quietly in the background while you focus on the things that matter most: your family, your faith, your health, your community. That's what real financial joy looks like – not more stuff, but more space to breathe, to give and to live fully.

Conclusion

If you'd like a structured way to put everything into motion, we've created an optional 90-Day Wealth Habit Challenge – a practical, interactive sprint that turns these pages into action.

Scan this QR code to download your free challenge workbook and digital dashboards.

Use it as a guide, a reset or a rhythm to return to whenever you need momentum. Your wealth journey doesn't end here, it begins. Because once habits take root, wealth becomes who you are, not just what you have.

Welcome to a life powered by *The Wealth Habit*. May it lead you to a life of financial joy.

Thank you from the bottom of our hearts for going on this journey with us. To God be the glory for the opportunity to write our second book. May it be a light to your feet, a blessing to you, your family and your generations to come. Pass it on to others.

Love, Ken and Mary 🖤

GLOSSARY

401(k) A workplace retirement savings plan mainly used in the US. Employees contribute part of their salary into investments, often with employer contributions added, to build long-term retirement wealth.

Active investing An approach where investors or fund managers frequently buy and sell assets to try to beat the market. It usually involves higher costs, more effort and greater risk than passive investing.

Arbitrage A strategy that seeks to profit from price differences for the same asset across different markets. True arbitrage opportunities are rare and usually short lived.

Asset Something you own that has the potential to grow in value or generate income over time, such as investments, property or businesses.

Bitcoin A decentralized digital currency that operates without a central authority. It uses blockchain technology and is known for price volatility, making it both innovative and risky.

Bond A loan made to a government or company. In return, the investor receives regular interest payments and their original capital back at maturity. Bonds are generally lower risk than shares.

Glossary

Bull market A period when markets are rising, and investor confidence is strong, often linked to economic growth and optimism.

Bear market A period of prolonged market decline, typically marked by falling prices and negative investor sentiment.

Compounding The process where growth builds on previous growth over time. Small, consistent actions compound into significant results when given enough time.

Diversification Spreading money across different assets to reduce risk. Diversification protects against any single investment causing major losses.

Equity Ownership in an asset. In investing, it usually means shares in a company. In property, it refers to the value owned after debt is subtracted.

ETF (Exchange-Traded Fund) A low-cost investment fund that holds a basket of assets and trades like a share on an exchange. Commonly used for diversification and passive investing.

FTSE All-Share A UK stock market index that tracks most companies listed on the London Stock Exchange, offering a broad view of the UK market.

ISA (Individual Savings Account) A UK tax-efficient account that allows savings or investments to grow without income or capital gains tax. Similar tax-free accounts exist in other countries.

Index A benchmark that tracks the performance of a group of assets, such as companies or bonds, to show how a market or sector moves over time.

Index fund A fund designed to track an index rather than outperform it. It offers diversification, low fees and steady long-term growth.

Inflation The gradual increase in prices over time, which reduces the purchasing power of money if it is not growing.

Liability A financial obligation or debt that requires repayment. Unmanaged liabilities can slow or reverse long-term wealth building.

Net worth The total value of what you own (assets) minus what you owe (liabilities). It is a snapshot of overall financial position, not income.

Passive investing An investment approach focused on matching market returns through low-cost index funds or ETFs, relying on consistency and compounding.

ROI (return on investment) A measure of how much profit or loss an investment generates compared to the amount invested.

Roth IRA (Individual Retirement Account) A US retirement account where contributions are made after tax, but future withdrawals are typically tax-free. Similar structures exist globally.

S&P 500 A major US stock market index tracking 500 large American companies, often used as a long-term performance benchmark.

SACCO (Savings and Credit Cooperative) A member-owned savings and lending cooperative, common in parts of Africa and emerging markets, designed to promote collective financial progress.

Share A unit of ownership in a company. Shareholders benefit from price growth and, in some cases, dividends.

SIPP (Self-Invested Personal Pension) A UK pension that allows individuals to choose and manage their own investments for retirement.

TFSA (Tax-Free Savings Account) A Canadian savings and investment account where growth and withdrawals are tax free. The concept mirrors tax-advantaged accounts used worldwide.

Volatility The degree to which prices rise and fall over time. Volatility is normal in markets and does not equal failure or long-term risk.

RESOURCES

Round-up and savings automation

Region	Example app(s)	Key features
UK	Monzo, Starling, Plum, Chip	Round-ups into 'pots' or micro-investing.
US	Acorns, Qapital, Oportun, Albert, Bank of America 'Keep the Change'	Round-ups and AI-driven savings rules.
Canada	KOHO, Moka, Wealthsimple	Nearest $1/2/5 round-ups into savings.
Australia	Raiz, ANZ Plus 'Round Ups', ING 'Everyday Round Up', Up Bank	ETF-based micro-investing.
New Zealand	ASB 'Save the Change', BNZ Rapid Save	Round-ups into savings 'spaces'.
Europe	Revolut, N26, bunq, Monese	Flexible multiples and 'vaults'.
Africa	TymeBank Save the Change (ZA), Kuda (NG), PiggyVest (NG)	Zero-fee goal-based savings buckets.
Middle East	YAP (UAE), meem (KSA), stc pay (KSA)	Spare-change 'vaults' and goal buckets.
Asia	Gojek Pay (ID), Paytm (IN), Revolut (SG)	Purchases rounded into savings or goals.

Investment automation

Region	Example app(s)	Key features
UK	Nutmeg, Wealthify, InvestEngine, Moneybox	Robo-advisor portfolios and auto-rebalancing.
US	Betterment, Wealthfront, M1 Finance, Ellevest	Goal-based robo-advisors with tax-loss harvesting.
Canada	Wealthsimple Invest, Nest Wealth, Questwealth	Automated ETF portfolios and human advisor overlay.
Australia	Stockspot, InvestSmart, Raiz Invest	AI-driven ETF picks and dynamic rebalancing.
New Zealand	Hatch Invest, Sharesies	Auto-reinvest dividends and recurring investment plans.
Europe	Scalable Capital, Raisin Invest	AI allocation and multi-market access.
Africa	Risevest (NG), Trove (NG), Chaka (NG)	USD-denominated automated portfolios.
Middle East	Sarwa, Wahed Invest, Wealthface, FinaMaze	Sharia-compliant robo-advisors and auto-rebalancing.
Asia	StashAway (SG), Syfe (SG), Upstox (IN)	Dynamic economic regime portfolios and goal planning.

NOTES

Chapter 1

1. https://institute.bankofamerica.com/content/dam/economic-insights/paycheque-to-paycheque-lower-income-households.pdf
2. https://www.sciencedirect.com/science/article/pii/S2214635017300291
3. https://pubmed.ncbi.nlm.nih.gov/5010404/
4. https://pubmed.ncbi.nlm.nih.gov/23063236/
5. https://pmc.ncbi.nlm.nih.gov/articles/PMC5125729/
6. https://www.ideas42.org/wp-content/uploads/2015/05/Applying-BE-to-Improve-Microsavings-Outcomes-1.pdf

Chapter 2

7. https://www.canada.ca/en/financial-consumer-agency/programs/research/online-intereventions-increase-young-womens-confidence-final-report.html
8. https://onlinelibrary.wiley.com/doi/abs/10.1002/ejsp.674
9. https://en.wikipedia.org/wiki/List_of_countries_by_GDP_(nominal)
10. https://sabeconomics.org/wordpress/wp-content/uploads/JBEP-2-2-6.pdf?
11. https://www.nestinsight.org.uk/millions-are-saving-more-for-tomorrow
12. https://www.nestinsight.org.uk/wp-content/uploads/2020/06/How-the-UK-Saves-the-effects-of-the-second-savings-rate-increase.pdf

Chapter 3

13 https://econjournals.com/index.php/ijefi/article/download/16578/8207/39121
14 https://pmc.ncbi.nlm.nih.gov/articles/PMC6594552/

Chapter 4

15 https://pmc.ncbi.nlm.nih.gov/articles/PMC7126161/
16 https://research.gold.ac.uk/28376/1/ANT_thesis_PuskasA_2020.pdf
17 https://law.bepress.com/cgi/viewcontent.cgi?article=6165&context=expresso
18 https://www.qualitative-research.net/index.php/fqs/article/view/1940/3620
19 https://en.wikipedia.org/wiki/Sudden_wealth_syndrome

Chapter 5

20 https://www.sciencedirect.com/science/article/pii/S2214804322001100
21 https://pmc.ncbi.nlm.nih.gov/articles/PMC10084287/
22 https://www.chicagobooth.edu/review/how-poverty-changes-your-mind-set
23 https://www.euronews.com/business/2024/05/13/housing-in-europe-how-do-homeownership-and-tenancy-rates-compare
24 https://www.frontiersin.org/journals/behavioural-economics/articles/10.3389/frbhe.2025.1379577/pdf
25 https://doi.org/10.1037/0033-2909.134.3.383
26 https://positivepsychology.com/3-steps-negativity-bias/
27 https://positivepsychology.com/gratitude-appreciation/

Chapter 6

28 https://ijirt.org/publishedpaper/IJIRT171072_PAPER.pdf
29 https://pmc.ncbi.nlm.nih.gov/articles/PMC9421032/

Notes

30 https://ijirt.org/publishedpaper/IJIRT171072_PAPER.pdf
31 https://longevity.stanford.edu/spent-resources-self-regulatory-resource-availability-affects-impulse-buying/
32 https://carlsonschool.umn.edu/sites/carlsonschool.umn.edu/files/2019-04/166714_2.pdf and https://academic.oup.com/jcr/article-abstract/37/5/902/1870112
33 https://www.insightdiy.co.uk/news/uk-consumers-spending-nearly-41bn-on-impulse-purchases-annually/14070.htm
34 https://capitaloneshopping.com/research/impulse-buying-statistics/ and https://www.invespcro.com/blog/impulse-buying/
35 https://ami.org.au/knowledge-hub/impulse-buying-surge-80-of-aussies-make-in-store-impromptu-purchases/
36 https://www.dacgroup.com/en-gb/insights/blog/strategy/retail-therapy-and-the-power-of-the-impulse-buy-2/
37 https://capitaloneshopping.com/research/impulse-buying-statistics/
38 https://www.invespcro.com/blog/impulse-buying/
39 https://www.warc.com/newsandopinion/news/chinas_gen_z_relies_on_social_media_for_shopping/39204
40 https://it-consultis.com/blog/social-shopping-in-china-the-rise-of-impulse-buying/
41 https://behavioralpolicy.org/wp-content/uploads/2017/05/BSP_vol1is1_Wood.pdf
42 https://www.jessicarosewilliams.com/journal/how-to-manage-emotional-spending-according-to-a-recovering-emotional-spender
43 https://www.tandfonline.com/doi/full/10.1080/10463283.2020.1808936#abstract and https://www.sciencedirect.com/science/article/abs/pii/S0065260106380021 and https://pmc.ncbi.nlm.nih.gov/articles/PMC4500900/
44 https://www.urban.org/sites/default/files/publication/101992/building-savings-ownership-and-financial-well-being_1_0.pdf
45 https://onlinelibrary.wiley.com/doi/10.1002/bdm.2376

Chapter 7

46 https://www.ajbell.co.uk/articles/investmentarticles/288084/which-countries-markets-have-recovered-liberation-day
47 https://www.behavioraleconomics.com/resources/mini-encyclopedia-of-be/choice-overload/
48 https://www.goodreads.com/quotes/8760232-if-you-don-t-find-a-way-to-make-money-while

Chapter 8

49 ONS pensions and savings data come from here: https://www.ons.gov.uk/peoplepopulationandcommunity/personalandhouseholdfinances/incomeandwealth/bulletins/totalwealthingreatbritain/april2020tomarch2022 and https://www.gov.uk/government/statistics/annual-savings-statistics-2024/commentary-for-annual-savings-statistics-september-2024 and https://www.flagstoneim.com/personal/learn/growing-your-savings/average-savings-by-age-uk

Chapter 9

50 https://www.apa.org/topics/personality/willpower
51 https://www.pnas.org/doi/10.1073/pnas.1706541114
52 https://news.cornell.edu/stories/2014/09/doing-makes-you-happier-owning-even-buying
53 https://shop.thehumblepenny.com/collections/all/products/budget-for-life

Chapter 10

54 https://www.princeton.edu/~ceps/workingpapers/213spears.pdf
55 https://onlinelibrary.wiley.com/doi/10.1002/smi.70050

Notes

Chapter 11

56   https://www.sciencedirect.com/science/article/abs/pii/S0148296312001816 , https://pmc.ncbi.nlm.nih.gov/articles/PMC10685127/
57   https://thedecisionlab.com/reference-guide/psychology/intention-action-gap
58   https://pmc.ncbi.nlm.nih.gov/articles/PMC3949005/

Chapter 12

59   Paraphrase of Genesis 41:34–36

Chapter 13

60   https://fortune.com/2014/07/07/arrillaga-silicon-valley/ and https://medium.com/@johnamemorial/john-arrillaga-1937-2022-ba11ee3818da and https://www.forbes.com/sites/kerryadolan/2022/01/25/silicon-valley-real-estate-billionaire-john-arrillaga-dies-at-age-84/
61   https://fortune.com/2014/07/07/arrillaga-silicon-valley/
62   Broad indices are giant baskets of hundreds or even thousands of companies, designed to represent the whole market rather than just one stock or sector.
63   https://www.spglobal.com/spdji/en/spiva/article/spiva-uk
64   https://www.spglobal.com/spdji/en/spiva/article/spiva-global/
65   https://www.planadviser.com/investors-bad-behavior-led-sharp-underperformance-2024/
66   https://www.berkshirehathaway.com/letters/2022ltr.pdf
67   https://www.berkshirehathaway.com/letters/2022ltr.pdf
68   https://www.investmentweek.co.uk/news/4379291/isa-millionaires-hits-nearly
69   https://www.ii.co.uk/ii-accounts/isa/guides/how-to-become-an-isa-millionaire
70   https://assets.publishing.service.gov.uk/media/656856b8cc1ec500138eef49/Gov.UK_Impact_of_AI_on_UK_Jobs_and_Training.pdf

Chatper 14

71 https://youtu.be/Ud3ElqsHD0g?si=d7-ElBPogYIUMHYj
72 https://youtu.be/3w6QGURs2FU?si=XfHBt1CnYf-oHvf-

Chapter 15

73 https://www.numbeo.com/cost-of-living/compare_cities.jsp?country1=United+Kingdom&city1=London&country2=United+Kingdom&city2=Manchester
74 https://www.numbeo.com/cost-of-living/compare_cities.jsp?country1=United+Kingdom&country2=Portugal&city1=London&city2=Lisbon
75 https://www.oecd.org/content/dam/oecd/en/publications/reports/2024/11/health-at-a-glance-europe-2024_bb301b77/b3704e14-en.pdf and https://www.oecd.org/en/data/tools/oecd-better-life-index.html
76 https://citizenremote.com/blog/digital-nomad-visa-countries/
77 https://www.numbeo.com/cost-of-living/compare_countries.jsp
78 https://www.numbeo.com/cost-of-living/comparison.jsp

Chapter 16

79 Joshua 13:1 (KJV)
80 https://www.bbc.co.uk/reel/video/p0g6q7wd/kakeibo-the-japanese-art-of-saving-money
81 https://www.bbc.com/pidgin/articles/cy947ykxx5eo
82 https://www.ipsos.com/en-za/stokvels-remain-untapped-human-banks-south-africa / https://www.youtube.com/watch?v=kJZcLQgfozw
83 https://www.morningstar.com.au/personal-finance/how-to-earn-1-7-more-a-year-than-the-average-investor

Notes

84 https://www.behavioraleconomics.com/resources/mini-encyclopedia-of-be/myopic-loss-aversion/

Chapter 17

85 https://giadzy.com/blogs/tips/pay-it-forward-in-naples-with-caffe-sospeso
86 https://www.cafonline.org/docs/default-source/inside-giving/wgi/wgi_2024_report.pdf
87 https://doi.org/10.1126/science.1150952
88 https://pmc.ncbi.nlm.nih.gov/articles/PMC5508200/
89 https://ggsc.berkeley.edu/images/uploads/GGSC-JTF_White_Paper-Generosity-FINAL.pdf and https://www.pnas.org/doi/10.1073/pnas.0604475103
90 https://positivepsychology.com/savoring/

Chapter 18

91 https://www.nature.com/articles/s41586-022-04996-4 / https://www.nytimes.com/interactive/2022/08/01/upshot/rich-poor-friendships.html / https://www.socialcapital.org/
92 https://www.nber.org/system/files/working_papers/w32186/w32186.pdf / https://theconversation.com/having-the-right-friends-may-hold-the-secret-to-building-wealth-according-to-new-study-on-socioeconomic-ties-239370
93 https://www.cse.wustl.edu/~m.neumann/fl2017/cse316/materials/strength_of_weak_ties.pdf / https://www.bbc.co.uk/worklife/article/20200701-why-your-weak-tie-friendships-may-mean-more-than-you-think
94 https://openjournals.libs.uga.edu/fsr/article/view/3341
95 https://www.youtube.com/watch?v=Pqftm3o5RdQ

Chapter 19

96 https://capuk.org/news-and-blog/free-help-with-money-worries
97 https://nfap.com/research/new-nfap-policy-brief-immigrant-entrepreneurs-and-u-s-billion-dollar-companies/
98 https://www.tenentrepreneurs.org/job-creators-2024
99 https://www.marketwatch.com/story/heres-the-good-news-if-theres-a-recession-nearly-half-the-fortune-500-was-created-during-times-of-economic-stress-morgan-stanley-says-11663156317
100 https://www.fidelity.com/learning-center/wealth-management-insights/3-things-to-know-about-recessions
101 https://www.jpmorganchase.com/institute/all-topics/business-growth-and-entrepreneurship/when-opportunity-knocks-how-economic-cycles-shape-entrepreneurial-ventures-and-their-success
102 https://www.weforum.org/publications/the-future-of-jobs-report-2025/digest/
103 https://www.reuters.com/world/uk/nature-loss-could-slow-uk-growth-12-by-2030s-report-says-2024-04-24
104 https://www.fidelity.com/learning-center/wealth-management-insights/3-things-to-know-about-recessions
105 https://www.fidelity.com/bin-public/060_www_fidelity_com/documents/DiscussionCycleGuide.pdf
106 https://www.bankofengland.co.uk/paper/2024/responses-to-the-digital-pound-consultation-paper
107 https://www.shepherdsfriendly.co.uk/resources/income-protection-gap-uk-2024/

ACKNOWLEDGEMENTS

We thank God for the opportunity to bring this second book to the world. May the work of our hands shine brightly, a light that cannot be hidden, for Your glory.

To our dear sons, Joshua and Elias: We love you, and we're proud of you. Thank you for helping to shape the book cover with your ideas and for encouraging us when writing got tough. May this book show you what's possible and may it be life-transforming for you, your future children and their children.

Ken

To my loving parents, Ogbuzuru Dr Ken Okoroafor and Ogbuefi Mrs Stella Okoroafor: Thank you for setting the example for me and sacrificing so much for the life I now live. I am who I am today because of you both. You've always been there to show me love, give wisdom and help me believe that I can achieve anything. I love you.

To my siblings, Jennifer, Pamela and Kingsley: We've been through so much together and managed to find light at the end of the tunnel. This book wouldn't be possible without all the experiences we shared and all your support. Thank you for believing in me and being there for our family always. I love you all, and may we always be united as a family.

Mary

Deepest gratitude to my loving parents, Mr Matthew Obadina and Mrs Martina Obadina, my pillars of unwavering support, inspiration, selfless love and prayers that have shaped my journey. Thank you for always reminding me to put God first, for believing in me, and for all the sacrifices you've made. I'm forever grateful.

To my siblings, Funmilola, Ade, Andrew and Shola: This book wouldn't be complete without acknowledging the people who have shaped me in more ways than I can express. I've watched, learned and benefited from your triumphs and the wisdom that comes with navigating the bumps along the way. Your mistakes became my lessons and your victories fuelled my aspirations. Thank you for your love and support. Love you.

To our extended family and friends: We love you more than you know. Thank you for continually supporting us, checking in on us and giving us feedback and ideas for our book. We also appreciate the practical love you've shown us, such as providing childcare on the many random occasions we needed it urgently. Our lives wouldn't be the same without our friendships.

To our editorial director, Emily Arbis: We love you. Thank you for believing in us. Without you, *The Wealth Habit* and *Financial Joy* would not exist. You're a dream come true for us.

To our literary agent, Oscar Janson-Smith: We always feel at peace working with you because we know you're after our best interest. Thank you for your wisdom in all our conversations. Long may we keep working together.

Acknowledgements

To our book cover designer, Steve Leard: You smashed it! We wanted a cover that was unique to us and timeless, and you achieved just that.

To our project editor and copyeditor, Victoria Lympus: Thank you for working exceptionally hard on this book and putting your heart into it. Every word in this book has received your blessing, and that's a special thing.

To our proofreader, Philippa Wilkinson: You've done an incredible job of making sure this book is complete. We're honoured to have you support this book with such attention to detail.

To our audio engineer, Carrie Hutchinson: Recording our audiobook is one of the most enjoyable aspects of writing this book. You made the whole process smooth and fun.

To our illustrator, Robert Brandt: You made all the frameworks in this book memorable and unique.

To our publicity manager, Emily Patience: Thank you for finding us amazing opportunities so that the world can read this book.

To our marketing managers, Charlotte Gill and Gracie Maddison: You've levelled up on the promo assets for *The Wealth Habit*, and for that, we're grateful. Everything from incredibly well filmed videos to static and moving assets. Thank you for your creativity and commitment to this work.

Finally, to you, the Wealth Builder holding this book: Thank you for choosing to build intentionally, one habit at a time. Our work and our community exist because of people like you: those who read our work, watch our videos, listen to our podcasts and walk this journey with us. Through your support, this work has become more than content or teaching; it has become purpose. For that, we are deeply grateful.

INDEX

1% daily improvement rule 36–7
    1% Compound Ladder 44–7
    applying 42–4
    case study 38
    embedding 44
    and exponential growth 39–42
    framework for achieving 44–7
    reflection exercise 47
80:20 rule 40–1, 197–8

A
abundance 82, 87–91, 296–7
accountability 130
    and decision making 77, 105, 186
    in families 281–4, 286
    global community practices 277–8
    social accountability 77, 105, 186, 244
    and trust 105, 186
accounts
    categorizing 121–2
    diversifying 331
    global considerations 268–9
    tax-free 122, 150, 172, 198, 217, 222–4

affirmations 31, 56, 61, 74
African traditions 4, 277–8, 298
analysis-paralysis mindset 14, 119
anti-fragile mindset 324–6, 337–8
    building 91, 196, 263, 279–81
    case study 324–5, 334–5
    developing new skills 141–8, 239–42, 328–9
    economic crises 326–8
    framework for achieving 332–4
    preparation for crises 329–32
    reflection exercise 336–7
artificial intelligence 125, 127, 222
    financial assistants 123, 128, 222, 346
    impact of 328–9, 334–5
    passive income ideas 143–8
    and side hustles 250–1
auto-rebalancing 123, 228, 346
automating investments 122–4, 127, 150–1, 218–21, 222–4, 346
    tools and strategies 125–8
automating savings 93, 108, 218–21, 222–4, 345
    AI-driven financial assistants 123, 128, 222, 346

benefits of 119–21, 173–4, 212
case study 124–5
cash flow 122–3, 126
categorizing accounts 121–2
compound growth 123–4
framework for changing 129–30
guardrails and checkpoints 124–5, 200
reflection exercise 130–1
reviewing 124, 151
tools and strategies 125–8

B

behavioural science
    and financial stress 86, 170
    habit formation 24–5, 27–30, 38, 62, 107–8
beliefs, internalized 25–6
    challenging 74
    and financial stress 85, 156
    and guilt 67–8
    The Money-Guilt Cure 75–7
    reframing 55–6, 58–61, 72–7, 87–91
beliefs, limiting 57, 58–9
belonging, sense of 5, 100, 288
Benartzi, Shlomo 41
bonuses 108, 123–4, 234, 237
the brain
    cognitive behavioural techniques 55–7
    and financial stress 86
    and generosity 296–8
    habit formation 27–31, 38, 62, 108
    and impulse buying 110
    neuroplasticity 86
    reward system 99, 296–7, 298
budgeting. see habits; micro-habits; money management
Buffett, Warren 121, 171, 214–15, 220, 221
burnout 6. see also financial stress

C

Caffè Sospeso 294–5
cash flow 9
    automating 122–3, 126
    passive income 141, 142–8, 149
celebrating success 21, 77, 93, 190
Central Bank Digital Currencies 331
change. see economic crises
Chetty, Raj 310
children and young people
    conversations with 89–90, 301
    cultural wealth 5, 301
    investment accounts 160, 331–2
choices. see also decision making; impulse buying
    and lifestyle 7, 22–5, 27, 256–7
    mindful spending 161–2, 277
    reframing 31
Clarion Events 307–8
Clear, James 29, 39
climate change. see economic crises
cognitive behavioural techniques 55–7
community 4–5, 318–19. see also networks; relationships
    celebrating others' success 91
    global practices 277–8, 285
    importance of 318
    isolation from 6–7, 100
    positive role models 56, 59
    and trust 149, 278, 295–6, 300
compound growth 123–4, 212
compound interest 134, 136–9
compounding, science of 27–8, 39–42
    1% Compound Ladder 44–7
    1% daily improvement rule 42–4
core index 225–6
cortisol 99
cost of living. see location and wealth
crises. see economic crises
cultural influences 5, 68, 71

Index

D
Davidson, Hilary 299
debt 7, 23, 299
decision fatigue 93, 119–21, 196
decision making
    and accountability 77, 105, 186
    and automation 119–21
    case study 182–3
    implementation intentions 107–8, 188
    'intention-action gap' 182–4
    and mindset 25–6
    pause and delay technique 184, 187–8, 189–90
    reflection exercise 189, 191
    reframing failure 189
    saving for the future 176
    strategies for 185–7
delayed gratification 26, 157–8, 173–4
digital nomad visas 261
digital tools 21, 186, 222
dividend reinvestment 123, 125, 151, 346
dollar-cost averaging 127, 219
dopamine and impulse buying 98, 99, 188
Duhigg, Charles 29
Dweck, Carol 54

E
economic crises
    anti-fragile mindset 324–6
    case study 324–5
    and change 328–9
    fear of loss and change 326
    opportunistic picks 226–7
    preparing for 329–32
    wealth-building opportunities 327–8
education and empowerment 74, 106, 334
emergency funds 121, 122, 124, 329–30
    accessibility of 221
    automating contributions 173–4
    benefits of 176–7
    case study 168–9, 177–8
    framework for achieving 175–8
    importance of 170–1
    reflection exercise 178–9
    setting up 172–3
emotions 21. *see also* guilt
    and decision making 182–4
    emotional eating 98
    and impulse buying 98, 100–2, 104, 107–11
    processing 56
employee mindset 13, 22–4
employment. *see* skills
environment. *see also* location and wealth
    changing 22, 24–5, 28
    design of 21
    and lifestyle choices 256–7
    positive role models 56, 59
equity funds 216, 220
esusu (savings plan) 277–8
ethics. *see* values
Exchange Traded Funds (ETFs) 127, 144, 151, 173, 223, 226
expenses, reviewing 92, 330, 333
exponential growth 39–42

F
families, accountability in 281–4, 286
fear 21, 59. *see also* economic crises; resilience
    of redundancy 23
    response to crises 324, 326
financial check-ins. *see* reviewing and monitoring
financial crises. *see* economic crises
Financial-Freedom Calendar 276, 281–5, 287, 288
Financial Joy Academy 15–16
financial mindset. *see* mindset
financial reviews. *see* reviewing and monitoring

Financial-Rhythm Method 285–7
financial security. *see* future, preparing for
financial stress 6–7, 82–4. *see also* economic crises
    and behaviour 86
    and internalized beliefs 85
    and mindset 84–7
Fogg, B.J. 29
freedom 4, 31–2, 161–2, 260, 264–5
future, preparing for 89. *see also* emergency funds; pensions; skills
    accessible accounts 172, 221
    automating contributions 173–4
    benefits of 176–7
    case study 168–9, 177–8
    children and young people 160, 331–2
    framework for achieving 175–8
    global examples 177–8
    importance of 170–1
    investments 172–3, 215–17
    reflection exercise 178–9
    strategies to set up 172–3

G

generosity 5, 59, 77, 89–90
    benefits of 299, 300, 301
    and boundaries 299–300
    in communities 298
    framework for achieving 300–1
    global rise in 295–6
    and long-term wealth 297–8
    micro-rituals 302
    and networks 312
    and neuroscience 296–7, 298
    'paying it forward' movement 294–5
    reflection exercise 302
    regular giving 298–300
    and relationships 309
    shifts mindset to abundance 296–7
    structuring 299–300

geographic arbitrage
    benefits of 262–3
    case study 258, 269–71
    framework for implementing 265–9
    quality of life 256–7, 259
    re-evaluation quiz 264–5
    reflection exercise 271–3
    strategies for 260–1
geopolitics. *see* economic crises
global equity index funds 220, 224, 225
global perspectives 4–5, 277–8
Global Wealth Habit. *see* location and wealth
The Golden Flow Model 198–200
golden-visas 261
Granovetter, Mark 311
gratitude 59, 73, 89–90
growth mindset 54–5
guardrails and checkpoints 124–5, 200, 299–300
guilt 21. *see also* joyful spending
    case study 66–7, 70–2
    causes 67–72
    framework for changing 75–7
    The Money-Guilt Cure 75–7
    reflection exercise 78–9
    reframing 72–3
    releasing 73–4

H

Habit Loop of Wealth 28–30, 32
habits 12, 24–5. *see also* micro-habits
    building 11, 22, 27–32, 38, 62, 108, 207, 339
    clarity of 21
    and consistency 27–8, 37, 42–7
    and core values 8, 9–10
    and identity 28–30
    and long-term wealth 24–7
    reinforcing 29, 61, 93–4
    success of 8–10, 29, 37

Index

happiness. *see* joyful spending
health and wellbeing 4, 6, 108–9, 299
The Humble Penny 15, 242

I

identity 7, 21, 27–30
    building 30–2, 38–9, 50–2, 53, 196
    fixed 57
    framework for changing 59–61
    and growth mindset 54–5
    reflection exercise 32, 62–3
    reframing 55–9
    wealth identity shift 59–61
Ijomah, Kingsley 334–5
immigrants, attitudes towards 326
impulse buying 24–5. *see also* decision making
    and accountability 77, 105, 186
    barriers to 105, 111, 187–8
    case study 98–9, 106–7
    digital tools 186
    and emotions 98, 100–2, 104, 107–11
    framework for resetting 109–11
    global nature of 100–2
    implementation intentions 107–8, 188
    'intention-action gap' 182–4
    pause and delay technique 184, 187–8, 189–90
    psychology of 99–103, 110
    reflection exercise 111–12, 189, 191
    reframing failure 189
    self-sabotage 102, 103
    statistics 100–1
    strategies for 185–7
    triggers 98, 100–4, 107–8, 110, 111
income. *see also* side hustles
    digital income 142–8
    income protection 331
    lifetime variability of 137–9
    multiple sources 9, 26, 151–2, 330
    passive 142–9
    single source dependency 23
    small increases in 43–4
inflation spikes. *see* economic crises
inherited wealth and guilt 70
insurance 331
integrity 7, 79, 214
intention. *see also* decision making
    daily habits 8
    saving habits 20–1, 41–2, 92
    spending habits 73, 163–5, 186
investment 24–5, 43, 150. *see also* The Wealth-Multiplier Effect
    1% daily improvement rule 42–7
    80:20 rule 40–1, 198–200
    automating 122–4, 127, 150–1, 218–21, 222–4, 346
    avoiding overwhelm 213–14
    barriers to 203–4, 217–18
    case study 212–14
    for children and young people 160, 331–2
    digital tools 222
    framework for increasing 224–7
    importance of 215–17
    micro-investing 108, 345
    opportunistic picks 226–7
    reflection exercise 228–9
    reviewing 124, 151
    and values 226
ISAs 150, 172, 198–200, 222–4, 225–6

J

Japan
    furusato nozei (home town tax) 298
    kakeibo (mindful spending) 277
Jennings, Sam 307–8
journalling 55, 77, 187, 190, 197
The Joy-Spend Radar 163–5
joyful spending 108–9, 156
    case study 156–7, 159–61
    framework for achieving 163–5

luxuries 157–8
and mindfulness 161–2
reflection exercise 165–6
strategies for 161–2, 164–5
and values 158–9

K
kakeibo (mindful spending) 277
Kenya: *harambee* gatherings 298
Kipchoge, Eliud 36–7

L
Labi, Valerie 324–5
language, power of 77, 88–9
learned helplessness 57
life partners 4–5
lifestyle 7, 22, 27, 256–7
building 12, 339, 340
and location 258
quality of life 256–7, 259, 339, 340
limiting beliefs 57
liquidity, advantages of 172, 224, 329–30
location and wealth 256–7, 259
benefits of mobility 262–5
case study 258, 269–71
framework for implementing 265–9
quality of life 256–7, 259
re-evaluation quiz 264–5
reflection exercise 271–3
strategies for 260–1
The Location-Leverage Loop 265–9
luxuries, cutting out 157–8

M
marriage 4–5
and accountability 281–4, 286
financial benefits of 314–16
shared finances and guilt 69
supportive 307–8
mentors 56, 59, 308
micro-habits
alternatives to spending 188

applying 42–4
automating 93
celebrating success 21, 77, 93, 190
and consistency 27–8, 37, 42–7
effectiveness of 37–9
embedding 44
and exponential growth 39–42
framework for achieving 44–7
and identity 38–9, 61
reflection exercise 47
reinforcing 29, 61, 93–4
triggers for 28–9, 31–2, 92
micro-investing 108, 345
mindfulness and spending 161–2, 277
mindset 32. *see also* anti-fragile mindset; identity
abundance mindset 87–91
analysis-paralysis mindset 14, 119
barriers to progress 13–14
building 11, 20–2
employee mindset 13
employee vs wealth mindsets 22–4
and financial decisions 25–6
growth mindset 54–5
and mobility 257
overnight-success mindset 14, 37
scarcity mindset 13, 57, 69, 74, 82–5, 87–95
wealth builder mindset 23–4, 28–32, 327–8
money 6–7
relationship with 3, 39, 72–3
and security 73
money management 20–1, 126
80:20 rule 40–1, 197–8
and automation 120–8
barriers to 203–4
and decision fatigue 119–20
micro-habits 37–9
monitoring 106, 124, 150, 151, 200
monitoring. *see* reviewing and monitoring
Munger, Charlie 316

Index

N
Nakawuki, Bena 317–18
negativity bias 86
networks
    building 309, 311–13, 318–19
    case study 307–8, 317–18
    and community 316–18
    digital tools 314
    and diversity 312
    and financial success 309–11
    framework for implementing 319–20
    and generosity 312
    importance of 306, 318
    reflection exercise 320–1
    strategies for 313–16
neuroplasticity 86
neuroscience
    and financial stress 86
    and generosity 296–8
    habit formation 27–31, 38, 62
    and impulse buying 98–103, 110

O
online shopping, controlling 24–5
overnight-success mindset 14, 37

P
pandemics. see economic crises
Pareto principle 40–1
passive income 141
    and artificial intelligence 142–8
    property income 149
patience 8, 26, 37–42, 280–1
pay yourself first rule 195
    80:20 rule 40–1, 197–8
    barriers to 203–4
    case study 201–3
    framework for achieving 198–200
    reflection exercise 204–6
pensions
    80:20 rule 198–200
    auto enrolment 42
    case study 201–3
    contributions 41–2
    SIPP (Self-Invested Personal Pension) 122, 135
perfectionism and guilt 70
phone apps 21
planning. see future, preparing for; joyful spending
positive thinking 56, 89–90
pound-cost averaging 127, 219
property income 149
psychology
    cognitive behavioural techniques 55–7
    and financial stress 86
    and habits 27–30, 38, 62
    and impulse buying 98–103, 110
    and limiting beliefs 57
purpose, sense of 5, 9, 21, 297–8

Q
quiet wealth 162

R
recessions. see economic crises
reinforcing habits 29, 61, 93–4. see also reviewing and monitoring
reinvestments 123, 150–1
relationships. see also networks
    building 309
    case study 307–8
    celebrating others' success 91
    erosion of 7
    and financial success 309–11
    and guilt 67–9
    importance of 306, 307–8
    investing spending in 108–9
    isolation from 6–7
    shared finances and guilt 69
remote-work passports 261
resilience
    building 91, 196, 263, 279–81

case study 324–5, 334–5
developing new skills 141–8, 239–42, 328–9
economic crises 326–8
framework for achieving 332–4
mindset 324–6
wealth-building opportunities 327–8
retail therapy. see impulse buying
reviewing and monitoring
automating savings 124, 151
Financial-Freedom Calendar 276, 281–5
Financial-Rhythm Method 285–7
framework for implementing 285–7
global practices 277–8
guardrails and checkpoints 124–5, 200, 299–300
importance of 277–8, 279–81
investment 124, 151
Japanese *kakeibo* practice 277
key habits to implement 281–4
reflection exercise 287–8
routines that work 284–7
South African *stokvel* practice 277–8
West African *esusu* practice 277–8
rewards. see joyful spending
robo-advisors 123, 222, 346
Ronaldo, Cristiano 239–40
round-up tools 126, 345

S
Save More Tomorrow™ 41
saving. see also emergency funds
80:20 rule 40–1, 197–200
AI-driven financial assistants 123, 128, 222, 346
automating. see automating savings
barriers to 203–4
and consistency 27–8, 37, 42–7
global community practices 277–8

micro-investing 108, 345
and self-control 24–5
small increases in 43, 92
Scarcity Loop
and financial stress 82–4
framework for escaping 91–5
and mindset 84–7
moving to abundance mindset 87–91
scarcity mindset 13, 57, 69
case study 82–4
challenging 74
and financial stress 84–5, 87
framework for escaping 91–4
reflection exercise 94–5
reframing 87–91
security. see future, preparing for
self-awareness 73–4, 88
self-compassion 56, 73–4
self-control, importance of 24–5
self-denial, dangers of 157–8
self-esteem 54
self-image 54, 55–6. see also identity
self-perception. see identity
self-sabotage 102, 103
self, sense of 7
self-worth 7, 57, 70
Set-And-Soar System 129–30
shame 21, 56, 59, 68
side hustles
and artificial intelligence 250–1
case study 232–3, 236
equity thinking vs salary 233–8
framework for achieving 250–2
increasing your value 242
knowing your value 235, 236–8
and mindset changes 243–9
reflection exercise 252
stacking rare skills 239–42
starting 243–9
SIPP (Self-Invested Personal Pension) 122, 135

skills. see also side hustles
    developing 141–8, 328–9, 330–1
    knowing your value 235, 236–8
    learning new skills 43–4
    stacking rare skills 239–42
Smith, Christian 299
social accountability 77, 105, 186, 244
social isolation 6–7
Sofoluke, Raphael 307–8
South African *stokvel* practice 277–8
spending. see also generosity; impulse buying; joyful spending
    and accountability 186
    aligning with values 156, 158–9
    analyse potential purchases 164
    conscious spending 73
    expenses 330, 333
    mindful spending 161–2, 277
    reviewing and monitoring 330, 333
spiritual emptiness 7
stock market 222–4, 225–7. see also investment
    automating investments 127, 220
    timing investments 118
stokvel (savings plan) 277–8
stress. see also financial stress
    and impulse buying 98, 99–103
subscription reviews 106
success, redefining 90
survival mechanisms. see guilt; impulse buying; scarcity mindset
survival mode 13, 156
    moving to abundance mindset 87–95

T
tax-free saving accounts 122, 150, 172, 198, 217, 222–4
tax-loss harvesting 127, 128, 346
technological change. see economic crises
Thaler, Richard 41
therapy and counselling 74
trade wars. see economic crises

trauma, financial 69, 74
treats. see joyful spending
triggers for saving 21, 28–9, 31–2, 92
triggers for spending 24
    categorizing 104–5
    emotional 98–103
TrueLayer 126
trust 8
    and accountability 105, 186
    importance of 149, 278, 295–6, 300, 306, 309
    self-trust 46, 47, 52, 192

U
ubuntu 4
UK Black Business Week 307–8
unworthiness 57

V
values
    aligning finances with 9–10, 73, 90, 226
    aligning spending with 158–9
    and daily habits 8
    erosion of 7
    and financial stress 82–4
    and inherited wealth 70
    limiting beliefs 57
    safeguarding 7
visualization 56, 59, 61, 74, 170, 176

W
Warmann, Martine 70–2
wealth 4–6. see also abundance; The Wealth-Multiplier Effect
    80:20 rule 40–1, 197–8
    benefits of 196–7
    and community 4–5
    and consistency 27–8, 37, 42–7
    cultural wealth 5
    and delayed gratification 26
    exponential growth 39–42

financial wealth 6–7
and freedom 4, 8, 31–2, 161–2, 260, 264–5
global perspectives 4–5
and identity 30–2, 53–62
increasing 327–8
and lifestyle choices 27
lifetime variability of 137–9
and mobility. see location and wealth
multiple income streams 9, 26, 151–2, 330. see also side hustles
and networks 309–11
pay yourself first rule 40–1, 195, 197–206
and purpose 5
quiet wealth 162
and relationships 309–11
reviewing and monitoring. see reviewing and monitoring
and self-control 24–5
and wellbeing 4, 108–9, 299
wealth builder mindset 23–4
achieving 30–2
and economic crises 327–8
framework for achieving 109–11
Habit Loop of Wealth 28–30
strategies for 107–9
wealth gap 139–41
wealth habit 8–10, 12
1% Compound Ladder 44–7
1% daily improvement rule 42–4
90-day challenge 341
and behavioural science 27–30
benefits of 10–13
Habit Loop of Wealth 28–30, 32
and long-term wealth 22–4
and mindset 20–4
The Wealth-Multiplier Effect 141
and artificial intelligence 143–8
case study 134–6
and compound interest 136–40
digital income 142–8
framework for implementing 149–52
passive income 142–9
reflection exercise 152–3
wealth gap 139–41
Wealth Trigger Reset 109–11
wellbeing 4, 6, 108–9, 263, 299
West African *esusu* practice 277–8
Westgate, Melissa 51–2
willpower depletion effect 158
windfalls, channeling 123–4, 220
working overseas 261
World Giving Index 295

ABOUT THE AUTHORS

Ken and Mary Okoroafor are a married couple with two children who achieved financial independence, 100% debt-free, by age 34. They are the award-winning founders of The Humble Penny and The Financial Joy Academy. Ken is a first-generation immigrant, Chartered Accountant, MBA and former CFO. Mary is an entrepreneur, born in London to hard-working immigrant parents of Nigerian heritage.

Website: www.thehumblepenny.com
Email: book@thehumblepenny.com
Socials: @TheHumblePenny